TURBO C®

User's Guide

**This manual was produced in its entirety with
Sprint: The Professional Word Processor,®
available from Borland.**

Borland International, Inc.
4585 Scotts Valley Drive
Scotts Valley, California 95066

10 9 8 7 6

Turbo C Runtime Library Source Code—
for professional programmers!

The Turbo C Runtime Library Source Code gives you a professional head start. It gives you a deeper understanding of Turbo C and better control over your program environment by giving you a close look at the inner workings of the compiler routines and functions.

The Turbo C Runtime Library allows you to customize the library of over 300 functions so that you can add or modify routines. Now you can handle those situations where the specific needs of your program are different from those assumed by the Turbo C Runtime Library. You can take advantage of the tightly coded and optimized Turbo C Library routines but not be limited by the assumptions they make.

Some compiler companies don't make library source code available; others have been known to charge thousands of dollars for it. The result is that many professionals have been forced to spend thousands of hours writing their own libraries just so they can know reliably how the library routines work. Borland makes it easy. We'll give you the source code to the hottest-selling compiler in the history of microcomputing for only $150.00!

Order your copy of the Turbo C Runtime Library source code today! Please fill in the order form and mail your payment direct to Borland: Turbo C Runtime Library Source Code, Borland International, 4585 Scotts Valley Drive, California 95066-9987. (The Borland Turbo C Runtime Library source code is available only direct from Borland.)

To Order Your Turbo C Runtime Library Source Code:

1. Please read and sign the Borland No-Nonsense Turbo C Runtime Library Source Code License Agreement on back. (To process your order, we must have your signature on this License. Your signed License will remain on file at Borland.)

2. Please send $150.00 and your signed License Agreement to Borland in the envelope provided.

3. Please indicate desired disk size: ☐ 5¼"   ☐ 3½"

Please print:

NAME: _____

COMPANY: _____

SHIPPING ADDRESS: _____

CITY: _____

STATE: _____ ZIP: _____

Please indicate method of payment:

☐ Check   ☐ Bank draft   ☐ VISA/MasterCard # | | | | | | | | | | | | | | | | | | | |

Expiration date: _____/_____

Name as it appears on the card: _____

Turbo C Runtime Library Source Code License	$150.00
California and Massachusetts residents add sales tax	$ _____
Outside USA add $10.00	$ _____
Total enclosed	$ _____

Price includes shipping to all US cities.

CODs and purchase orders WILL NOT be accepted by Borland. Outside USA make payment by bank draft, payable in US dollars, drawn on a US bank.

BOR 0343B

Borland International, 4585 Scotts Valley Drive, Scotts Valley, CA 95066-9987

How Borland Gives You The Unique Opportunity To License
The Turbo C Runtime Library Source Code!

Once again Borland provides you with a unique opportunity. As an experienced C programmer, you know how important it is to have access to the source code for the Turbo C Runtime Library. We are making Turbo C's Runtime Library source code available for your use for only $150.00.

This is an exceptional opportunity for you to gain a better understanding of your code and to optimize the performance of your Turbo C programs.

Order your copy of the Turbo C Runtime Library source code today. Because of its extreme value and confidentiality, the Turbo C Runtime Library source code is only available direct from Borland International. Please fill in the order form on the other side of this page and mail your payment, so you can take advantage of this special offer!

Turbo C Runtime Library Source Code
Borland's No-Nonsense License Agreement!

Borland International, Inc. ("Borland") is offering you a license to the source code to the Turbo C Runtime Library portion of Turbo C (the "Source Programs"), including updates that may later be supplied by Borland at additional cost, but not including the source code of the 8087 emulator.

The Source Programs are protected by both United States copyright law and international treaty provisions. Therefore, you must treat the Source Programs just like a book, with the following single exception: Borland authorizes you to make archival copies of the Source Programs for the sole purpose of backing-up your programs and protecting your investment from loss.

By saying, "just like a book," Borland means, for example, that the Source Programs may be used by any number of people and may be freely moved from one computer workstation to another, so long as there is **no possibility** of them being used at one computer workstation while they are being used at another. Just as a book can't be read by two different people in two different places at the same time, neither can the Source Programs be used by two different people in two different places at the same time. (Unless, of course, Borland's copyright has been violated.)

You may use the Source Programs to support your licensed copies of Turbo C. This means you may include the Source Programs in your own development copies of Turbo C-based programs, but you can only distribute copies of them in executable form. You may not distribute any part of the actual Turbo C Runtime Library source code. You are not, of course, restricted from distributing your own source code.

You may modify the Source Programs, but the modified source code, regardless of the extent of the modifications, shall always remain Borland's source code. You may not remove or modify Borland's copyright and other proprietary rights notices. You may not distribute any part of the Source Programs, regardless of the extent of the modifications, and you may not transport any of the Source Programs to another computer operating system or environment. **You shall be responsible for all claims, liability, and damages arising from your own modifications and the products which include them.**

All rights not specifically granted in this license are reserved by Borland.

LIMITED WARRANTY

With respect to the physical diskette and physical documentation, Borland warrants the same to be free of defects in materials and workmanship for a period of sixty (60) days from the date of purchase. In the event Borland receives written notice from you of defects in materials or workmanship within such 60-day period, Borland will replace the defective diskette or documentation. **If you need to return a product, call the Borland Customer Service Department to obtain a return authorization number.**

The remedy for breach of this limited warranty shall be limited solely to replacement diskettes and documentation and shall not include any other damages. **Borland will not be liable for consequential, special, indirect, or other similar damages or claims,** including loss of profits or any other commercial damage, even if our agents have been advised of the possibility of such damages, and in no event will Borland's liability for any damages to you or any other person ever exceed the price paid for the license to use the Source Programs, regardless of any form of the claim.

Borland specifically disclaims all other warranties, expressed or implied. Specifically, **Borland makes no warranty that the Source Programs are fit for any particular purpose. Any implied warranty of merchantability is limited to the sixty-day duration of the limited warranty covering the physical diskettes and documentation only (not the Source Programs), and is otherwise expressly and specifically disclaimed.**

This limited warranty gives you specific legal rights; you may have others which vary from state to state. Some states do not allow the exclusion of incidental or consequential damages, or the limitation on how long an implied warranty lasts, so some of the above may not apply to you.

GOVERNING LAW AND GENERAL PROVISIONS

This license agreement shall be construed, interpreted, and governed by the laws of the state of California. If any provision of this Agreement is found void, invalid or unenforceable, it will not affect the validity of the balance of this Agreement, which shall remain valid and enforceable according to its terms. **In the event any remedy hereunder is determined to have failed of its essential purpose, all limitations of liability and exclusion of damages set forth herein shall remain in full force and effect.** This agreement may only be modified in writing signed by you and an authorized representative of Borland.

I have read the foregoing and understand it. Any questions that have occurred to me have been answered to my satisfaction.

SIGNATURE: _____

NAME: _____

COMPANY (if any): _____

DATE: _____

TURBO C SERIAL #: _____

Borland's shipment of the product shall constitute its acceptance of this Agreement.

To order your Turbo C Runtime Library source code, see the other side of this page.

Table of Contents

Chapter 6. Notes for Turbo Pascal Programmers   149

Turbo C is for C programmers who want a fast, efficient compiler; for Turbo Pascal programmers who want to learn C with all the "Turbo" advantages; and for anyone just learning C who wants to start with a fast, easy-to-use implementation.

The C language is the structured, modular, compiled, general-purpose language traditionally used for systems programming. It is portable—you can easily transfer application programs written in C between different computers. You can use C for almost any programming task, anywhere. But while traditional C compilers plod along, Turbo C flies through compilation (7000 lines per minute) and gives you more time to test and perfect your programs.

The Turbo C Package

Your Turbo C package consists of four distribution disks and the two-volume documentation set—the *Turbo C User's Guide* (this book) and the *Turbo C Reference Guide*. The distribution disks contain all the programs, files, and libraries you need to create, compile, link, and run your Turbo C programs; they also contain sample programs, a stand-alone MAKE utility, a context-sensitive help file, and additional C documentation not covered in these guides.

The user's guide is designed as a handbook and guide for the novice (and a useful refresher course for the pro). The reference guide is first and foremost a detailed list and explanation of Turbo C's extensive library routines. It also contains information on utilities (CPP, MAKE and TLINK), the Turbo C editor, error messages, command-line options, Turbo C syntax, and customization. Unless you are already a pro, you will probably want to begin with the user's guide before wading into the thicker waters of the reference guide.

Requirements

Turbo C runs on the IBM PC family of computers, including the XT and AT, along with all true IBM compatibles. Turbo C requires DOS 2.0 or higher and at least 384K of RAM; it will run on any 80-column monitor. One floppy disk drive is all that's required, although we recommend two floppy drives or a hard disk with one floppy drive.

It includes floating-point routines that let your programs make use of an 8087 (or 80287) math coprocessor chip, or will emulate the chip if it is not available. The 8087 (or 80287) can significantly enhance performance of your programs, but is not required.

The Turbo C Implementation

Turbo C supports the Draft-Proposed American National Standards Institute (ANSI) C standard, fully supports the Kernighan and Ritchie definition, and includes certain optional extensions for mixed-language and mixed-model programming that allow you to exploit your PC's capabilities.

Volume I: The User's Guide

Volume I introduces you to Turbo C, shows you how to create and run programs, and includes background information on topics such as compiling, linking, error-tracking, and project making. Here is a breakdown of the chapters in the user's guide:

Chapter 1: Getting Started describes the contents of the four distribution disks and tells you how to load the Turbo C files and libraries into your system. It also suggests how you should go about using the rest of the user's guide.

Chapter 2: The Turbo C Integrated Development Environment explains Turbo C's menus and text editor and shows you how to use the editor to create and modify C source files.

Chapter 3: Putting It All Together—Compiling and Running shows how to use the Turbo C Run command, and explains how to "make" (rebuild) a program's constituent files, plus guides you through running your first program.

Chapter 4: Programming in Turbo C introduces you to some of the basic steps involved in creating and running Turbo C programs and takes you through a set of short, progressive sample programs.

Chapter 5: More About Programming in Turbo C provides summary explanations of additional C programming elements including arrays, pointers, structures, and statements.

Chapter 6: Notes for Turbo Pascal Programmers uses program examples to compare Turbo Pascal to Turbo C, describes and summarizes the significant differences between the two languages, and gives some tips on avoiding programming pitfalls.

Chapter 7: Interfacing Turbo C with Turbo Prolog shows how to interface modules written in Turbo C with Turbo Prolog programs and provides several examples that demonstrate the process.

Chapter 8: Turbo C Language Reference lists all aspects and features of this implementation that differ from Kernighan and Ritchie's definition of the language, and details the Turbo C extensions not given in the current draft of the ANSI C standard.

Chapter 9: Advanced Programming in Turbo C provides details about the start-up code, memory organization in the different memory models, pointer arithmetic, assembly-language interface, and using floating-point.

Volume II: The Reference Guide

Volume II, the *Turbo C Reference Guide*, is written for experienced C programmers; it provides implementation-specific details about the language and the run-time environment. In addition, it describes each of the Turbo C functions, listed in alphabetical order. These are the chapters and appendixes in the programmer's reference guide.

Chapter 1: Using Turbo C Library Routines summarizes Turbo C's input/output (I/O) support, and lists and describes the #include (.h) files.

Chapter 2: The Turbo C Library is an alphabetical reference of all Turbo C library functions. Each definition gives syntax, include files, related functions, an operative description, return values, and portability information for the function.

Appendix A: The Turbo C Interactive Editor gives a more thorough explanation of the editor commands—for those who need more information than that given in Chapter 2.

Appendix B: Compiler Error Messages lists and explains each of the error messages and summarizes the possible or probable causes of the problem that generated the message.

Appendix C: Command-Line Options lists the command-line entry for each of the user-selectable TCC (command-line compiler) options.

Appendix D: Turbo C Utilities discusses three utilities included in the Turbo C package; CPP—the preprocessor, MAKE—the program builder, and TLINK—the Turbo Link utility. The section on CPP summarizes how the C preprocessor functions. The section on MAKE documents how to use MAKE for rebuilding program files. The section on TLINK summarizes how to use the command-line version of Turbo C's built-in Turbo Linker.

Appendix E: Language Syntax Summary uses modified Backus-Naur Forms to detail the syntax of all Turbo C constructs.

Appendix F: Customizing Turbo C takes you on a walk through the installation program (TCINST), which lets you customize your keyboard, modify default values, change your screen colors, etc.

Recommended Reading

You will find these documents useful additions to your Turbo C manuals:

- The most widely known description of C is found in *The C Programming Language* by Brian W. Kernighan and Dennis M. Ritchie (New Jersey: Prentice-Hall, 1978).

- The ANSI Subcommittee X3J11 on Standardization of C is presently creating a formal standard for the language, and Turbo C supports this upcoming ANSI C standard.

- *Using Turbo C* and *Advanced Turbo C* by Herbert Schildt (Berkeley: Osborne/McGraw Hill) are both good tutorials for learning to use Turbo C to its fullest extent.

If you are learning C for the first time, we recommend that you use Turbo C to work through the exercises in Kernighan and Ritchie. If you are experienced with C, you should have little difficulty using Turbo C.

Typographic Conventions

All typefaces used in this manual were produced by Borland's Sprint: The Professional Word Processor, on an Apple LaserWriter Plus. Their uses are as follows:

`Monospace type`	This typeface represents text as it appears on the screen (or in your program) and anything you must type (such as command-line options).
`< >`	Angle brackets in text or DOS command lines enclose optional input or data that depends on your system, which should not be typed verbatim. Angle brackets in the function reference section enclose the names of include files.
Boldface	Turbo C function names (such as **printf**) are shown in boldface when mentioned within text (but not in program examples).
Italics	Italics indicate variable names (identifiers) within sections of text and emphasize certain words (especially new terms).
`Bold monospace`	This typeface represents Turbo C keywords (such as `char`, `switch`, `near`, and `cdecl`).
Keycaps	This special typeface indicates a key on your keyboard. It is often used when describing a particular key you should type, e.g., "Press *Esc* to exit a menu."

Borland's No-Nonsense License Statement

This software is protected by both United States Copyright Law and International Treaty provisions. Therefore, you must treat this software *just like a book* with the following single exception: Borland International authorizes you to make archival copies of Turbo C for the sole purpose of backing up your software and protecting your investment from loss.

By saying, "just like a book," Borland means, for example, that this software may be used by any number of people and may be freely moved from one computer location to another so long as there is **no possibility** of its being used at one location while it's being used at another. Just like a book that can't be read by two different people in two different places at the same time, neither can the software be used by two different people in two different places at the same time. (Unless, of course, Borland's copyright has been violated.)

Acknowledgments

In this manual, we refer to several products:

- Turbo Pascal, Turbo Prolog and Sprint: The Professional Word Processor are registered trademarks of Borland International Inc.
- WordStar is a trademark of MicroPro Inc.
- IBM PC, XT, and AT are trademarks of International Business Machines Inc.
- MS-DOS is a registered trademark of Microsoft Corporation.
- UNIX is a registered trademark of ATT.

How to Contact Borland

The best way to contact Borland is to log on to Borland's Forum on CompuServe: Type GO BOR from the main CompuServe menu and select "Enter Language Products Forum" from the Borland main menu. Leave your questions or comments there for the support staff to process.

If you prefer, write a letter detailing your comments and send it to:

Technical Support Department
Borland International
4585 Scotts Valley Drive
Scotts Valley, CA
95066, USA

As a last resort, if you cannot write to us for some reason, you can telephone our Technical Support department. Please have the following information handy before you call:

- product name and version number
- computer make and model number
- operating system and version number

1

Getting Started

Your Turbo C package actually includes two different versions of the C compiler: the Integrated Environment version and a separate, stand-alone command-line version. When you install Turbo C on your system, you copy files from the distribution disks to your working floppies or to your hard disk. There is no copy protection, and you do not need to run any installation programs. The distribution disks are formatted for double-sided, double-density disk drives and can be read by IBM PCs and close compatibles. For reference, we include a list of the distribution files in this chapter.

As we explained in the "Introduction," you should make a complete working copy of the distribution disks when you receive them, then store the original disks away in a safe place. Do *not* run Turbo C from the distribution disks; they are your original (and only) back-ups in case anything happens to your working files.

If you are not familiar with Borland's No-Nonsense License Statement, now is the time to read the agreement in the "Introduction" (it's also at the front of this book) and mail us your filled-in product registration card.

In This Chapter ...

We start this chapter with a complete list of the files on the Turbo C 5-1/4" distribution disks. Then we give instructions for loading Turbo C on systems with 5-1/4" floppy disk drives or hard disk drives. We end this chapter with some recommendations on which chapters you will want to read next, based on your programming language experience.

Summary of 5-1/4" Distribution Disks

The Turbo C package comes with four 5-1/4" distribution disks. The files on these disks are organized in such a way that you can set up Turbo C on your system with a minimum of disk-swapping (floppy-flipping).

Disk 1: The Integrated Environment

This disk contains the core files for Turbo C: the integrated-environment version of Turbo C, the Turbo C help files, and up-to-the-minute notes and errata on the package. These are the files on Distribution Disk #1:

TC.EXE	Turbo C integrated environment
TCHELP.TCH	The Turbo C help file
README	A last-minute update file for your information
README.COM	Program to read the README file
TCINST.COM	The Turbo C customization program
HELLO.C	The classic "Hello, World" source code

Disk 2: Command-Line Version & Utilities

This disk contains the command-line version of Turbo C and the other utilities that command-line afficionados will want to use. Refer to Appendixes C and D in the *Turbo C Reference Guide* for information about using these programs.

TCC.EXE	The command-line version of Turbo C
TLINK.EXE	The Turbo Linker program
CPP.EXE	The C preprocessor as a separate executable program
MAKE.EXE	The Turbo C MAKE utility
TOUCH.COM	The Turbo C file re-dating utility
CNVTCFG.EXE	A program to convert configuration files

Files for building start-up:

BUILD-C0.BAT	Batch file for building the start-up code modules
C0.ASM	Assembler source for start-up code
RULES.ASI	Assembler include file for start-up code
SETENVP.ASM	Assembler source code for preparing the environment
SETARGV.ASM	Assembler source code for parsing the command line

Miscellaneous files:

MAIN.C	An alternate main file.

Disk 3: Include Files & Libs I

This disk contains the floating-point libraries, the *header files*, and the run-time libraries for the tiny, small, and large memory models.

Floating-point files:

87.LIB	Floating point coprocessor (8087/80287) library
EMU.LIB	Floating point emulation library

Include (header) files:

ALLOC.H	Memory management functions
ASSERT.H	Debugging macro header file
BIOS.H	BIOS header file
CONIO.H	Direct DOS console I/O
CTYPE.H	The character classification macros
DIR.H	Structures, macros, and functions for directories and path names
DOS.H	Interfacing with DOS and the 8086
ERRNO.H	System call error number mnemonic file
FCNTL.H	File control information file
FLOAT.H	Floating-point parameters file
IO.H	Input/Output structures and declarations
LIMITS.H	Environmental parameters file
MATH.H	Declarations of various math functions
MEM.H	Memory manipulation functions
PROCESS.H	Process management structures and declarations
SETJMP.H	Declarations for **setjmp** and **longjmp**
SHARE.H	File sharing file

SIGNAL.H	Signal definitions file
STDARG.H	Variable arguments header file
STDDEF.H	Commonly used types and macros file
STDIO.H	The standard I/O header file
STDLIB.H	Declarations for some "standard" routines
STRING.H	String manipulation routines file
TIME.H	Time of day function header file
VALUES.H	Symbolic names for machine-dependent constants
SYS\STAT.H	Subdirectory containing STAT.H—an auxiliary I/O header file

Run-time libraries for the tiny, small, and large memory models:

C0T.OBJ	Tiny-model start-up object
C0S.OBJ	Small-model start-up code
CS.LIB	Small- and tiny-model library routines
MATHS.LIB	Small- and tiny-model math routines
C0L.OBJ	Large-model start-up code
CL.LIB	Large-model library routines
MATHL.LIB	Large-model math routines

MicroCalc Files:

MCALC.DOC	MicroCalc documentation
MCALC.C	MicroCalc main program source code
MCALC.H	MicroCalc header file
MCALC.PRJ	MicroCalc project file
MCOMMAND.C	MicroCalc commands source code
MCDISPLY.C	MicroCalc screen display source code
MCINPUT.C	MicroCalc input routines source code
MCPARSER.C	MicroCalc input parser source code
MCUTIL.C	MicroCalc utilities source code
MCMVSMEM.C	MicroCalc direct screen memory write source code
MCMVSMEM.OBJ	Compiled version of MCMVSMEM—will link with any memory model

Note: Instructions for compiling and running MicroCalc are given in Appendix G in the *Turbo C Reference Guide*.

Disk 4: Libs II

This disk contains the run-time libraries for the compact, medium, and huge memory models, and some miscellaneous files.

Run-time libraries for the compact, medium, and huge memory models:

C0C.OBJ	Compact-model start-up code
CC.LIB	Compact-model library routines
MATHC.LIB	Compact-model math routines
C0M.OBJ	Medium-model start-up code
CM.LIB	Medium-model library routines
MATHM.LIB	Medium-model math routines
C0H.OBJ	Huge-model start-up code
CH.LIB	Huge-model library routines
MATHH.LIB	Huge-model math routines

Miscellaneous Files:

CPINIT.OBJ	Initialization code for linking Turbo C and Turbo Prolog.
MATHERR.C	Source file for alternate **matherr** function
FILECOMP.C	Example Turbo C program to compare files
GETOPT.C	Source code for routine that parses options in command line
BAR.C	Example function to be used with PBAR.PRO
PBAR.PRO	Example Turbo Prolog program to be used with BAR.C

Installing Turbo C on Your System

Your Turbo C package includes all the files and programs necessary to run both the integrated-environment and command-line versions of the compiler, along with start-up code and library support for six memory models and 8087 coprocessor emulation. Which files you copy depends on which version and which memory model you will be using for your application.

Note: We assume that you are already familiar with DOS, particularly the `copy`, `mkdir`, and `chdir` commands, which you need for setting up Turbo C on your system.

If you do not already know how to use these DOS commands, refer to your DOS Reference Manual before starting to set up Turbo C on your system.

Read This Before Setting Up Turbo C

You are not required to set up Turbo C the way we explain in this chapter, but the method we give is logical and easy to use because it takes advantage of DOS's subdirectory capabilities.

For hard-disk systems, the method we give has you place the Turbo C files as follows:

1. the Turbo C program files in a directory called TURBOC
2. the include files (header files) in a subdirectory called TURBOC\INCLUDE
3. the library files in a another subdirectory called TURBOC\LIB.

For floppy-disk systems, the method we give has you place the Turbo C files as follows:

1. the Turbo C program files directly on the floppy disk
2. the include files (header files) in a floppy-disk subdirectory called \INCLUDE
3. the library files in a another floppy-disk subdirectory called \LIB.

When you use subdirectories to organize your files, it is easiest to use Turbo C with a configuration file. You will use either TCCONFIG.CFG (if you're using TC—the Integrated Environment version of Turbo C), or TURBOC.CFG (if you're using TCC—command-line Turbo C). The configuration file tells Turbo C where to look to find the INCLUDE and LIB subdirectories. You will find information about the configuration files in the section " Writing the Configuration File" in this chapter.

If you don't want to use subdirectories when you set up Turbo C on your system, refer to the section "If You Don't Want to Use Subdirectories" in this chapter.

Setting Up Turbo C on a Floppy Disk System

How you set up Turbo C to run from floppies depends on whether your computer system has one or two floppy disk drives. Obviously, having two drives makes life easier, but using Turbo C with just one drive is perfectly possible. Here's how to go about it....

Using Turbo C with One Floppy

If your computer system has only one floppy drive, you should just use the Turbo C Integrated Environment (the menu-driven version called TC.EXE on your distribution disk). Even though you have only one disk drive, you will have to create two separate floppies—a program disk and a work disk.

Your Program Disk

Onto one floppy, copy the following files:

- TC.EXE
- TCHELP.TCH

If you're not familiar with DOS, refer to your DOS manual for information about the copy command.

Your Work Disk

Your work disk, of course, will contain your program source, and object and executable files. We also recommend (though it's not necessary) setting up two separate subdirectories on this floppy: \INCLUDE for your include files and \LIB for your library files. (Your DOS manual has more information on setting up subdirectories with the `mkdir` and `chdir` commands).

Note: If you choose to set up these two subdirectories and you use TCC, you must specify the include directory with the `-I` option and the library directory with the `-L` option (see Appendix C for more on command-line options). If you're using TC, you must set up the include and library directories from within the **Options/Environment** menu.

Into the \INCLUDE subdirectory copy the include files from distribution disk 3 (*.H and SYS\STAT.H).

Into the \LIB subdirectory copy the following library files:

- C0x.OBJ
- EMU.LIB
- FP87.LIB
- MATHx.LIB
- Cx.LIB

Note that the *x* in these files stands for the first letter of the particular memory model you're using. In other words, if you're using the *large* memory model, you would substitute an *L* for the *x*'s. In that case, you would copy C0L.OBJ, MATHL.LIB, and CL.LIB into the \LIB subdirectory.

To run Turbo C from a single floppy drive, first insert the program disk into the disk drive and type `tc`. Once the program has loaded into memory, remove the program disk and insert your work disk. If you need on-line help, though, re-insert the program disk before pressing *F1*.

Using Turbo C with Two Floppies

If your computer system has two floppy disk drives, you have the choice of running the Turbo C Integrated Environment or the Turbo C command-line version. You will need two different sets of floppies to run each of these versions.

To Run the TC Version

To run the Integrated Environment version of Turbo C (the menu-driven version called TC.EXE), you should follow the preceding steps for setting up a program disk and a work disk for a single disk system. But instead of swapping one disk for the other, you can insert the program disk in drive A and the work disk in drive B.

To Run the TCC Version

To run the command-line version of Turbo C (called TCC.EXE), you need to create two new disks—one for drive A, one for drive B.

On the disk for drive A, copy the following:

- TCC.EXE
- TLINK.EXE
- a subdirectory called \LIB
- a subdirectory called \INCLUDE

Into the \LIB subdirectory on this disk, copy the following files:

- C0x.OBJ
- EMU.LIB
- FP87.LIB
- MATHx.LIB
- Cx.LIB

Note that the x in these files stands for the first letter of the particular memory model you're using. In other words, if you're using the Large memory model, you would substitute an L for the x's. In that case, you would put C0L.OBJ, MATHL.LIB, and CL.LIB into the \LIB subdirectory.

Into the \INCLUDE subdirectory on this disk, copy all the include files (the .H files as found on distribution disk 3).

On the disk for drive B (your work disk), copy all the .C, .OBJ, and .EXE files that you create with the command-line version of Turbo C.

Setting Up Turbo C on a Hard Disk

Using Turbo C on a hard disk allows you to switch easily from the Integrated Environment version (TC.EXE) to the command-line version (TCC.EXE).

You should first create a subdirectory off your root directory and call it \TURBOC. Into this subdirectory go all the program files, all your own files, and any .C files that you create with Turbo C.

Then off of the \TURBOC subdirectory, create two further subdirectories: \LIB and \INCLUDE.

Into the \LIB subdirectory go all the library and start-up files (that is, all the .LIB and C0x.OBJ files).

Into the \INCLUDE subdirectory go all the header files (.H files) as found on distribution disk 3.

When using TC, remember that you must set up the include and library directories from within TC's **Options/Environment** menu. For TCC, specify the include directory with the -I command line option, and the library directory with the -L option.

Setting Up Turbo C on a Laptop System

If you have a laptop computer (one with an LCD or plasma display), in addition to following the procedures given in the previous sections, you should set your screen parameters before using Turbo C. The Turbo C Integrated Development Environment version (TC.EXE) works best if you enter MODE BW80 at the DOS command line before running Turbo C.

Alternatively, you can install TC for a black and white screen using the Turbo C installation program, TCINST. (Refer to Appendix F in the *Turbo C Reference Guide*.) With this installation program, you should select "Black and White" from the **Screen Modes** menu.

If You Don't Want to Use Subdirectories

Using Turbo C with subdirectories is optional, so if you don't want to use them to organize your Turbo C files, you can put all the files in one directory on the appropriate disk.

On a Hard Disk System

We recommend that you create a directory called TURBOC on your hard disk, then copy all the Turbo C files to that directory. If you don't know how to make a directory, refer to the mkdir command in your DOS manual.

TC On a Floppy Disk System

If you're using the Integrated Environment version of Turbo C (TC.EXE) with only floppy-disk drives, but choose not to use subdirectories, you will still need to create two disks (your program disk and you work disk).

We describe how to do this in "Setting Up Turbo C on a Floppy Disk System" in this chapter. The difference is that, without subdirectories, you will copy the files you need (as listed in that section) directly to the work disk, without setting up \INCLUDE or \LIB on that disk.

TCC On a Floppy Disk System

If you don't want to use subdirectories, have two floppy-disk drives, and are using command-line Turbo C (TCC.EXE), follow the directions in "To Run the TCC Version" in this chapter, **with the following exceptions:**

- instead of setting up \INCLUDE on the disk for drive A, just copy the include (header) files directly to the disk
- instead of setting up \LIB on the disk for drive A, just copy the specified library files directly to the disk

Writing the Configuration File

The Integrated Development Environment version of Turbo C includes a built-in configuration file named TCCONFIG.TC. When you save compiler options, Turbo C automatically writes those options into TCCONFIG.TC, the configuration file.

If you choose to create your own configuration file for use with the command-line version of Turbo C (TCC), you need to follow this procedure:

1. With an ASCII editor, create a file called TURBOC.CFG that contains the following line:

   ```
   -LC:\TURBOC\LIB -IC:\TURBOC\INCLUDE
   ```

   (This assumes that your library directory is C:\TURBOC\LIB and your include files directory is C:\TURBOC\INCLUDE.)
2. Decide where to store TURBOC.CFG, taking the following information into consideration. When TCC starts, it looks for TURBOC.CFG in the current directory. If it doesn't find it there *and* if you're running DOS 3.x, it then looks in the start directory (where TCC.EXE resides). Note that this configuration file is not the same as TCCONFIG.TC, which is the default Integrated Environment version of a configuration file.

How to Use MicroCalc

When you want to compile and run MicroCalc (a spreadsheet program given in several files on distribution disk 3), refer to Appendix G in the *Turbo C Reference Guide*.

Where to Now?

Now that you have loaded the Turbo C files and libraries onto the appropriate floppy disks or hard disk directories, you are ready to start digging into this guide and using Turbo C. But, since this user's guide is written for three different types of users, certain chapters are written with your particular Turbo C programming needs in mind. Take a few moments to read the following, then take off and fly with Turbo C speed!

Programmers Learning C

If you are just now learning the C language, you will want to read Chapters 4 and 5. These are written in tutorial fashion and take you through the process of creating and compiling your first C programs. If you are not sure how to use the Integrated Development Environment, you will need to read Chapter 2. When you are ready to run programs, Chapter 3 shows you how.

Experienced C Programmers

If you are an experienced C programmer, you should have little difficulty porting your programs to this implementation. You will want to read Chapter 8, "Advanced Programming in Turbo C," next for a summary of how Turbo C compares to Kernighan and Ritchie and to the draft ANSI C standard. When you are ready to port or create C programs with Turbo C, you will need to read Chapter 3, "Putting It All Together—Compiling and Running," and Chapter 9, "Advanced Programming in Turbo C."

Turbo Pascal Programmers

Chapter 6, "Notes for Turbo Pascal Programmers," is written specifically for you; in it, we provide some examples that compare Turbo Pascal programs with equivalent Turbo C programs, and we elaborate on some of the significant differences between the two languages.

If you have programmed with Turbo Pascal, you are familiar with the seven basic elements of programming. To get up to speed with Turbo C, you will want to read Chapters 2, 4, and 5. (If you have used another menu-driven Borland product, such as SideKick or Turbo Basic, you will only need to skim Chapter 2.)

Turbo Prolog Programmers

If you have used Turbo Prolog and would like to know how to interface your modules with Turbo C, you should read Chapter 7.

2

The Turbo C Integrated Development Environment

Turbo C is much more than just a fast C compiler; it is a fast, efficient C compiler with an easy-to-learn and easy-to-use Integrated Development Environment. With Turbo C, you don't need to use a separate editor, compiler, linker, and Make software in order to create and run your C programs. All these features are built right into Turbo C, and they are all accessible from one clear and simple display—the Turbo C main screen.

In This Chapter ...

This chapter is divided into two sections: Part I, "Using the Menu System," and Part II, "The Menu Commands."

In Part I, "Using the Menu System," we

- describe the components of the Turbo C main screen
- explain how to use the Turbo C main menu selections
- demonstrate how to get into the Edit window and use the editor (editor commands are covered in Appendix A, "The Turbo C Interactive Editor"

In Part II, "The Menu Commands," we

■ examine and explain each menu item's function
■ summarize the compile-time options

What You Should Read

If you are not familiar with using menu-driven software, you will want to read Part I first. If you are well-versed in working with menu-driven products, such as SideKick or Turbo Prolog, you may want to skip Part I and turn directly to Part II.

How To Get Help

Turbo C, like other Borland products, gives context-sensitive on-screen help at the touch of a single key. You can get help at any point within any Turbo C menu.

To call up Help, press *F1*. The Help window details the functions of the item on which you're currently positioned. Any Help screen may contain a *keyword* (a highlighted item) on which you can get more information. Use the arrow keys to move to any keyword and press *Enter* to get more detailed Help on the selected item. You can use the *Home* and *End* keys to go to the first and last keywords on the screen, respectively.

If you want to return to a previous Help screen while either in or out of the Help system, press *Alt-F1*. (You can back up through 20 previous Help screens.) To get to the Help Index, press *F1* again once you're in the Help system. To exit from Help and return to your menu selection, press *Esc* (or any of the *hot keys* described in the next section).

Part I: Using the Menu System

When you load Turbo C (type `tc` and press *Enter* at the DOS prompt), the start-up screen includes the main screen and product version information (pressing *Alt-F10* any time will bring up this version information). When you press any key, the version information disappears but the main screen remains (see Figure 2.1). Look closely at the main screen; it consists of four parts: the main menu, the Edit window, the Message window, and the Quick Reference (Quick-Ref) Line.

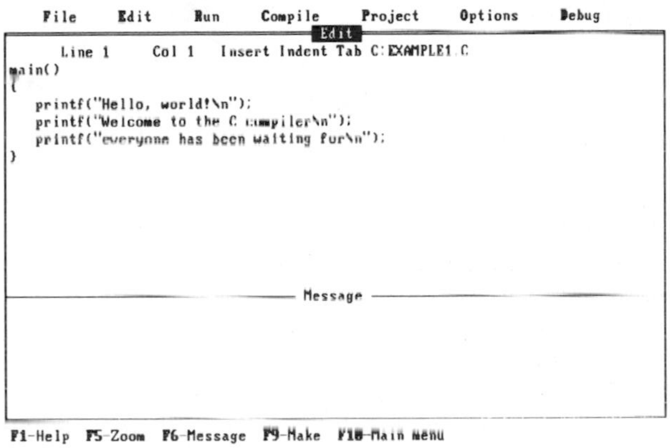

Figure 2.1: Turbo C's Main Screen

To gain familiarity with the Turbo C system, here are some navigating basics:

From within a menu:

- Use the highlighted capital letter to select a menu item, or use the arrow keys to move to the option and press *Enter*.
- Press *Esc* to exit a menu.
- Press *Esc* when in the main menu to go to the previously active window. (When active, the window will have a double bar at its top and its name will be highlighted.)
- Press *F6* to get from any menu level to the previously active window.

- Use the *Right* and *Left* arrow keys to move from one pull-down menu to another.

From anywhere in Turbo C:

- Press *F1* to get information about your current position (help on running, compiling, etc.).
- Press *F10* to invoke the main menu.
- Press *Alt* plus the first letter of any *main* menu command (F, E, R, C, P, O, D) to invoke the specified command. For example, from anywhere in the system pressing *Alt-E* will take you to the Edit window; *Alt-F* takes you to the File menu.

From within the Edit or Message window:

- Press *F5* to zoom/unzoom.
- Press *F6* to switch windows.

Note: To exit Turbo C and return to DOS, go to the File menu and select **Quit** (press *Q* or move the selection bar to **Quit** and press *Enter*). If you select **Quit** without saving your current work file, the editor will query whether you want to save it or not.

Before we describe the various menu options available to you, there are a number of *hot keys* (short cuts) you should be aware of. Hot keys are keys set up to perform a certain function. For example, as discussed previously, pressing *Alt* and the first letter of a main menu command will take you to the specified option's menu or perform an action (see Figure 2.2 for a graphic example). The only other *Alt*/first-letter command is *Alt-X*, which is really just a short cut for **File/Quit**.

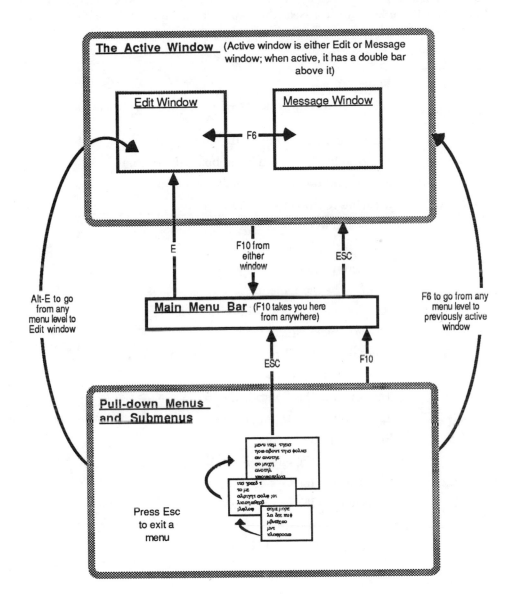

Figure 2.2: A Sample Use of Hot Keys

Table 2.1 lists all of the hot keys you can use while in Turbo C. Remember that when these keys are pressed, their specific function is carried out no matter where you are in the Turbo C environment.

Table 2.1: Turbo C's hot keys

Key(s)	Function
F1	Brings up a Help window with info about your current position
F2	Saves the file currently in the Editor
F3	Lets you load a file (an input box will appear)
F5	Zooms and unzooms the active window
F6	Switches to the active window
F7	Takes you to the previous error
F8	Takes you to the next error
F9	Performs a "make"
F10	Invokes the main menu
Alt-F1	Brings up the last Help screen you referenced
Alt-F3	Lets you pick a file to load
Alt-F9	Compiles to .OBJ (the file loaded in the Editor)
Alt-F10	Displays the version screen
Alt-C	Takes you to the **C**ompile menu
Alt-D	Takes you to the **D**ebug menu
Alt-E	Puts you in the Editor
Alt-F	Takes you to the **F**ile menu
Alt-O	Takes you to the **O**ptions menu
Alt-P	Takes you to the **P**roject menu
Alt-R	Runs your program
Alt-X	Quits Turbo C and takes you to DOS

Menu Structure

Figure 2.3 shows the complete structure of Turbo C's main menu and its successive pull-down menus. There are three general types of items on the Turbo C menus: commands, toggles and settings.

Commands perform a task (running, compiling, storing options, and so on).

Toggles switch a Turbo C feature *on* or *off* (Link map, Test stack overflow, and so on) or cycle through and select one of several options by repeatedly pressing the *Enter* key till you reach the item desired (such as Instruction set or Calling convention).

Settings allow you to specify certain compile-time and run-time information to the compiler, such as directory locations, names of files, macro definitions, etc.

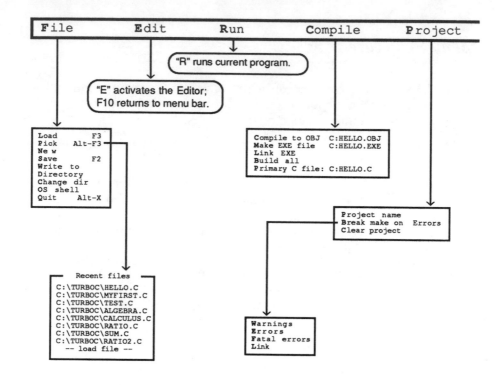

```
  File          Edit          Run          Compile          Project
```

"R" runs current program.

"E" activates the Editor;
F10 returns to menu bar.

```
Load        F3
Pick     Alt-F3
New
Save        F2
Write to
Directory
Change dir
OS shell
Quit     Alt-X
```

```
Compile to OBJ   C:HELLO.OBJ
Make EXE file    C:HELLO.EXE
Link EXE
Build all
Primary C file: C:HELLO.C
```

```
Project name
Break make on  Errors
Clear project
```

```
        Recent files
C:\TURBOC\HELLO.C
C:\TURBOC\MYFIRST.C
C:\TURBOC\TEST.C
C:\TURBOC\ALGEBRA.C
C:\TURBOC\CALCULUS.C
C:\TURBOC\RATIO.C
C:\TURBOC\SUM.C
C:\TURBOC\RATIO2.C
   -- load file --
```

```
Warnings
Errors
Fatal errors
Link
```

Navigating in Turbo C

From within a menu:
- The initial (highlighted) letter always selects the menu item.
- Use Esc to exit a menu. (From the main menu, use Esc to return to the previously active window.)
- F6 goes from any menu level to the previously active window (either the Edit or Message window).

From anywhere in Turbo C:
- Alt plus the first letter of any main menu command (F, E, R, C, P, O, D) invokes that command. E.g, Alt-E goes from anywhere into the Edit window; Alt-F pulls down the File menu.
- F1 calls up context-sensitive help information.
- F10 takes you to the main menu.
- Alt-X quits Turbo C.

Figure 2.3: Turbo C's Menu Structure

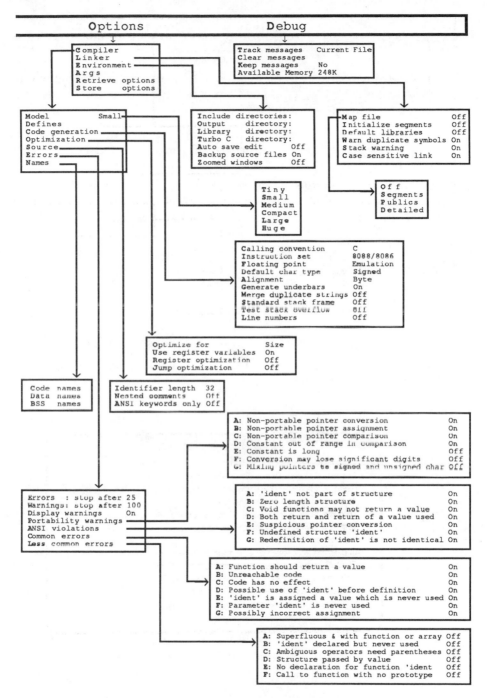

Figure 2.4: Turbo C's Menu Structure, continued

Menu-Naming Conventions

In this book, we will refer to all menu items by an abbreviated name. The abbreviated name for a given menu item is represented by the sequence of letters you type to get to that item from the main menu. For example:

- At the main menu, the menu offering compile-time options related to error messages is **Options/Compiler/Errors**; we'll tell you to select **O/C/Errors** (press *O C E*, in that order).

- At the main menu, the menu for specifying the name of the Include directories is the **Options/Environment/Include** directories; we'll tell you to select **O/E/Include** (press *O E I*, in that order).

The Main Menu

File   Edit   Run   Compile   Project   Options   Debug

Figure 2.5: Turbo C's Main Menu Bar

At the top of the main screen is the Turbo C main menu bar (see Figure 2.5), which offers seven selections:

File   Handle files (loading, saving, picking, creating, writing to disk), manipulates directories (listing, changing), quitting the program, and invokes DOS.

Edit   Lets you create and edit source files.

Run   Automatically compiles, links, and runs your program.

Compile   Compiles and makes your programs into object and executable files.

Project   Allows you to specify what files are in your program and manage your project.

Options   Allows you to select compiler options (such as memory model, compile-time options, diagnostics, and linker options) and define macros. Also records the Include, Output, and Library file directories, saves compiler options, and loads options from the configuration file.

Debug   Allows you to track your errors or manage error messages.

Note that two main menu items have only one option: Edit simply invokes the editor; Run simply runs your programs. Several of the other menu items, however, lead to pull-down menus with many options and/or subsequent menus.

The Quick-Ref Lines

Whether you're in one of the windows or one of the menus, a default Quick-Ref line appears at the bottom of the screen. This line provides at-a-glance function-key help for your current position.

To see a summary of what other key combinations do in a different setting, hold down the *Alt* key for a few seconds. The Quick-Ref line changes to describe what function will be performed when you combine other keys with this key.

When you're in the main menu, the default Quick-Ref line looks like this:

```
F1-Help  F5-Zoom  F6-Edit  F9-Make  F10-Main Menu
```

When you hold down the *Alt* key, a summary of *Alt* key combinations is displayed. It looks like this:

```
Alt-F1-Last help  Alt-F3-Pick  Alt-F9-Compile    Alt-X-Exit
```

The Edit Window

In this section, we describe the components of the Turbo C Edit window and explain how to work in the window.

First, to get into the Edit window, go to the Edit option on the main menu and press *Enter* (or press E from anywhere on the main menu). To get into the Edit window from anywhere in the system, including from the Message window, just press *Alt-E*. (Remember, *Alt-E* is just a short cut for *F10 E*.) Once you're in the Edit window, notice that there are double lines at the top of it and its name is highlighted—that means it's the active window.

Besides the body of the Edit window, where you can see and edit several lines of your source file, the Turbo C Edit screen has two information lines you should note: an Edit status line and the Quick-Ref line.

The Edit status line at the top of the Edit window gives information about the file you are editing, where in the file the cursor is located, and which editing modes are activated:

`    Line    Col    Insert    Indent    Tab    C:FILENAME.EXT`

`Line n`	Cursor is on file line number *n*.
`Col n`	Cursor is on file column number *n*.
`Insert`	Insert mode is *on*; toggle Insert mode *on* and *off* with *Insert* or *Ctrl-V*. See Appendix A for an explanation of Insert and Overwrite mode.
`Indent`	Autoindent is *on*. Toggle it *off* and *on* with *Ctrl-O I*. See Appendix A for an explanation of autoindent.
`Tab`	Tab mode is *on*. Toggle it *on* and *off* with *Ctrl-O T*.
`C:FILENAME.EXT`	The drive (C:), name (FILENAME), and extension (.EXT) of the file you are editing.

The Quick-Ref line at the bottom of the screen displays which hot keys perform what action:

`F1-Help    F5-Zoom    F6-Message    F9-Make    F10-Main menu`

To select one of these functions, press the listed key:

`F1-Help`	Opens a Help window that provides information about the Turbo C editor commands.
`F5-Zoom`	Makes the active window full screen. Toggle *F5* to get back to the split-screen environment.
`F6-Message`	In this case, *F6* takes you to the Message window; in general, *F6* switches between windows. Press it once more to make the Edit window active again.
`F9-Make`	Makes your .EXE file.
`F10-Main menu`	Invokes the main menu.

The editor uses a command structure similar to that of SideKick's Notepad and Turbo Pascal's editor; if you're unfamiliar with the editor these products use, Appendix A describes the editor commands in detail. Page 35 lists some of the most commonly used commands.

If you're entering code in the editor while you're in Insert mode, you can press *Enter* to end a line (the editor has no word-wrap). The maximum line width is 248 characters; the Edit window is 77 columns wide. If you type past column 77, the window scrolls as you type. The Edit window's status line gives the cursor's location in the file by line and column.

After you've entered your code into the Edit window, press *F10* to invoke the main menu. Your file will remain onscreen; you need only press *E* (for Edit) at the main menu to return to it.

Quick Guide to Editor Commands

Here is a summary of the editor commands you will use most often:

- Scroll the cursor through your text with the *Up/Down, Left/Right,* and *PgUp/PgDn* keys.
- Delete a line with *Ctrl-Y.*
- Delete a word with *Ctrl-T.*
- Mark a block with *Ctrl-K B* (beginning) and *Ctrl-K K* (end).
- Move a block with *Ctrl-K V.*
- Copy a block with *Ctrl-K C.*
- Delete a block with *Ctrl-K Y.*

See Appendix A for a more detailed explanation of the editor commands.

How to Work with Source Files in the Edit Window

When you invoke the Edit window before loading a particular file, the Turbo C editor automatically names the file NONAME.C. At this point you have all the features of the editor at your fingertips. You can

- create a new source file either as NONAME.C or another file name
- load and edit an existing file
- pick a file from a list of edit files, and then load it into the Edit window
- save the file seen in the Edit window
- write the file in the editor to a new file name
- alternate between the Edit window and the Message window for finding and correcting compile-time errors

While you are creating or editing a source file, but before you have compiled it, you do not need the Message window. So you can press *F5* to zoom the Edit window to full screen. Press *F5* again to unzoom the Edit window (return to split-screen mode).

Creating a New Source File

To create a new file, select either of the following methods:

- At the main menu, select File/New, then press *Enter*. This opens the Edit window with a file named NONAME.C.

- At the main menu, select File/Load. The Load File Name prompt box opens; type in the name of your new source file. (Pressing the shortcut *F3* from within the Edit window will accomplish the same thing.)

Loading an Existing Source File

To load and edit an existing file, you can select two options: File/Load or File/Pick.

If you select File/Load at the main menu, you can

- Type in the name of the file you want to edit; paths are accepted—for example, C:\TURBOC\TESTFILE.C.

- Enter a mask in the Load File Name prompt box (using the DOS wildcards * and ?), and press *Enter*. Entering *.* will display all of the files in the current directory as well as any other directories. Directory names are followed by a backslash (\). Selecting a directory displays the files in that directory. Entering C:*.C, for example, will bring up *only* the files with that extension in the root directory.

    Press the *Up/Down* and *Left/Right* arrow keys to highlight the file name you want to select. Then press *Enter* to load the selected file; you are placed in the Edit window.

- At the main menu, invoke the editor by pressing *E*. This opens the Edit window with the current edit file (or with the default file name NONAME.C if no other edit file has been loaded).

If you select File/Pick (see the discussion of the Pick option later in this chapter), you can

- Press *Alt-F* then *P* to bring up your pick list (or press the short cut *Alt-F3*).

- Use the *Up* and *Down* arrow keys to move the selection bar to the file of your choice.

Pick lets you quickly pick the name of a previously loaded file.

Saving a Source File

- From anywhere in the system, press *F2*.
- From the main menu, select **File/Save**.

Writing an Output File

You can write the file in the Editor to a new file or overwrite an existing file. You can write to the current (default) directory or specify a different drive and directory.

At the main menu, select **File/Write to**. Then, in the New Name prompt box, enter the full path name of the new file name:

```
C:\DIR\SUBDIR\FILENAME.EXT
```

and press *Enter*.

- C: (optional) is the drive.
- \DIR\SUBDIR\ represent optional directories.
- FILENAME.EXT is the name of the output file and its extension (the extension .C is assumed; append a period (.) at the end of your file name if you don't want an extension name).

Press *Esc* once to return to the main menu, twice to go back to the active window (the editor). You can also press *F6* or *Alt-E*.

If FILENAME.EXT already exists, the editor will verify that you want to overwrite the existing file before proceeding.

The Message Window

You will use the Message window to view diagnostic messages when you compile and debug your source files. Turbo C's unique error-tracking feature lists each compiled file's warnings and error messages in the Message window and simultaneously highlights the corresponding position of the appropriate source file in the Edit window (depending upon the settings in the **Debug** menu). Turbo C's error-tracking feature is more fully discussed in Appendix C, "Command-line Options."

When the cursor is in the Message window, the Quick-Ref line looks like this:

F1-Help F5-Zoom F6-Edit F9-Make F10-Main menu

To use one of these features, press the desired key:

F1-Help   Opens a Help window that summarizes the Turbo C error-tracking feature.

F5-Zoom   Expands the Message window to full screen.

F6-Edit   Makes the Edit window active.

F9-Make   Makes the .EXE file.

F10-Main menu   Invokes the main menu.

Part II: The Menu Commands

The main menu contains the major selections you'll use to load, edit, compile, link, debug, and run Turbo C programs. The seven selections include **File**, **Edit**, **Run**, **Compile**, **Project**, **Options**, and **Debug**, each of which will be described here. A few of the options within the main menu pull-downs are actually for use in advanced programming; they are described in more detail in Chapter 3.

Note: The references to "make" in this chapter refer to Project-Make, not to the stand-alone MAKE utility. Project-Make is a program building tool similar to MAKE; refer to Chapter 3 for more on Project-Make. The MAKE utility is described in Appendix D in the *Turbo C Reference Guide*.

The File Menu

The File pull-down menu offers various choices for loading existing files, creating new files, and saving files. When you load a file, it is automatically placed in the editor. When you finish with a file, you can save it to any directory or file name. In addition, from this pull-down you can change to another directory, temporarily go to the DOS shell, or exit Turbo C.

Figure 2.6: The File Menu

Load

Loads a file. You can use DOS-style masks to get a listing of file choices, or you can load a specific file. Simply type in the name of the file you want to load. **Note**: If you enter an incorrect drive or directory, you'll get an error box onscreen. You'll get a verify box if you have an unsaved, modified file in the editor while you're trying to load another file. In either case, the hot keys are disabled until you press the key specified in the error or verify box.

Pick

Lets you pick a file from a list of the previous eight files loaded into the Edit window. The file selected is then loaded into the Editor and the cursor is positioned at the location where you last edited that file. If you select the "`--load file--`" item from the pick list, you'll get a Load File Name prompt box exactly as if you had selected File/Load or *F3*. *Alt-F3* is a short cut to get this list.

You can toggle *on* the Load/save pick list option from within Turbo C's installation program (TCINST) to have Turbo C automatically save the current pick list when you exit Turbo C and then reload that file upon reentering the program. If this option is toggled *off* when you exit Turbo C, your pick list will not be saved.

New

Specifies that the file is to be a new one. You are placed in the editor; by default, this file is called NONAME.C. (You can change this name later when you save the file.)

Save

Saves the file in the Editor to disk. If your file is named NONAME.C and you go to save it, the editor will ask if you want to rename it. From anywhere in the system, pressing *F2* will accomplish the same thing.

Write to

Writes the file to a new name or overwrites an existing file.

Directory

Displays the directory and file set you want (to get the current directory, just press *Enter*). *F4* allows you to change the wildcard mask.

Change dir

Displays the current directory and allows you to change to a specified drive and directory.

OS shell

Leaves Turbo C temporarily and takes you to the DOS prompt. To return to Turbo C, type `exit`. This is useful when you want to run a DOS command without quitting Turbo C.

Quit

Quits Turbo C and returns you to the DOS prompt.

The Edit Command

The Edit command invokes the built-in screen editor.

You can invoke the main menu from the editor by pressing *F10* (or *Alt* and the first letter of the main menu command you desire). Your source text remains displayed on the screen; you need only press *Esc* or *E* at the main menu to return to it (or press *Alt-E* from anywhere).

The Run Command

Run invokes Project-Make, then runs your program using the arguments given in **Options/Args**. (Project-Make is a program building tool similar to the stand-alone MAKE utility; see Chapter 3.) After your program has finished running, you'll get a `Press any key` message; at that point you can press *Alt-V* to get the value returned by the main function.

Note: You can run your executable Turbo C programs from DOS by simply typing the file name (no extension is necessary) at the DOS prompt.

The Compile Menu

You will use the items on the Compile menu to Compile to an .OBJ file, to Make an EXE file, to Link EXE, to Build all, or to set a Primary C file.

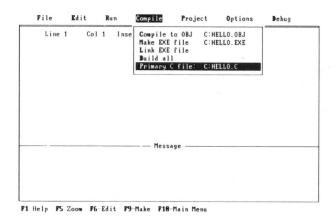

Figure 2.7: The Compile Menu

Compile to OBJ

This menu item is a command. It always displays the name of the file to be produced; for example, `C:EXAMPLE.OBJ`. When selected, it compiles the file. The .OBJ file name listed is derived from one of two names, in the following order:

- the Primary C file name, or if none is specified
- the name of the last file you loaded into the Edit window.

Make EXE file

This menu item is a command that invokes Project-Make. This item always displays the name of the .EXE file to be produced; for example, `C:EXAMPLE.EXE`. When selected, it makes the file.

The .EXE file name listed is derived from one of three names, in the following order:

- the project file (.PRJ) specified in the Project/Project name menu item, or if none is specified
- the Primary C file name, or if none is specified
- the name of the last file you loaded into the Edit window.

Link EXE

Takes the current .OBJ and .LIB files and links them without doing a make; this produces a new .EXE file.

Build all

Rebuilds all of the files in your project regardless of whether they are out of date or not. This option is similar to make except that it is unconditional; make rebuilds only the files that aren't current.

Primary C file:

Use this option to specify which .C file will be compiled to .OBJ (or .EXE if no project name is defined) when you enter the Compile/Compile to OBJ command (*Alt-F9*). (If no project is defined, use the Compile/Make EXE option, *F9*; see the earlier discussion of this option.)

The Primary .C file option is useful (but not required) when you're compiling a single .C file that includes multiple header (.H) files. If an error is found during compilation, the file containing the error (which might be a .C file or a .H file) is automatically loaded into the editor so that you can correct it. (Note that the .H file is *only* automatically loaded if you have changed the default debug settings to Debug/Track messages...All files; using the default settings will not cause an autoload to occur.) The primary .C file is then recompiled when you press *Alt-F9*, even if it is not in the Editor.

When Turbo C is compiling, a window pops up to display the compilation results. When compiling/making is complete, press any key to remove this compiling window. If any errors occurred, you are automatically placed in the Message window at the first error (which is highlighted). This Compile command and its options are explained in more detail in Chapter 3.

The Project Menu

The selections in this pull-down menu allow you to combine multiple source and object files to create finished programs. For more information on **Project**, refer to Chapter 3.

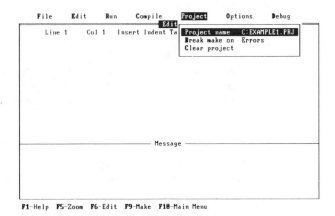

Figure 2.8: The Project Menu

Project Name

Selects a project file containing the names of the files to be compiled and/or linked. The project name is given to the .EXE and .MAP files when they are created.

Break make on

Permits you to specify whether the make should stop after compiling a file that has **Warnings, Errors, Fatal** errors, or before **Linking**.

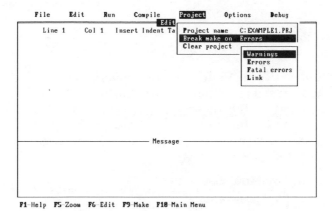

Figure 2.9: The Project/Break Make On Menu

Clear project

Clears the project name and resets the Message window.

The Options Menu

The **O**ptions menu contains settings that determine how the Integrated Environment works. The settings affect things like compiler and linker options, library and include directories, program run-time arguments, and so on. The items on this menu, described in this section, are three commands that call up more menus, one setting, and two commands that perform managerial tasks, as follows:

- Compiler (calls up more menus)
- Linker (calls up more menus)
- Environment (calls up more menus)
- Args (setting)
- Retrieve options (performs task)
- Save options (performs task)

Figure 2.10: The Options Menu

Compiler

These options allow you to specify particular hardware configurations, memory models, debug techniques, code optimizations, diagnostic message control, and macro definitions. The items in this menu, described in the next several pages, are as follows:

- Model
- Defines
- Code generation
- Optimization
- Source
- Errors
- Names

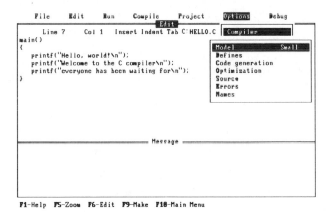

Figure 2.11: The Options/Compiler Menu

The Model Menu

These selections are the different memory model switches available in Turbo C. The memory model chosen determines the default method of memory addressing. If you select Compiler/Model, the options Tiny, Small, Compact, Medium, Large, and Huge appear in a menu. The default memory model is Small, so normally the word "Small" appears to the right of the menu choice Model. Refer to Chapter 9 for more information about these memory models.

Figure 2.12: The O/C/Model Menu

The Defines Menu Item

Selecting **D**efines opens up a macro definition box in which you can pass macro definitions to the preprocessor. Multiple "defines" can be separated by semicolons (;). Values can be optionally assigned with an equal sign (=).

Leading and trailing spaces are stripped, but embedded spaces are left intact. If you want to include a semicolon in a macro, you must place a backslash (\) in front of it.

Here's a macro that defines the symbol *BETA_TEST*, sets *ONE* to 1, and *COMPILER* equal to the string *TURBOC*:

```
BETA_TEST; ONE = 1; COMPILER = TURBOC
```

The Code Generation Menu

These options tell the compiler to prepare the object code in various ways.

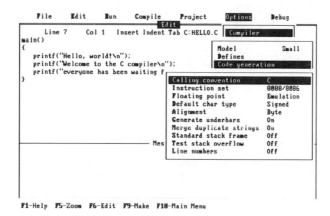

```
     File     Edit     Run     Compile     Project   [Options]   Debug
    ┌─────────────────────────────[Edit]─────────────────────────────┐
    │   Line 7    Col 1   Insert Indent Tab C:HELLO.C │[Compiler   ]  │
    │main()                                     ┌────────────────────┐│
    │{                                          │ Model         Small ││
    │   printf("Hello, world!\n");              │ Defines             ││
    │   printf("Welcome to the C compiler\n");  │[Code generation   ] ││
    │   printf("everyone has been waiting f┌──────────────────────────┐
    │}                                      │ Calling convention    C  │
    │                                       │ Instruction set    8088/8086
    │                                       │ Floating point   Emulation
    │                                       │ Default char type   Signed
    │                                       │ Alignment          Byte
    │                                       │ Generate underbars   On
    │                                       │ Merge duplicate strings On
    │                                       │ Standard stack frame Off
    │                              ─── Mes│ Test stack overflow  Off
    │                                       │ Line numbers        Off
    │                                       └──────────────────────────┘
    │                                                                 │
    │                                                                 │
    └─────────────────────────────────────────────────────────────────┘
    F1-Help  F5-Zoom  F6-Edit  F9-Make  F10-Main Menu
```

Figure 2.10. The O/C/Code Generation Menu

Calling convention:

Causes the compiler to generate either a C calling sequence or a Pascal (fast) calling sequence for function calls. The differences between C and Pascal calling conventions are in the way each handles stack cleanup, number and order of parameters, case and prefix (underbar) of external identifiers.

Do not change this option unless you're an expert and have read Chapter 9 on advanced programming techniques.

Instruction set:

Permits you to specify a different target CPU; this is a toggle between an 8088/8086 instruction and an 80186/80286 instruction. The default generates 8088/8086 code. Turbo C can generate extended 80186 instructions. You will also use this option when generating 80286 programs running in the unprotected mode, such as with the IBM PC AT under MS-DOS 3.x.

Floating point:

Allows for three options:

8087/80287, which generates direct 8087 in-line code

Emulation, which detects whether you have an 8087 and uses it if you do—otherwise, it emulates the 8087 just as accurately but at a slower pace

None, which assumes you're not using floating point. (If None is selected and you use floating-point calculations in your program, you will get link errors.)

Default char type:

Toggles between Signed and Unsigned `char` declarations. If you select Signed, the compiler will treat all `char` declarations as if they were `signed char` type; and vice versa for selecting Unsigned. The default value is Signed.

Merge duplicate strings:

This optimization merges strings when one string matches another; this produces smaller programs.

Alignment:

This allows you to toggle between word-aligning and byte-aligning. When word-aligning, non-character data aligns at even addresses. When byte-aligning, data can be aligned at either odd or even addresses, depending on which is the next available address. Word-alignment increases the speed with which 8086 and 80286 processors fetch and store the data.

Standard stack frame:

Generates a standard stack frame (standard function entry and exit code). Helpful when you use a debugger—simplifies the process of tracing back through the stack of called subroutines.

Test stack overflow:

Generates code to check for a stack overflow at run time. Although this costs space and time in a program, it can be a real life saver; a stack overflow can be a difficult bug to track down.

Generate underbars:

By default, this option is toggled *on*.

Don't change this unless you're an expert and have read Chapter 9 on advanced programming techniques.

Line numbers:

Includes line numbers in the object file (for use by a symbolic debugger). This increases the size of the object file but will not affect size or speed of the executable program.

Since the compiler may group common code from multiple lines of source text together during jump optimization or reorder lines (which makes line-number tracking difficult), we recommend turning *off* **Jump** optimization when using this option.

The Optimization Menu

These options allow you to optimize your code to your own programming needs.

Figure 2.14: The O/C/Optimization Option

Optimize for:

Changes Turbo C's code generation strategy. Normally the compiler uses **O**ptimize for…Size, choosing the smallest code sequence possible. With this item toggled to **O**ptimize for…Speed, the compiler will choose the *fastest* sequence for a given task.

Use register variables:

Suppresses or enables the use of register variables. With this option *on*, register variables are automatically assigned for you. With this option *off*, the compiler does not use register variables even if you have used the `register` keyword (see Appendix C in the *Turbo C Reference Guide* for more details).

Generally, you can keep this option *on* unless you are interfacing to preexisting assembly code that does not support register variables.

Register optimization:

Suppresses redundant load operations by remembering the contents of registers and reusing them as often as possible.

Note: You should exercise caution when using this option because the compiler cannot detect if a register has been modified indirectly by a pointer. Refer to Appendix C in the *Turbo C Reference Guide* for a detailed explanation of this limitation.

Jump optimization:

Reduces the code size by eliminating redundant jumps and reorganizing loops and switch statements. The loop reorganizations can speed up tight inner loops.

The Source Menu

The items on this menu govern how the compiler treats your source code during the initial phases of the compilation.

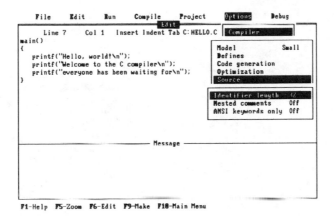

Figure 2.15: The O/C/Source Menu

Identifier length:

Specifies the number of significant characters in an identifier. All identifiers are treated as distinct only if their first *N* characters are distinct. This includes variables, preprocessor macro names, and structure member names. The number given can be any value from 1 to 32; the default is 32.

Nested comments:

Allows you to nest comments in Turbo C source files. Nested comments are not normally allowed in C implementations, and they are not portable.

ANSI Keywords Only:

Toggle to *on* when you want the compiler to recognize only ANSI keywords and treat any Turbo C extension keywords as normal identifiers. These keywords include **near, far, huge, asm, cdecl, pascal, interrupt, _es, _ds, _cs, _ss,** and the register pseudovariables (_AX, _BX, ...). This option also defines the symbol **__STDC__** during compiles.

The Errors Menu

With the selections from this menu, you govern how the Turbo C compiler deals with and responds to diagnostic messages.

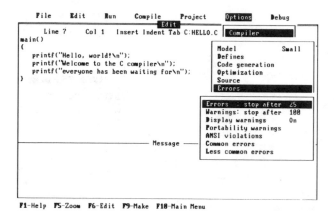

Figure 2.16: The O/C/Errors Menu

Errors: stop after:

This causes compilation to stop after 25 errors have been detected. However, 25 is only the default; you can enter any number from 0 to 255. Entering 0 will cause compilation to continue indefinitely.

Warnings: stop after:

Selecting this option causes the compilation to stop after 100 warnings have been detected. However, 100 is only the default; the legal range is 0 to 255, where entering 0 will cause compilation to continue indefinitely or until the error limit has been reached.

Display warnings:

By default, this is set to *on*, which means that any or all of the following warning types can be displayed if selected:

Portability warnings

ANSI violations

Common errors

Less common errors

When this item is *off*, none of the warnings will be displayed. These warning messages are discussed in more detail in Appendices B and C in the *Turbo C Reference Guide*.

Figure 2.17: Displaying the Common Errors

The Names Menu

With the items in this menu, you can change the default segment, group, and class names for Code, Data, and BSS sections.

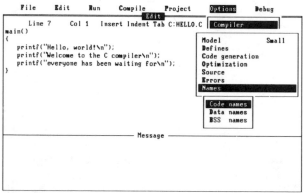

Figure 2.18: The O/C/Names Option

When you select one of these items, the asterisk (*) on the next menu that appears tells the compiler to use the default names.

Don't change this option unless you are an expert and have read Chapter 9 on advanced programming techniques.

Linker

The items in this menu deal with setting options for the linker. Refer to Appendix D in the *Turbo C Reference Guide* for more information about these settings.

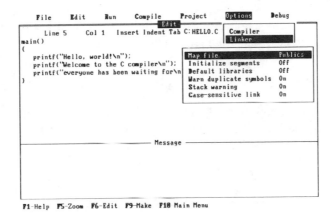

Figure 2.19: The Options/Linker Menu

Map file

Selects the type of map file to be produced. For values other than **Off**, the map file is placed in the output directory defined in **O/E/Output** directory. By default, this is set to the **Off** option; your other choices are **Segments**, **Publics**, and **Detailed**.

Initialize segments

Tells the linker to initialize uninitialized segments. (This is normally not needed.)

Default libraries

When you're linking with modules that have been created by a compiler other than Turbo C, the other compiler may have placed a list of default libraries in the object file.

If this option is *on*, the linker will try to find any undefined routines in these libraries as well as the default libraries supplied by Turbo C.

If this option is *off*, only the default libraries supplied by Turbo C will be searched; any defaults in .OBJ files will be ignored.

Warn duplicate symbols

Turns *on* and *off* the Linker warning for duplicate symbols in object and library files. The default is *off*.

Stack warning

Disables the `No stack specified` message generated by the linker.

Case-sensitive link

Turns *on* and *off* case sensitivity during linking. Normally, this option will be *on*, since C is a case-sensitive language.

Environment

This menu's entries tell Turbo C where to find the files it needs to compile, link, and provide Help. Some miscellaneous options permit you to tailor the Turbo C working environment to suit your programming needs.

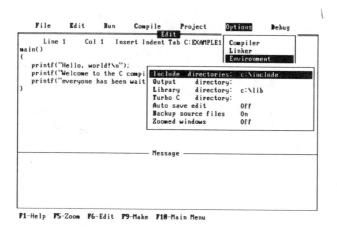

Figure 2.20: The Options/Environment Menu

Include directories

Specifies the directories that contain your standard include files. Standard include files are those given in angle brackets (<>), such as `#include` *<myfile.h>*. Multiple directories are separated by semicolons (;). See Chapter 3 for more information about this option.

Output directory

Your .OBJ, .EXE, and .MAP files are stored here; Turbo C looks for them here when doing a **Make** or **Run**. If the entry is blank, this implies that the files are stored in the current directory. (If they aren't, you'll get errors when you try to do a **Run** or **Make**.)

Library directory

Specifies the directory that contains your Turbo C start-up object files (CO?.OBJ) and run-time library routines (.LIB files).

Turbo C directory

This is used by the Turbo C system to find the configuration file (.TC) and the help file (TCHELP.TCH). For Turbo C to find your default configuration file (TCCONFIG.TC) at startup (if it's not in your current directory), you must install this path with TCINST, the external installation program.

Auto save edit

Helps prevent loss of your source file by automatically saving your edit file (if it's been modified) when you use **Run** or **OS** shell.

Backup source files

By default, Turbo C automatically creates a backup of your source file when you do a **Save**. It saves the backup copy using the same file name and a .BAK extension. This activity can be turned *off* and *on* with this option.

Zoomed windows

Zoomed *on* expands the Edit and Message windows to full screen. You can still switch between them, but only one window at a time will be visible. Zoomed *off* returns to the split-screen environment containing both the Edit and Message windows.

Args

This setting allows you to give your running programs command-line arguments exactly as if you had typed them on the DOS command line (redirection is not supported). It is only necessary to give the arguments here; the program name is omitted.

Retrieve options

Loads the configuration file previously saved with the Store options command.

Store options

Saves all your selected Compiler, Linker, Environment, Debug, and Project options in a configuration file (the default file is TCCONFIG.TC). On start-up, Turbo C looks in the current directory for TCCONFIG.TC; if the file's not found, then Turbo C looks in the Turbo directory for the same file.

The Debug Menu

The selections in this menu allow you to tailor your compilation for debugging. The information presented here is just an overview; refer to Chapter 3 for more details about error tracking and these selections.

Figure 2.21: The Debug Menu

Track messages

Turbo C will track errors in the editor when you scroll through the Message window. This three-way toggle tells Turbo C which files to track in.

The default (Track...Current file) will only track errors in the file currently in the editor. Track...All files will load and track in every file for which there is a message. You can also turn tracking *off*.

Clear messages

Clears the error messages from the Message window.

Keep messages

This is a toggle; when it is *on*, Turbo C saves the error messages currently in the Message window, appending any messages from further compiles to the window. When a file is compiled, any messages for that file are removed from the Message window and new messages are added to the end. When this toggle is *off*, messages are automatically cleared before a compile or make.

Available memory

This item is provided for your information only; it is not selectable. It indicates the amount of memory you have left for compilation.

3

Putting It All Together—Compiling and Running

Turbo C provides a flexible environment for C program development; it comes with default option settings to get you started, but you can easily change these defaults to best meet your programming needs. Turbo C also provides various support tools to perform the routine chores associated with program development, such as error tracking and file-system management.

If you are not familiar with Borland's easy-to-use Integrated Environment, you should look over Chapter 2 before compiling and running your programs through Turbo C's menu system. It is a logical and easy system to learn, and it won't take long to understand.

In This Chapter...

Because you can compile and run your Turbo C programs either from the Integrated Environment or from a standard DOS command line, we discuss both processes in this chapter. However, because the Integrated Environment is a complete package, powerful and easy to use, we think you will want to know about it first.

We begin this chapter with a discussion of how you compile and link Turbo C source files through the Integrated Environment to produce executable programs. Turbo C's interactive error-tracking feature assists you in debugging and perfecting your programs; we demonstrate it in the discussion of compiling and linking.

After we show you how to compile and remove errors from your source files, we provide additional information on how to set the compiler and linker options to fit your program.

Then we demonstrate how to run your programs from the Integrated Environment; we also introduce Turbo C's built-in Project facility, Project-Make, and demonstrate how to use it.

After showing you how to run programs within the Integrated Environment, we explain how to use command lines for compiling, linking, making (rebuilding), and running your Turbo C programs. In addition to the Integrated Environment version of Turbo C, your package includes stand-alone compiler, linker, and MAKE utilities. Specific details on these stand-alone programs are given in Appendices C and D.

Compiling and Linking from the Integrated Environment

Building a new program in the Turbo C Integrated Development Environment usually entails going through the following steps.

1. Set environment options so the compiler and linker know where to find and store things.
2. Load the program you want to build into the editor. (Note: If the program consists of more than one module, you need to create a project file that lists the names of your modules.)
3. Build the executable program file.

The exact content of these general steps differs depending on whether you're working with one file or several files as your source.

Building a Single-Source Program

For the moment let's assume you're building the single source file program provided on disk (HELLO.C). Later we will explain how to build programs from more than one module. There are six steps necessary—from starting Turbo C to running the program.

Step 1: Load Turbo C

Load Turbo C by typing `tc` on the DOS command line.

There are several ways you can tell DOS where to find the Turbo C program:

- TC.EXE can be in the current directory
- TC.EXE can be in another directory and that directory is in the DOS path (see PATH in your DOS manual).
- TC.EXE can be in another directory and, in 3.x versions of DOS, you can type the path name to TC.EXE directly on the command line; for example, `\TURBOC\TC`.

The Integrated Environment will accept two command-line arguments: a file name of the file to be loaded into the editor, and a /c switch immediately followed by another file name. These two arguments can be in any order. Thus,

```
tc hello /cmyconfig
```

will place HELLO.C in the editor and will load the configuration file MYCONFIG.TC. (Note that there is no space between the `/c` switch and the file name and that the default extension .C is assumed for the edit file and the default extension .TC is assumed for the configuration file.)

Step 2: Select the example program

Select the drive and directory that contain the example program. Do this by going to the pull-down file menu by pressing *Alt-F* (or one of the other methods described in Chapter 2). Then select **Change dir** and type in the name of the directory that contains the example program. This directory becomes the current directory.

(**Note:** When the New Directory prompt box comes up, it lists the current directory. You can use this to check what directory you are in; simply press *Esc* to get back to the menus without changing the current directory.)

Step 3: Set up your working environment

Set up and save your working environment by pressing *Alt-O* to quickly invoke the **Options** command from the main menu bar. Select Environment to call up a pop-up submenu. You will need two of the items on this submenu: Include directories, Library directory.

Select Include directories, then type the name of the drive and directory that contains the Turbo C standard include files (.H files) and press *Enter*.

Now select Library directory, and type in the name of the drive and directory that contains the Turbo C library and start-up files.

(If you wish, you may set the **O**utput directory in the same submenu in the same way. If you do select an output directory, all compiler and linker output will be written to that directory instead of to the current directory. In our example case, this is not necessary.)

For most simple cases, this is all the setup necessary for building C programs.

You can save these settings in a configuration file that can be automatically loaded when you start Turbo C. When starting, Turbo C looks in the current directory for a file called TCCONFIG.TC, which it loads if found. Thus, when working on a particular program it is useful to have a default configuration file in the same directory as the program and to start Turbo C from that directory. However, if the configuration file is not found in the current directory Turbo C looks in the Turbo C directory. So you can keep one general purpose configuration file in the Turbo C directory and specify ones in the source directories that use different settings. **Note:** You must use the TCINST installation program to set the Turbo directory.

Press *Esc* to get back to the **O**ptions menu. Select **S**tore options to write the current options to disk. The default file, TCCONFIG.TC, will be written to the current directory. If you wish, you can give the configuration file another name by typing in the new name and pressing *Enter*. If you do this, however, you will need to *explicitly* load this configuration file, either on the TC command line with the /c switch, or by using the **O**ptions menu item **R**etrieve options.

Step 4: Load the example into the editor

Press *F3* (load file) to read in the example program. You can explicitly type in the name of the program, or you can use a wildcard (*.C) to get a list of file names, use the cursor keys to move to the file you want, and then press *Enter* to read it. After the file is loaded, the Edit window is active and you can edit the source file (editing the source file isn't necessary in this example, however).

The file should look like this:

```
#include <stdio.h>

main ()
{
    printf("Hello world\n");
}
```

Step 5: Build the executable file

The Compile menu tells you the name of the file that will be compiled and the name of the EXE that will be built. When no project name is defined, Turbo C assumes it can build an executable file with the information you have already given it. It looks first at the Primary C file and then at the last file you loaded in the editor to determine what the executable file name is. It then proceeds as if you had defined a project file with only that one name in it (more on project files later).

In this simple case of a single file program, you can compile, link, and run the program without building a project file. To build an executable file, you must compile the source and link the object file with the standard start-up and libraries. Though there are other approaches, the easiest way to do this is to press *F9* (Make) or select the Compile menu and press *Enter* on the Make EXE file option.

Step 6: Run the program

At this point, you should have an executable program. To run it, press *Alt-R* or select Run on the main menu. (**Note:** You can run your executable program from the DOS command line by simply typing the file name, minus its extension.)

Debugging

Tracking and fixing errors in programs is always one of the more frustrating aspects of programming. One of the best reasons to use the Turbo C Integrated Environment, however, is to fix syntax errors and evaluate any warnings the compiler gives you. Turbo C collects compiler and linker messages in a buffer and then displays them in the Message window. This lets you look at the messages all at once while still giving you direct access to your source.

To try this out, add some syntax errors to the example program. Remove the # from the include statement on the first line. Next take out the trailing quotation mark in the **printf** string on the fifth line. The now-buggy file should look like this:

```
include <stdio.h>

main ()
{
    printf("Hello world\n);
}
```

Now compile the file again by pressing *Alt-F9* (Compile). The Compiling window will tell you how many errors and warnings you have introduced (there should be three errors and no warnings).

The Message Window

When you see the message `Press any key` in the Compiling window, just press the space bar. You will be taken to the Message window where a highlight bar is placed on the first error or warning. Since the first error occurred in the file that is currently in the editor, you will also see a highlighted line in the Edit window. This marks the place in your source code where the compiler generated the error or warning.

At this point you can use the cursor keys to move the Message window's highlight bar up and down to view other messages. Notice how the highlight bar in the Edit window tracks where the compiler thinks each error occurred in your source. When you place the highlight bar on the "compiling" message, the editor shows you the last place you were in that file.

If the text in the Message window is too long to see, you can use the left and right arrow keys to scroll the message horizontally. To view more messages at once, you can zoom the Message window by pressing *F5* (Zoom). When the Message window is zoomed, you cannot see the Edit window, so no tracking occurs. For now, leave the windows in split-screen mode.

Correcting a Syntax Error

To correct an error, place the Message window highlight bar on the first error message and then press *Enter*. Your cursor shifts to the Edit window and is placed at the spot that generated the error message. Notice that the status line of the editor shows the message you selected (this is useful when you work in zoomed mode). You can now correct the error that generated the message. (You'll have to put back the # in the first line that you took out earlier.)

Since there is more than one error message, there are two ways to proceed to fix the next error.

The first method is to return to the Message window by pressing *F6* (Message) and selecting the next message you want to fix, as previously described.

However, you do not need to return to the Message window to get to the next error. Instead, you can simply press *F8* (Next error) and the editor will place the cursor at the location of the error listed next in the message window. Note that the message shown in the status line and the highlighted line in the Message window change as you move from one error to the next. You can also move backward by pressing *F7* (Previous error).

There are certain advantages to both these methods, and usually circumstances dictate which method is preferable. Sometimes one silly mistake in the source can confuse the compiler, producing many messages. In this case, selecting and fixing the first message makes the next few error messages moot. When this happens, it is more convenient to use method one—to return to the Message window after fixing the first error, to scroll down to the next meaningful message, then to select it. In other cases, however, you may wish to check each message in sequence; pressing *F8* (Next error) in this case is more effective.

Remember that *F7* and *F8* (Previous error and Next error) are *hot keys*, i.e., they work from anywhere within Turbo C. Thus if you are in the Message window and you press *F8* (Next error), you don't get the message that is currently highlighted but the one after it. (If you want to select the current message, press *Enter.*) If there are no further compiler messages, *F8* (Next error) has no effect. **Note:** Linker messages are not selectable and will not track in your source.

In the course of fixing syntax errors, it is often necessary to add and delete text. The editor keeps track of this: When you proceed to the next error, it correctly positions the cursor on the error. You don't need to remember line numbers or to keep track of added or deleted lines of text.

Using Multiple Source Files

One of the great things about Turbo C is its ability to handle separate compilation of multiple source files. And Turbo C's Project-Make facility makes it even nicer.

In the earlier example, there was only one source file so that you could use the **Compile/Make** option to make an executable file without having to define a project file. When building a program from multiple C source files, however, it is necessary to tell Turbo C exactly which files are involved; i.e., to create a project file.

Don't panic. Creating a project file is as simple as listing the names of your C source files. Even though you will see that you can pack a lot of power into making a project, for now, let's start simple—with a two-file program.

A basic case is to have a main program file and a support file that defines functions or data that is referenced from the main file. For example, the main file called MYMAIN.C might look like this:

```
#include <stdio.h>
main (int argc, char *argv[])
{
  char *s;

  if (argc > 1)
    s = argv[1];
  else
    s = "the universe";

  printf("%s %s.\n",GetString(),s);

}
```

And the support file called MYFUNCS.C might look like this:

```
char ss [] = "The restaurant at the end of";

char *GetString(void)
{
   return ss;
}
```

These two files now give you something to work with to build a project file. As you can probably guess, the project file simply contains two lines naming the files to be compiled and linked. Call the project file MYPROG.PRJ. It looks like this:

```
mymain
myfuncs
```

That's all. Turbo C assumes any file without an extension is a .C file (though you may add the .C if you want to). Also, the order is not important except that it determines the order in which files are compiled. The following project file would have the same end result:

```
myfuncs
mymain
```

Notice that the name of the project file (MYPROG.PRJ) is not the same as the name of the main file (MYMAIN.C). The two names could have been the same (but not the extensions), but they do not have to be. The important thing to remember is that the name of your executable file (and any map file produced by the linker) will be based on the project file's name. In this case the executable file will be MYPROG.EXE (and possibly a map file called MYPROG.MAP).

Also note that you can specify complete path names for any of the files listed in the project file. In this way, you can build a program without having all the source files in the same directory.

Go ahead and type in the three files described previously, MYMAIN.C, MYFUNCS.C, and MYPROG.PRJ.

Building a Multi-Source File Program

Now that you have a project file, all you need to do is tell Turbo C what project you want to make. This is done by entering the name of the project file on the project menu. Press *Alt-P* to get to the Project menu and select **Project name**. You can explicitly type in the name of your project file or you can use wildcards to find it in a list of file names from a directory. (But remember, if you haven't saved the file, it won't be on disk.) Once your project name is entered, you can simply press *F9* (Make) to make the executable file. To run this program, press *Alt-R* (Run).

Note that running a program includes doing a "make." This means that pressing *Alt-R* can initiate a compile and link cycle if the files in the project need to be recompiled. This means you could have omitted the explicit make (*F9*).

Error Tracking Revisited

In the example of a single-file source, you saw that syntax errors that generate compiler warning and error messages can be viewed and selected from the Message window. Likewise, the Message window also handles errors from multiple-file compilations (or "makes").

To see this, introduce some syntax errors into the two files, MYMAIN.C and MYFUNCS.C. From MYMAIN.C, remove the first angle bracket in the first line and remove the *c* in `char` from the fifth line. These changes should generate three errors and three warnings in MYMAIN.

Now load MYFUNCS.C and remove the first *r* from "return" in the fifth line. This change will produce two errors and two warnings.

Editing these files makes them out of date with respect to their object files, so doing a make will recompile them. Since you want to see the effect of tracking in multiple files, you need to modify the criterion that Project-Make uses to decide when to stop. This is done by setting a toggle *on* in the Project menu.

Stopping a Make

There are several reasons why the make cycle stops in Turbo C. Obviously, Project-Make stops once an executable file has been produced. But Project-Make will also stop to report some type of error.

For example, Project-Make will always stop if it can't find one of the source files (or one of the dependency files—to be discussed later) listed in the project file. Also, you can force Project-Make to stop by pressing *Ctrl-Break*.

A make can also stop when the compiler generates messages. You can choose the type of message you want it to stop on by setting the toggle option in the **Project** menu called **Break** make on. This toggle defaults to **Break** make on...Errors—which is normally the setting you'll want to use. However, you can have a make stop after compiling a file with warnings, or with errors, or with fatal errors, or have it stop before it tries to link.

The usefulness of each of these modes is really determined by the way you like to fix errors and warnings. If you like to fix errors and warnings as soon as you see them, you should set the **Break** make on toggle to **Warnings** or maybe to **Errors**. If you prefer to get an entire list of errors in all of the source files before fixing them up, you should set the toggle to **Fatal errors** or to **Link**.

Syntax Errors in Multiple Source Files

To demonstrate errors in multiple files, set the **Break** make on toggle to Fatal errors. To do this, press *Alt-P* to get to the **Project** menu, and select **Break** make on. Now select **Fatal** errors from the submenu.

At this point, you should have introduced syntax errors into MYMAIN.C and MYFUNCS.C. Press *F9* (Make) to "make the project." The Compiling window will show the files being compiled and the number of errors and warnings in each file and the total for the make. When the `Press any key` message flashes, press the space bar.

Your cursor should now be positioned on the first error or warning in the Message window. And if the file that message refers to is in the editor, there will be a highlight bar in the Edit window showing you where the compiler detected a problem. Again, you can scroll up and down in the Message window to view the different messages. Note that there is a "Compiling" message for each source file that was compiled. These messages are not errors or warnings but serve to separate as "file boundaries," separating the various messages generated by each file.

When you scroll down past a file boundary, the Edit window may or may not track in the next file, depending on the setting of the **Track** messages toggle in the **Debug** menu. The default value is to track only in the current file.

Thus, moving to a message that refers to a file other than the one in the editor causes the Edit window's highlight bar to turn off. If you select one of these messages (that is, press *Enter* on it), the file it refers to will be loaded into the editor and you will be placed in the editor with the cursor on the error. If you then return to the Message window by pressing *F6* (Message), tracking will resume in that file.

But by setting the **Track** messages toggle to **All** files, you can track messages across file boundaries. This means that when you scroll through the Message window, Turbo C will automatically load the file into the editor so you can see where each message refers. Try it.

You can also turn tracking off completely, by setting the **Track** messages toggle to Off. In this case, you simply select the message you wish to work on and then press *Enter*. The file the message refers to will then be loaded into the editor with the cursor placed on the error.

Note that *F7* and *F8* (Previous error and Next error) are not affected by the setting of the **Track** messages toggle. These hot keys will always find the next or previous error and will load the file if necessary.

Keeping and Getting Rid of Messages

Normally, whenever you start to make a project, the Message window is cleared out to make room for new messages. Sometimes, however, it is desirable to keep messages around between makes.

Consider the following example: You might have a project that has many source files and you have **B**reak make on set to stop on Errors. In this case, you may get several warning messages in several files, but then one file contains an error so that the make stops. You fix that error and want to find out if the compiler will accept the fix. But if you just do a make or compile again, you will lose your earlier warning messages, which you may yet want to look at. How can you avoid this? All you have to do is to turn on the **K**eep messages toggle in the **D**ebug menu.

When the **K**eep messages toggle is on, messages are not cleared out when you start up a make. The only messages removed are the ones that result from the files you *re*compile. Thus, the old messages for a given file are replaced with any new messages that the compiler may generate.

If at some point you are done with the messages, you can get rid of them by selecting **C**lear messages on the **D**ebug menu. This zaps all the current messages. Turning off **K**eep messages and running another make will also get rid of any old messages.

It's a good idea to get into the habit of clearing the messages when you change projects. To facilitate this, there is a short cut in the **P**roject menu, called **C**lear project, that clears both the project name and the current messages. After selecting **C**lear project, you can define a new project or compile and run single-file programs by simply loading them into the editor or defining the **P**rimary C file name.

The Power of Project Making

In the last description of making a project, you dealt with the most basic situation: just a list of C source file names. Project-Make provides a lot of power to go beyond this simple situation. To see this you need to understand how a make works.

Make works by comparing the date of the source file with the date of the object file generated by the compiler. This comparison of creation dates defines several *implicit dependencies* in a simple project list.

Given the earlier example using MYPROG.PRJ, you have the following dependencies:

MYMAIN.OBJ   is dependent on   MYMAIN.C
MYFUNCS.OBJ   is dependent on   MYFUNCS.C
MYPROG.EXE   is dependent on   MYMAIN.OBJ, MYFUNCS.OBJ, and MYPROG.PRJ

This means the object file MYMAIN.OBJ is out-of-date if MYMAIN.C is newer than MYMAIN.OBJ; thus MYMAIN.C will be recompiled. Notice the executable file is always dependent on all object files in the project and on the project file itself. This latter fact means that if any of the objects or if the project file MYPROG.PRJ itself has a newer date than MYPROG.EXE, the make function will relink MYPROG.EXE. These implicit dependencies arise from the simple list of file names of the C files in your project.

Explicit Dependencies

However, bigger projects require a more sophisticated make facility that allows you to specify explicit dependencies. This is useful when a particular C source file depends on other files. It is common for a C source to include several header files (.H files) that define the interface to external routines. If the interface to those routines changes, you would like the file that uses those routines to be recompiled. This is done with explicit dependencies.

For example, say you have a main program file, MYMAIN.C, that includes a header file MYFUNCS.H. Make will recompile MYMAIN.C and MYFUNCS.C if MYFUNCS.H changes—if you specify the following dependencies in your project file:

```
MYMAIN.C (MYFUNCS.H)
MYFUNCS  (MYFUNCS.H)
```

Notice that this project file makes the MYFUNCS.C file dependent on the MYFUNCS.H file. This is a good consistency check for your files. So now you have the same implicit dependencies as well as some explicit dependencies, like so:

MYMAIN.OBJ   is dependent on   MYMAIN.C, and MYFUNCS.H
MYFUNCS.OBJ   is dependent on   MYFUNCS.C, and MYFUNCS.H
MYPROG.EXE   is dependent on   MYMAIN.OBJ, MYFUNCS.OBJ, and MYPROG.PRJ

Any C file listed in a project file can have as many explicit dependencies as it needs. Simply place the files you want the C source to be dependent on in parentheses, separated by blanks, commas, or semicolons.

For example if you want MYMAIN.C to be dependent on MYFUNCS.H, YOURS.H, and OTHER.H, you would type

```
MYMAIN.C (MYFUNCS.H, YOURS.H, OTHER.H)
```

That is all there is to dependencies. This method gives you the power of more traditional makes without all the hassle of a complicated make syntax.

What? More Make Features?

There are two other features that add to the power of the make function. The first lets you specify external object and library files to be linked into your project, and the second lets you override the standard start-up and libraries.

External Object and Library Files

From time to time, you might want to use some routines that came from another source, such as assembly language or from another compiler. Or maybe you have some library files that perform special functions not provided in the standard libraries. In these cases, you can include the name of the object or library files in your project with an explicit extension. Like so (note that the order when listing files is not important):

```
MYMAIN  (MYFUNCS.H)
MYFUNCS (MYFUNCS.H)
SPECIAL.OBJ
OTHER.LIB
```

When Project-Make sees a file with an explicit .OBJ extension, it simply includes that file in the list of files to be linked together. It does not try to compile it or find its source. Similarly, a name in your project file with a .LIB extension gets put into the list of libraries that the linker searches when trying to resolve external references. Again, it does not try to compile or build the library.

Note that these types of files cannot have explicit dependency lists (they will be ignored if they do). However, feel free to include these names in your C source dependency list like any other file you want your source to depend on.

For example:

```
MYMAIN  (MYFUNCS.H, SPECIAL.OBJ)
MYFUNCS (MYFUNCS.H, OTHER.LIB)
SPECIAL.OBJ
OTHER.LIB
```

What this means is that if for some reason these .OBJ or .LIB files become updated, the C source will be recompiled.

Overriding the Standard Files

In some cases, it is necessary to override the standard start-up or libraries. This is usually reserved for the heavy hackers, and is not a common practice for beginners. But if you ever feel the need, here is how to do it.

To override the start-up file, you must place a file called C0*.OBJ as the *first* name in your project file—where the asterisk (*) can be filled out to any DOS name (for example C0MINE.OBJ). The critical parts are that the name start with C0, that it is the first file in your project, and that it have an explicit .OBJ extension.

To override the standard library, all you need to do is to place a special library name anywhere in the list of names in your project file. The name of the library must start with a C, be two characters in length, and have an explicit .LIB extension. For example, CX.LIB or C1.LIB.

When the standard library is overridden, Make does not try to link in the math libraries as based on the Floating point toggle in the O/C/Code generation menu. If you wish to have these libraries linked in when you override the standard library, you must explicitly include them in your project file.

Compiling and Linking from a Command Line

In addition to using the Integrated Environment, you can run your Turbo C programs with the old-fashioned type of command-line interface. While the Integrated Environment mode is best for developing and running your programs, you may sometimes prefer to use the command line; in some advanced programs, the command-line interface may be the only way to do something intricate. For example, if your Turbo C programs include in-line assembly code, you will need to use the command-line version of Turbo C (TCC) rather than TC, the Integrated Environment version.

TCC compiles C source files and links them together into an executable file. It works similarly to the UNIX CC command. TCC will also invoke MASM to assemble .ASM source files. Note that to *compile only* you have to use the -c option at the command line.

The TCC Command Line

To invoke Turbo C from the command line, enter `tcc` at the DOS prompt and follow it with a set of command-line arguments. Command-line arguments include compiler and linker options, and file names. The generic command-line format is

```
tcc [option option option ...] filename filename ...
```

Options on the Command Line

Each command-line option is preceded by a dash (-), and separated from the `tcc` command, other options, and following file names by at least one space. You can explicitly turn a command-line option *off* by following the option with a dash. (For example, -K- explicitly turns the **unsigned chars** option *off*.) Turbo C's command-line options are described in Appendix C.

File Names on the Command Line

After the list of options, type file names on the command line. The compiler compiles files according to the following set of rules:

filename	compile *filename.c*
filename.c	compile *filename.c*
filename.xyz	compile *filename.xyz*
filename.obj	include as object at link time
filename.lib	include as library at link time
filename.asm	invoke MASM to assemble to .OBJ

The compiler will then invoke the linker and supply the linker with the names of the appropriate C start-up file and standard C libraries.

The Executable File

Normally, the compiler derives the name of the executable file from the first source or object file name supplied on the command line. The executable program is given that first file name with the .EXE extension.

If you want to specify a different name for the executable file, use the -e option. After the `tcc` command and before any file names, enter -e *immediately followed* by the name you want to give the executable file (no white space between the *e* and the file name).

Some Example Command Lines

The following example illustrates proper syntax for invoking Turbo C with a DOS command line:

```
tcc -IB:\include -LB:\lib -etest start.c body.obj end
```

For this example command line, the command `tcc` invokes Turbo C at the DOS prompt. Turbo C then interprets the command-line options as meaning

- The include directory is B:\INCLUDE (`-IB:\include`).
- The libraries are in the B:\LIB directory (`-LB:\lib`).
- The executable result should be placed in a file called TEST.EXE (`-etest`).

Turbo C interprets the listed files to mean that this program consists of

- a source file called START.C to be compiled
- an object file called BODY.OBJ to be included at link time
- another source file called END.C to be compiled

Here is another example of a Turbo C compile-time command line:

```
tcc -IB:\include -LB:\lib2 -mm -C -K s1 s2.c z.asm mylib.lib
```

This compile-time command line directs Turbo C to

- look for the include files in the B:\INCLUDE directory (`-IB:\include`)
- look for the libraries in the B:\LIB2 directory (`-LB:\lib2`)
- use the Medium memory model (`-mm`)
- allow nested comments (`-C`)
- make **char**s unsigned (`-K`)

Turbo C interprets the list of file names to mean that

- The source files called S1.C and S2.C are to be compiled.
- The file Z.ASM is to be assembled (using MASM).
- The executable file will be named S1.EXE.
- The library file MYLIB.LIB is to be linked in at link time.

The TURBOC.CFG File

You can set up a list of options in a configuration file called TURBOC.CFG, which can be used in addition to options entered on the command line. This configuration file contains options as they would be entered on the command line.

You create the TURBOC.CFG file using any standard ASCII editor or word processor (such as the Turbo Editor in the Integrated Environment version). You can list options (separated by spaces) on the same line or list them on separate lines. Then, when you compile your program from the command line, Turbo C uses the options supplied in TURBOC.CFG, in addition to the ones given on the command line.

When TCC starts, it looks for TURBOC.CFG in the current directory. If it doesn't find it there *and* if you're running DOS 3.x, it then looks in the start directory (where TCC.EXE resides). Note that this configuration file is not the same as TCCONFIG.TC, which is the default Integrated Environment version of a configuration file.

Options given on the command line override the same options specified in TURBOC.CFG. This ability to override configuration file options with command-line options is an important one. If, for example, your configuration file contains several options, including the -a option (which you want to turn *off*), you can still use the configuration file but override the -a option by listing -a- in the command line.

How are command-line options and TURBOC.CFG options combined and overridden? Conceptually, the TURBOC.CFG file's list of options is split into two parts: the -I options, and all the other options in the file. The -I options are then appended to the right of the command-line options, and the remaining TURBOC.CFG options are inserted on the left of the command line's list of options (immediately after the tcc command).

Command-line options are evaluated from left to right; any option duplication on the right overrides the same option on the left. Because of the way the command line and TURBOC.CFG are combined, with the TURBOC.CFG -I options on the extreme right, the include directories specified in the command line are the first ones that Turbo C searches for in the include files. This gives the -I directories on the command line priority over those in the configuration file—which is what you want.

The MAKE Utility

Turbo C's stand-alone MAKE utility, a more powerful version of Project-Make, permits you to describe source and object file dependencies; it is based on the UNIX MAKE utility. The MAKE utility evaluates those dependencies to ensure that the files are correctly compiled and linked.

What is the advantage to using a MAKE utility? As with Project-Make, you do not have to keep track of which program components have changed since you last compiled them. Stand-alone MAKE is more powerful than Project-Make, however, because it is a general-purpose program builder. Before linking your complex program's object files, MAKE recompiles any files that need to be updated. Then it simply incorporates the newly compiled files with those that did not need to be recompiled and creates a new, executable program file.

You should read Appendix D (in the *Turbo C Reference Guide*) for more information on MAKE. That appendix contains a detailed explanation of the stand-alone MAKE utility.

Running Turbo C Programs from the DOS Command Line

To run executable Turbo C programs from the DOS command line, simply type the executable file name at the DOS prompt. It is not necessary to include the .EXE extension. For example, to execute the program TEST.EXE, you would just type `test` at the DOS prompt and press *Enter*. The TEST program would then run (execute).

All Together Now: Get a Move On with Turbo C

Now that you have seen how to compile, link, run, and make your Turbo C programs, both with the Integrated Environment and through standard command lines, you are ready to put Turbo C through its paces. As you expand your knowledge about the language and about this implementation, you will want to refer to the second volume of this handbook, the *Turbo C Reference Guide*, for information about the run-time environment, the library files, advanced programming techniques, and Turbo C's implementation of the C language.

If you know Turbo Pascal or Turbo Prolog, you will also want to read Chapters 6 and 7 6 and 7, respectively, for some tips on how to use either of these languages with this fast, powerful C programming package.

C   H   A   P   T   E   R

4

Programming in Turbo C

Have you ever programmed in C before? You may have heard various stories about how C is a difficult language to learn. Nonsense. It is true that some C programmers delight in writing obscure programs that are difficult to read and debug, but there's nothing that says you have to do the same. The basic elements of the C programming language are easy to understand and use.

In This Chapter ...

We will teach you the basic elements of the C language in this chapter, and show you how to use them in your programs. The next chapter, "More About Programming in Turbo C," teaches more about C, while Chapter 9, "Advanced Programming in Turbo C," tells all about memory models, interrupts, assembly-language programming, and other advanced topics.

Of course, we can't teach you everything about programming in C in one or two chapters; there are entire books about that. Two very good new books are on the market for programmers learning C: *Using Turbo C* and *Advanced Turbo C*, both by Herbert Schildt (published by Osborne-McGraw Hill).

Before you work through this chapter, you should read Chapter 2, "The Turbo C Integrated Development Environment," and learn how to use the menus and text editor in Turbo C. You should also have installed Turbo C (made working copies of your Turbo C disks or copied the files onto your hard disk) as described in Chapter 1. Also, be sure that you've created the file TCCONFIG.TC as described in that same chapter; otherwise, Turbo C won't know where the library (\LIB) and include (\INCLUDE) files are.

Once you've done all that, then sit down, turn on your computer (if it isn't already on), and get ready to learn about programming in Turbo C.

Creating Your First Turbo C Program

Tradition has it that your first C program should always be the *Hello, world* program found in the classic work, *The C Programming Language* by Kernighan and Ritchie. Start by typing (from the DOS prompt) the command:

```
tc hello.c
```

This gets you into the Integrated Development Environment version of Turbo C, creates a file named HELLO.C (if it doesn't already exist), and puts you into the Turbo C editor. Now, type in the following program:

```
main()
{
    printf("Hello, world\n");
}
```

Having entered this program, you should save it to disk before going any further; after all, if you should crash your computer system, you'd hate to lose all this work. To save your first Turbo C program to the disk, you can press *F2* or you can select **S**ave from the File menu by pressing *F10 F S*.

Compiling It

Having saved this program, you must do two things before you can run it: compile it and then link it.

To compile your file, you press *Alt-F9* (hold down the *Alt* and *F9* keys at the same time). A second way to compile your file is to explicitly return to the main menu (press *F10*), select *C* to get to the **C**ompile menu, and then press *C* again (for **C**ompile to OBJ).

When compilation is done (which should only take a second or two), a flashing message on-screen will say Success: Press any key. When you press a key, the window will disappear, and your menu bar will be active.

If you've had any warnings or errors, they'll appear in the Message window at the bottom of the screen. You shouldn't get any; so if you do, check to be sure that you've typed the program in exactly as given, then compile it again.

Running It

Once you've compiled without any errors, you're ready to run your program. Since the menus are active, you can just press *R* (for **Run**). If you've gone back into the editor, you can press *Alt-R*; or you can bring up the menus again (press *F10*), then press *R* to select the **Run** command. A new linking window will come up, showing you that Turbo C is now linking in whatever library routines it needs.

Did you get any errors? If you did, it's probably because you haven't told Turbo C where the library files are. If you're still seeing the Linking window, make it go away (press any key), press *F10* then *O* to bring up the Options menu (or use the *Alt-O* short-cut).

Press *E* to select the Environment command, then press *L* to choose the Library directory command. When the Library directory window comes up, type in the complete path name of the subdirectory where you've stored your library files—it's probably A:\TURBOC\LIB or C:\TURBO\LIB—and press *Enter*.

Press *Esc* to make the Environment menu go away, then press *S* (for Store options). A Config File prompt box will come up, with the name TCCONFIG.TC in it. Just press *Enter*, if Turbo C asks if you want to overwrite TCCONFIG.TC, type *Y*.

Finally, press *Esc* to make the Options menu go away, and press *R* to run again.

At this point, Turbo C should successfully link your program. This means that for your program to run Turbo C copies in the necessary subroutines from the run-time libraries. The default memory model is **Small** (see Chapter 9 for more details on memory models), so Turbo C will link in the library routines from CS.LIB.

Having linked your program, Turbo C then runs it. The screen clears, the message Hello, world appears at the top of the screen, and the message Press any key to return to Turbo C... appears at the bottom. Press any key, and the Turbo C display reappears. Congratulations—you've just created your first Turbo C program!

What Happened?

Now get out of Turbo C and look at what you've created. Select the Quit command from the File menu.

At the DOS prompt, type `dir hello.*` and press *Enter*. You'll get a list of files that looks something like this:

```
HELLO.C      42    1-01-80   9:25p
HELLO.OBJ    221   1-01-80   9:26p
HELLO.EXE    4486  1-01-80   9:26p
```

The first file, HELLO.C, contains the text (the *source code*) of your program. You can display it on the screen; just enter (at the DOS prompt) the command `type hello.c`. As you can see, it isn't very big—only 42 bytes long.

The second file, HELLO.OBJ, contains the binary machine instructions (the object code) produced by the Turbo C compiler. If you use the DOS `type` command to display this file on the screen, you'll get mostly gibberish.

The last file, HELLO.EXE, is the actual *executable program* produced by the Turbo Linker. It not only contains the code in HELLO.OBJ, but also has all the necessary support routines (such as **printf**) that the linker copied in from the library file. To run any executable file, you just type its name at the DOS prompt, without the .EXE extension.

At the DOS prompt, type `hello` and press *Enter*. The message `Hello, world` will appear on the screen, and the DOS prompt will come back again. You've now written a working Turbo C program that you can give away to all your friends (who are undoubtedly dying for such a program).

Modifying Your First Turbo C Program

Get back into Turbo C by typing `tc hello.c` at the DOS prompt. You'll find yourself back in the Turbo C editor, with your program already loaded in.

Now you'll modify it so that you can interact with it a little. Edit your program so that it now looks like this:

```
main()
{
   char    name[30];

   printf("What's your name?   ");
   scanf("%s",name);
   printf("Hello, %s\n",name);
}
```

You've added three lines to your program. The first line (char name[30];) declares a variable named *name*, which can hold a string of up to 29 characters (letter, digit, punctuation, etc.). The second added line calls **printf** to write out the message What's your name?. The third added line calls **scanf** to read your name into the variable *name*.

Save your modified program by pressing *F2* or *F10 F S*. Press *F10* to invoke the main menu, then press *R* (for **Run**). Note that Turbo C is smart enough to know that you have modified your program, so it recompiles the program before running it.

This time, when your program runs three things happen: the screen clears, the message What's your name? appears at the top, and the cursor sits waiting after the question mark. Type in your name and press *Enter*. The program now says Hello, <your_name>. Note that it only read the first name you typed in; you'll learn why later in this chapter. For now, press any key on the keyboard to return to Turbo C.

As you write programs, you might make errors or receive warnings. An *error* is a mistake in your program that prevents Turbo C from creating object code. A *warning* is just that: a message to point out a possible problem. Errors and warnings are listed in the Message window. There are many different errors and warnings; they are covered in more detail in Appendix C.

Sending Your Output to a Printer

Are you wondering how to send your "Hello, World" program to a printer instead of to the screen? We'll show you how here, but we won't go into the details of how this works yet; you have plenty to learn for now, and we want to save some of the fun for later.

Modify your program to look like this:

```
#include <stdio.h>

main()
{
   FILE *printer;

   printer = fopen("PRN","w");
   fprintf(printer,"Hello, World\n");
   fclose(printer);
}

/*
   Note: If your system uses LPT1 or LPT2, you  can replace
   PRN with either of those to specify your printer.
*/
```

Note that this time we've used the **fprintf** function instead of **printf**, and we've prefaced the program with an #include directive. As you gain more expertise with Turbo C and venture into the *Turbo C Reference Guide*, you'll learn more about these elements we've added.

Writing Your Second Turbo C Program

Now modify your program to create a new one. Get into the Edit window (press *F10 E* or *Alt-E*) and change your program so that it looks like this:

```
main()
{
   int  a,b,sum;

   printf("Enter two numbers:  ");
   scanf("%d %d",&a,&b);
   sum = a + b;
   printf("The sum is %d \n",sum);
}
```

You have made five changes to the original program. You have

- replaced the line defining *name* with one defining other variables (*a*, *b*, and *sum*, all integers)
- changed the message in the **printf** statement
- changed the format string and variable list in the **scanf** statement
- added the assignment statement sum = a + b;
- changed the format string and argument list in the final **printf** statement

Don't let the percent signs (%), ampersands (&), and backslashes (\)
confuse you; we'll explain what they mean soon.

Writing to Disk

Now, do *not* press the *F2* function key. If you do, this program will be saved
as HELLO.C (you are going to save it under a different name).

Instead, press *F10* to get to the main menu. Press *F*, then *W* to bring up the
File/Write to command. Turbo C will ask you to type in the new name for
this program; type `sum.c` and press *Enter*. Your second program has now
been saved on disk as SUM.C. Press *F10* to invoke the main menu again.

Running SUM.C

Press *R* to select the **Run** command. Turbo C will compile your program. If
there are any errors, go back into the editor and be sure that what you've
typed in matches exactly what is given in the example.

Once there are no errors, Turbo C will link in the appropriate library
routines and then run your program. The screen will clear and this message
will appear at the top:

```
Enter two values:
```

Your program is waiting for you to enter two integer values, separated by
blanks and/or tabs and/or carriage returns. Be sure to press *Enter* after
typing the second value. Your program now prints the sum of those two
values, then waits for you to press any key before returning to Turbo C.

Congratulations! You've now written two completely different Turbo C
programs using several of the basic elements of programming. Wondering
what those elements are? You can find out by reading the next section of
this chapter before going on to Chapter 5.

The Seven Basic Elements of Programming

The purpose of most programs is to solve a problem. Programs solve problems by manipulating information or data. You've got to:

- get the information into the program
- have someplace to keep it
- give the instructions to manipulate it
- get it back out of the program to the user (you, usually)

You can organize your instructions so that:

- some are executed only when a specific condition (or set of conditions) is *true*
- others are repeated a number of times
- others are broken off into chunks that can be executed at different locations in your program

We've just described the seven basic elements of programming: *input, data types, operations, output, conditional execution, loops,* and *subroutines*. This list is not comprehensive, but it does describe those elements that programs usually have in common.

Most programming languages have all these; many, including C, have additional features as well. But when you want to learn a new language quickly, you can find out how that language implements these seven elements, then build from there. Here's a brief description of each element:

Output means writing information to the screen, to a disk, or to an I/O port.

Data Types are constants, variables, and structures that contain numbers (integer and real), text (characters and strings), or addresses (of variables and structures).

Operations assign one value to another, combine values (add, divide, etc.), and compare values (equal, not equal, etc.).

Input means reading values in from the keyboard, from a disk, or from an I/O port.

Conditional Execution refers to executing a set of instructions if a specified condition is *true* (and skipping them if it is *false*).

Loops execute a set of instructions some fixed number of times or while some condition is *true*.

Subroutines are separately named sets of instructions that can be executed anywhere in the program just by a reference to the name.

Now we'll take a look at how to use these elements in Turbo C.

Output

It may seem funny to talk about output first, but a program that does not somehow output information isn't of much use. That output usually takes the form of information written to the screen (words and pictures), to a storage device (floppy or hard disk), or to an I/O port (serial port, printer port).

The printf Function

You've already used the most common output function in C: the **printf** routine. The purpose of **printf** is to write information to the screen. Its format is both simple and flexible:

```
printf(<format string>,<item>,<item>,...);
```

The Format String

The format string is just a string that begins and ends with double quotes ("like this"); **printf**'s purpose is to write that string to the screen. First, though, **printf** substitutes any additional items listed into the string, according to the format commands found in the string itself. For example, your last program had the following **printf** statement:

```
printf("The sum is %d \n",sum);
```

The %d in the format string is a *format specification*. All format specifications start with a percent sign (%) and are (usually) followed by a single letter, indicating the type of data and how the data is to be formatted.

You should have exactly one item listed for each format specification. If the item is of a data type that doesn't directly correspond to the format specification, then Turbo C will attempt to make an appropriate conversion. The items themselves can be variables, constants, expressions, function calls. In short, they can be anything that yields a value appropriate to the corresponding format specification.

The %d used in this specification says that it expects an integer. Here are some other commonly used format specifications:

- %u (unsigned integer)
- %p (pointer value)
- %f (floating point)
- %e (floating point in exponential format)
- %c (character)
- %s (string)
- %x or %X (integer in hexadecimal format)

You can set the field width by placing it between the % and the letter; for example, a decimal field of width 4 would be %4d. The value will then be printed out right-justified (with leading blanks), so that the total field width is 4.

If you need to print a percent sign, just insert %%.

The \n in the string isn't a format specification. It is known (for historical reasons) as an *escape sequence*, and it represents a special character being inserted into the string. In this case, the \n inserts a newline character, so that after the string is written out, the cursor moves to the start of a new line.

A complete list of all escape sequences can be found in Chapter 8, but a few of the more commonly used ones include:

- \f (formfeed or clear screen)
- \t (tab)
- \b (backspace)
- \xhhh (insert the character represented by ASCII code *hhh*, where *hhh* = 1 to 3 hexadecimal digits)

And if you need to print a backslash, just insert \\. If you want more detail on how **printf** works, turn to the **printf** entry in the *Turbo C Reference Guide*.

Other Output Functions: puts and putchar

There are two other output functions that you might be interested in: **puts** and **putchar**. The function **puts** writes a string to the screen followed by a newline character.

For example, you could rewrite HELLO.C as

```
main()
{
    puts("Hello, world");
}
```

Note that we dropped the \n at the end of the string; it isn't needed, since **puts** adds one.

On the other hand, the function **putchar** writes a single character to the screen and does not add a \n. The statement `putchar(ch)` is equivalent to `printf("%c",ch)`.

Why might you want to use **puts** and/or **putchar** instead of **printf**? One good reason is that the routine that implements **printf** is rather large; unless you need it (for numeric output or special formatting), you can make your program both smaller and quicker by using **puts** and **putchar** instead. For example, the .EXE file created by compiling the version of HELLO.C that uses **puts** is much smaller than the .EXE file for the version that uses **printf**.

Data Types

When you write a program, you're working with some kind of information, most of which falls into one of four basic types: *integers, floating-point numbers, text,* and *pointers*.

Integers are the numbers you learned to count with (1, 5, –21, and 752, for example).

Floating-point numbers have fractional portions (3.14159) and exponents (2.579×10^{24}). These are also sometimes known as *real* numbers.

Text is made up of characters (*a, Z, !, 3*) and strings ("This is only a test.").

Pointers don't hold information; instead, each one contains the address of some location in the computer's memory that *does* hold information.

Float Type

C supports these four basic data types in various forms. You've already used two of them: integers (**int**) and characters (**char**). Now you will modify your last program to use a third type: floating point (**float**).

Get into the Turbo C editor and change your program to look like this:

```
main()
{
    int    a,b;
    float  ratio;

    printf("Enter two numbers:  ");
    scanf("%d %d",&a,&b);
    ratio = a / b;
    printf("The ratio is %f \n",ratio);
}
```

Save this as RATIO.C by bringing up the menus and selecting the File/Write to command. Then press *R* to compile and run the program. Enter two values (such as 10 and 3) and note the result (3.000000).

You were probably expecting an answer of 3.333333; why was the answer just 3? Because *a* and *b* are both of type **int**, so the result of *a/b* was of type **int**. That was converted to type **float** when you assigned it to *ratio*, but the conversion took place after the division, not before.

Go back and change the type of *a* and *b* to **float**; also change the format string "%d %d" in **scanf** to "%f %f". Save the code (press *F2*), then compile and run. The result is now 3.333333, as you expected.

There's also a large version of type **float**, known as **double**. As you might have guessed, variables of type **double** are twice as large as variables of type **float**. This means that they have more significant digits and a larger range of exponents. The specific sizes and ranges of values for these types in Turbo C can be found in Chapter 8.

The Three ints

In addition to the type **int**, C supports **short int** and **long int**, usually abbreviated as **short** and **long**. The actual sizes of **short**, **int**, and **long** depend upon the implementation; all that C guarantees is that a variable of type **short** will not be larger (that is, will not take up more bytes) than one of type **long**. In Turbo C, these types occupy 16 bits (**short**), 16 bits (**int**), and 32 bits (**long**).

Unsigned

C allows you to declare certain types (**char**, **short**, **int**, **long**) to be **unsigned**. This means that instead of having negative values, those types only contain non-negative values (greater than or equal to zero).

Variables of those types can then hold larger values than signed types. For example, in Turbo C a variable of type **int** can contain values from –32768 to 32767; one of type **unsigned int** can contain values from 0 to 65535. Both take up exactly the same amount of space (16 bits, in this case); they just use it differently. Again, see Chapter 8 for specific details.

Defining a String

C does not support a separate string data type, but it does provide two slightly different approaches to defining strings. One is to use a *character array*; the other is to use a *character pointer*.

Using a Character Array

Select the Load command from the File menu and bring your edited version of HELLO.C back in. Now edit it to appear as follows:

```
main()
{
    char  msg[30];

    strcpy(msg,"Hello, world");
    puts(msg);
}
```

The [30] after *msg* tells the compiler to set aside space for up to 29 characters, that is, an array of 29 **char** variables. (The 30th space will be filled by a *null character*—a \0—often referred to in this user's guide as a *null terminator*.) The variable *msg* itself doesn't contain a character value; it holds the address (some location in memory) of the first of those 29 **char** variables.

When the compiler finds the statement strcpy(msg,"Hello, world"); it does two things:

- It creates the string "Hello, world", followed by a null (\0) character (ASCII code 0) somewhere within the object code file.
- It calls a subroutine named **strcpy**, which copies the characters from that string, one at a time, into the memory location pointed to by *msg*. It does this until it copies the null character at the end of the "Hello, world" string.

When you call puts(msg), you pass the value in *msg*—the address of the first letter it points to—to **puts**. Then **puts** checks to see if the character at that address is the null character. If it is, then **puts** is finished; otherwise,

puts prints that character, adds one (1) to the address, and checks for the null character again.

Because of this dependency on a null character, strings in C are known as being *null terminated*: a sequence of characters followed by the null character. This approach removes any arbitrary limit on the length of strings; instead, a string can be any length, as long as there is enough memory to hold it.

Using a Character Pointer

The second method you can use to define strings is a *character pointer*. Edit your program to look like this:

```
main()
{
   char    *msg;

   msg = "Hello, world";
   puts(msg);
}
```

The asterisk (*) in front of *msg* tells the compiler that *msg* is a pointer to a character; in other words, *msg* can hold the address of some character. However, the compiler sets aside no space to store characters and does not initialize *msg* to any particular value.

When the compiler finds the statement msg = "Hello, world\n"; it does two things:

- As before, it creates the string "Hello, world\n", followed by a null character somewhere within the object code file.
- It assigns to the starting address of that string—the address of the character *H*—to *msg*.

The command puts(msg) works just as it did before, printing characters until it encounters the null character.

There are some subtle differences between the array and pointer methods for defining strings, which we'll talk about in the next chapter.

Identifiers

Up until now, we've cheerfully given names to variables without worrying about whatever restrictions there might be. Let's talk about those restrictions now.

The names you give to constants, data types, variables, and functions are known as *identifiers*. Some of the identifiers used so far include:

char, int, float	predefined data types
main	main function of program
name, a, b, sum, msg, ratio	user-defined variables
scanf, printf, puts	predeclared functions

Turbo C has a few rules about identifiers; here's a quick summary:

- All identifiers must start with a letter (*a...z* or *A...Z*) or an underscore (_).
- The rest of an identifier can consist of letters, underscores, and/or digits (0...9). No other characters are allowed.
- Identifiers are *case-sensitive*. This means that lowercase letters (*a...z*) are *not* the same as uppercase letters (*A...Z*). For example, the identifiers *indx*, *Indx*, and *INDX* are different and distinct from one another.
- The first 32 characters of an identifier are significant.

Operations

Once you get that data into the program (and into your variables), what are you going to do with it? Probably manipulate it somehow, using the operators available. And C has got lots and lots of operators.

Assignment Operator

The most basic operation is *assignment*, as in `ratio = a / b` or `ch = getch()`. In C, assignment is a single equal sign (=); the *value* on the right of the equal sign is assigned to the *variable* on the left.

You can stack up assignments, such as `sum = a = b`. In a case like this, the order of evaluation is right to left, so that *b* would be assigned to *a*, which in turn would be assigned to *sum*, giving all three variables the same value (namely, *b*'s original value).

Unary and Binary Operators

C supports the usual set of binary arithmetic operators:

- multiplication (*)
- division (/)
- modulus (%)
- addition (+)
- subtraction (–)

Turbo C supports *unary minus* (a + (-b)), which performs an arithmetic negation; as an ANSI extension, Turbo C also supports *unary plus* (a + (+b)).

Increment (++) and Decrement (– –) Operators

C has some special unary and binary operators as well. The most well known unary operators are *increment* (++) and *decrement* (--). These allow you to use a single operator that *adds 1 to* or *subtracts 1 from* any value; the addition or subtraction can be done in the middle of an expression, and you can even decide whether you want it done before or after the expression is evaluated. Consider the following lines of code:

```
sum = a + b++;
sum = a + ++b;
```

The first says, "Add *a* and *b* together, assign the result to *sum*, and increment *b* by one." The second says, "Increment *b* by one, add *a* and *b* together, and assign the result to *sum*."

These are very powerful operators, but you have to be sure you understand them correctly before using them. Modify SUM.C as follows, then try to guess what its output will be before you run it.

```
main()
{
   int    a,b,sum;
   char   *format;

   format = "a = %d   b = %d   sum = %d \n";
   a = b = 5;
   sum = a   + b;  printf(format,a,b,sum);
   sum = a++ + b;  printf(format,a,b,sum);
   sum = ++a + b;  printf(format,a,b,sum);
   sum = --a + b;  printf(format,a,b,sum);
   sum = a-- + b;  printf(format,a,b,sum);
   sum = a   + b;  printf(format,a,b,sum);
}
```

Bitwise Operators

For bit-level operations, C has the following operators:

- shift left (<<)
- shift right (>>)
- AND (&)
- OR (|)
- XOR (^)
- NOT (~)

These allow you to perform very low-level operations on values. To see the effect of these operators, type in and run this program:

```
main()
{
    int   a,b,c;
    char  *format1,*format2;

    format1 = " %04X %s %04X = %04X\n";
    format2 = " %c%04X = %04X\n";
    a = 0x0FF0;  b = 0xFF00;
    c = a << 4;  printf(format1,a,"<<",4,c);
    c = a >> 4;  printf(format1,a,">>",4,c);
    c = a & b;   printf(format1,a,"& ",b,c);
    c = a | b;   printf(format1,a,"| ",b,c);
    c = a ^ b;   printf(format1,a,"^ ",b,c);
    c = ~a;      printf(format2,'~',a,c);
    c = -a;      printf(format2,'-',a,c);
}
```

Again, see if you can guess the output of this program before running it. Note that field-width specifiers have been used to nicely align the output; the %04X specifier says that we want the output to use leading zeros, to be four digits wide, and to be in hexadecimal (base 16).

Combined Operators

C allows you to use a little shorthand when writing expressions that contain multiple operators. You can combine the assignment operator (=) with the operators discussed so far (unary, binary, increment, decrement, and bitwise).

Just about any expression of the form

```
<variable> = <variable> <operator> <exp>;
```

can be replaced with

```
<variable> <operator>= <exp>;
```

Here are some examples of such expressions and how they can be
condensed:

```
a = a  +  b;      is condensed to   a  +=  b;
a = a  -  b;      is condensed to   a  -=  b;
a = a  *  b;      is condensed to   a  *=  b;
a = a  /  b;      is condensed to   a  /=  b;
a = a  % b;       is condensed to   a  %=  b;
a = a  << b;      is condensed to   a <<=  b;
a = a  >> b;      is condensed to   a >>=  b;
a = a  &  b;      is condensed to   a  &=  b;
a = a  |  b;      is condensed to   a  |=  b;
a = a  ^  b;      is condensed to   a  ^=  b;
```

Address Operators

C supports two special address operators: the *address-of* operator (&) and
the *indirection* operator (*).

The & operator returns the address of a given variable; if *sum* is a variable
of type **int**, then &*sum* is the address (memory location) of that variable.
Likewise, if *msg* is a pointer to type **char**, then **msg* is the character to
which *msg* points.

Type in the following program and see what you get.

```
main()
{
    int    sum;
    char   *msg;

    sum = 5 + 3;
    msg = "Hello, there\n";
    printf(" sum = %d   &sum = %p \n",sum,&sum);
    printf("*msg = %c    msg = %p \n",*msg,msg);
}
```

The first line prints out two values: the value of *sum* (8) and the address of
sum (assigned by the compiler). The second line also prints out two values:
the character to which *msg* points (*H*) and the value of *msg*, which is the
address of that character (also assigned by the compiler).

Input

C has several input functions; some take input from a file or an input stream, others from the keyboard. When you need detailed information about the Turbo C input functions, refer to ...**scanf**, **read**, and Chapter 8.

The scanf Function

For interactive input, you'll probably use **scanf** most of the time. **scanf** is the input equivalent of **printf**; its format is

```
scanf(<format string>,<addr>,<addr>,...)
```

scanf uses many of the same %<letter> formats that **printf** does: %d for integers, %f for floating-point values, %s for strings, and so on.

However, there is one important difference with **scanf**: The items following the format string must be addresses, not values. The program SUM.C contains the following call:

```
scanf("%d %d",&a,&b);
```

This call tells the program that it expects you to type in two decimal (integer) values separated by a space; the first will be assigned to *a* and the second to *b*. Note that it uses the address-of (&) operator to pass the addresses of *a* and *b* to **scanf**.

Whitespace

The space between the two %d format commands actually means more than just a space. It means that you can have any amount of *whitespace* between the values. What is whitespace? Any combination of blanks, tabs, and newlines. C compilers and programs typically ignore whitespace in most circumstances.

But what if you wanted to separate the numbers with a comma instead of a blank? Then you could change the line to read:

```
scanf("%d,%d",&a,&b);
```

This allows you to enter the values with a comma between them.

Passing an Address to scanf

What if you want to input a string? Type in and run the following program:

```
main()
```

```
    {
    char    name[30];

    printf("What is your name:  ");
    scanf("%s",name);
    printf("Hello, %s\n",name);
    }
```

Since *name* is an array of characters, the value of *name* is the address of the array itself. Because of that, you don't use the & operator in front of *name*; you simply say `scanf("%s",name)`.

Note that we used the array approach (`char name[30];`) rather than the pointer approach (`char *name;`). Why? Because the array declaration actually sets aside memory to hold the string, while the pointer declaration does not. If we wanted to use `char *name`, then we'd have to explicitly allocate memory for *name*.

Using gets and getch for Input

Using **scanf** to input strings introduces another problem, though. Run your program again, but this time type in your full name. Note that the program only uses your first name in its reply. Why? Because, to **scanf**, the blank you typed after your first name signalled the end of the string you were entering.

There are two possible solutions to this. Here's the first:

```
    main()
    {
    char    first[20],middle[20],last[20];

    printf("What is your name:  ");
    scanf("%s %s %s",first,middle,last);
    printf("Hello, Dr. %s, or should I say %s?\n",last,first);
    }
```

This, of course, assumes that you have some middle name; in this example, **scanf** won't continue until you've actually typed in three strings. But what if you want to read in the entire name as a single string, blanks and all?

Here's the second solution:

```
    main()
    {
    char    name[60];

    printf("What is your name:  ");
    gets(name);
    printf("Hello, %s\n",name);
    }
```

The function **gets** reads in everything you type until you press *Enter*. It does not store the *Enter* in the line; but it does stick a null character (\0) at the end.

Finally, there's the function **getch**. It reads a single character from the keyboard without echoing it to the screen (unlike **scanf** and **gets**). Note that it doesn't take *ch* as a parameter; instead **getch** is a function of type `char`, and its value can be assigned directly to *ch*.

Conditional Statements

There are some operators we haven't talked about yet: *relational* and *logical* operators. Also, there are some complexities about expressions that we saved for this discussion of conditional (*true* or *false*) statements.

Relational Operators

Relational operators allow you to compare two values, yielding a result based on whether the comparison is *true* or *false*. If the comparison is *false*, then the resulting value is 0; if *true*, then the value is 1. Here's a list of the relational operators in C:

>	greater than
>=	greater than or equal to
<	less than
<=	less than or equal to
==	equal to
!=	not equal to

Why would you care if something were *true* or *false*? Load and run the program RATIO.C and see what happens when you enter 0 for the second value. Your program prints a `Divide by zero` error message and halts.

Now make the following changes to your program and run it again.

```
main()
{
   float  a,b,ratio;

   printf("Enter two numbers:  ");
   scanf("%f %f",&a,&b);
   if (b == 0.0)
      printf("The ratio is undefined\n");
   else {
      ratio = a / b;
      printf("The ratio is %f \n",ratio);
   }
}
```

The statement on the two lines after the call to **scanf** is known as an *if statement*. You can read it as: "If the value of the expression (*b* == 0.0) is *true*, immediately call **printf**. If the value of the expression is *false*, assign *a/b* to *ratio*, then call **printf**."

Now if you enter 0 as the second value, your program prints the message

```
The ratio is undefined
```

waits for you to press any key, then returns to Turbo C. If the second value is non-zero, the program calculates and prints out the ratio, then waits for you to press a key—all through the magic of the `if` statement.

Logical Operators

There are also three logical operators: AND (&&), OR (| |), and NOT (!). These are not to be confused with the bitwise operators (&, |, ~) previously described. These logical operators work with logical values (*true* and *false*), allowing you to combine relational expressions.

How do they differ from the corresponding bitwise operators?

■ These logical operators always produce a result of either 0 (*false*) or 1 (*true*), while the bitwise operators do true bit-by-bit operations.

■ The logical operators && and | | will *short circuit*. Suppose you have the expression `exp1 && exp2`. If *exp1* is *false*, then the entire expression is *false*, so *exp2* will never be evaluated. Likewise, given the expression `exp1 | | exp2`, *exp2* will never be evaluated if *exp1* is *true*.

More About Expressions

Before we go on to loops, we have a few more comments about expressions. Things like `(b == 0.0)` and `(a <= q*r)` are pretty straightforward. However, C allows you to make things more complicated than that. Much more complicated. We won't show you how complicated, but we'll give you a few hints.

Assignment Statements

Any assignment statement enclosed in parentheses is an expression that has the same value as that which was being assigned.

For example, the expression `(sum = 5+3)` has the value 8, so that the expression `((sum = 5+3) <= 10)` would always yield a value of *true* (since 8 <= 10).

More exotic is this example:

```
if ((ch=getch()) == 'q')
    puts("Quitting, huh?\n");
else
    puts("Good move; we'll have another go at it\n");
```

Can you figure out what this does? When your program hits the expression `((ch=getch()) == 'q')`, it stops until you press a character, assigns that character to *ch*, then compares that same character to the letter *q*. If the character you pressed equals *q*, then the message `"Quitting, huh?"` is printed on the screen; otherwise, the other message (`"Good move..."`) is printed.

The Comma Operator

You can use the comma operator (,) to put multiple expressions inside a set of parentheses. The expressions are evaluated left to right, and the entire expression assumes the value of the last one evaluated. For example, if *oldch* and *ch* are both of type **char**, then the expression

```
(oldch = ch, ch = getch())
```

assigns *ch* to *oldch*, gets a character from the keyboard and assigns it to *ch*, and then assumes the (assigned) value of *ch*.

For example:

```
ch = 'a';
if((oldch = ch, ch = 'b') == 'a')
    puts("aye");
else
    puts("bee");
```

The if Statement

Look again at the **if** statement in the previous examples. The **if** statement takes the following generic format:

```
if(value)
    statement1;
else
    statement2;
```

where *value* is any expression that resolves to (or can be converted to) an integer value. If *value* is non-zero (*true*), then *statement1* is executed; otherwise, *statement2* is executed.

We must explain two important points about **if-else** statements in general.

First, the `else statement2` portion is optional; in other words, this is a valid **if** statement:

```
if (value)
    statement1;
```

In this case, *statement1* is executed if and only if *value* is non-zero. If *value* is zero, then *statement1* is skipped, and the program continues.

Second, what if you want to execute more than one statement if a particular expression is *true* (or *false*)? Answer: Use a *compound statement*. A compound statement consists of

■ a left brace ({)

■ some number of statements, each ending with a semicolon (;)

■ a right brace (})

The ratio example uses a single statement for the **if** clause

```
if (b == 0.0)
    printf("The ratio is undefined\n");
```

and a compound statement for the **else** clause

```
else {
    ratio = a / b;
    printf("The ratio is %f \n",ratio);
}
```

You might also notice that the body of your program (the function **main**) is simply a compound statement.

Loops

Just as there are statements (or groups of statements) that you want to execute conditionally, there are other statements that you may want to execute repeatedly. This kind of construct is known as a *loop*.

There are three basic kinds of loops (though two are just special cases of the other one): the **while** loop, the **for** loop, and the **do...while** loop. We'll cover them in that order.

The while Loop

The **while** loop is the most general loop and can be used to replace the other two; in other words, a **while** loop is all you need, and the others are just there for your convenience. Load up HELLO.C and modify it as follows:

```
#include <stdio.h>
main()
{
    int   len;

    len = 0;
    puts("Type in a sentence, then press <Enter>");
    while (getchar() != '\n')
        len++;

    printf("\nYour sentence was %d characters long\n",len);
}
```

This program lets you type in a sentence, counting the number of keystrokes, until you press *Enter* (\n). It then tells you how many characters (not counting the *Enter*) you typed.

The format of the **while** statement is:

```
while (expression)
    statement
```

where *expression* resolves to a zero or nonzero value, and *statement* is either a single or a compound statement.

The **while** loop evaluates *expression*. If it's *true*, then *statement* is executed, and *expression* is evaluated again. If *statement* isn't *true*, the **while** loop is finished and the program continues on.

Take a look at another example of the **while** loop, based on HELLO.C:

```
main()
{
   char   *msg;
   int    indx;

   msg = "Hello, world";
   indx = 1;
   while (indx <= 10) {
      printf("time #%2d:  %s\n",indx,msg);
      indx++;
   }
}
```

When you compile and run this program, it prints out the following lines:

```
time # 1:  Hello, world
time # 2:  Hello, world
time # 3:  Hello, world
```

and so on, down to

```
time #10: Hello,  world
```

The **printf** statement was executed exactly ten times, with *indx* going from 1 to 10 during those ten executions.

If you think about it, you may see a way to write that loop a little tighter:

```
indx = 0;
while (indx++ < 10)
   printf("time #%2d:  %s\n",indx,msg);
```

Study this second **while** loop until you understand why it functions exactly the same way as the first version. Then go on and learn about the **for** loop.

The for Loop

The **for** loop is the one found in most major programming languages, including C. However, the C version of the **for** loop is very flexible and very powerful, as you'll see.

The basic idea is that you execute a set of statements some fixed number of times while a variable (known as the *index variable*) steps through a range of values.

For example, modify the previous program to read as follows:

```
main()
{
    char    *msg;
    int     indx;

    msg = "Hello, world";
    for (indx = 1; indx <= 10; indx++)
        printf("time #%2d:  %s\n",indx,msg);
}
```

As you can see when you run it, this does the same thing as both **while** loops already shown and, in fact, is precisely equivalent to the first one. Here's the generic format of the **for** loop statement:

```
for (exp1; exp2; exp3)
    statement
```

As with **while**, the **for** statement executes just one statement, but that statement can be a compound statement ({...}).

Note what's inside the parentheses following the word **for**; there are three sections separated by semicolons.

- *exp1* is usually an assignment to the index variable.
- *exp2* is a test for loop continuation.
- *exp3* is usually some modification of the index variable.

The generic **for** loop is equivalent to the following code:

```
exp1;
while (exp2) {
    statement;
    exp3;
}
```

You can leave out any or all of the expressions, though the semicolons must remain. If you leave out *exp2*, it is assumed to have a value of 1 (*true*), so the loop never terminates (this is known as an *infinite loop*).

On the other hand, you can use the comma operator to put in multiple expressions for each expression.

For example, try these modifications on HELLO.C:

```
main()
{
   char  *msg;
   int   up,down;

   msg = "Hello, world";
   for (up = 1, down = 9; up <= 10; up++, down--)
      printf("%s: %2d down, %2d to go\n",msg,up,down);
}
```

Note that the first and last expressions in this **for** loop have two expressions each, initializing and modifying the variables *up* and *down*. You can make these expressions arbitrarily complex. (Perhaps you have heard the legends of C hackers who crammed most of their programs into the three expressions of a **for** statement, leaving only a few statements for the loop to execute.)

The do...while Loop

The final loop is the **do...while** loop. Modify RATIO.C as follows:

```
main()
{
   float  a,b,ratio;
   char   ch;

   do {
      printf("Enter two numbers:  ");
      scanf("%f %f",&a,&b);
      if (b == 0.0)
         printf("The ratio is undefined\n");
      else {
         ratio = a / b;
         printf("The ratio is %f \n",ratio);
      }
      printf("Press 'q' to quit, any other key to continue");
   } while ((ch = getch()) != 'q');
}
```

This program calculates a ratio, then asks you to press a key. If you press *q*, the expression at the bottom is *false* and the loop ends. If you press some key other than *q*, the expression is *true* and the loop repeats.

Here's the generic format for the **do...while** loop:

```
do statement while (exp);
```

The main difference between the **while** loop and the **do...while** loop is that the statements in the **do...while** loop always execute at least once. This is similar to the **repeat...until** loop in Pascal, with one major difference: The **repeat** loop executes *until* its condition is *true*; **do...while** executes *while* its condition is *true*.

Functions

You've learned how to execute code *conditionally* and *iteratively*. Now, what if you want to perform the same set of instructions on different sets of data or at different locations in your program? Answer: You put those statements into a *subroutine*, which you then call as needed.

In C, all subroutines are known as *functions*. In theory, every function returns some value. In practice, the values returned by many functions are ignored, and more recent definitions of C (including the draft ANSI C standard and Turbo C) allow you to declare functions of type **void**, which means they don't return values at all. Never.

In C, you can both *declare* and *define* a function. When you declare a function, you let the rest of your program know about it so that other functions (including **main**) can call it. When you define a function, you give the actual code for the function itself. For example, consider this rewrite of RATIO.C:

```
/* Function declarations */

void  get_parms(float *p1, float *p2);
float get_ratio(float dividend, float divisor);
void  put_ratio(float quotient);

const float    INFINITY = 3.4E+38;

/* Main function:  starting point for program */

main()
{
   float   a,b,ratio;
   do {
       get_parms(&a,&b);                                   /* Get parameters */
       ratio = get_ratio(a,b);                             /* Calculate ratio */
       put_ratio(ratio);                                   /* Print answer out */
       printf("Press q to quit, any other key to continue ");
   } while (getch() != 'q');
}
/* End of main */

/* Function definitions */
```

```
void  get_parms(float *p1,float *p2)
{
   printf("\nEnter two numbers:  ");
   scanf("%f %f",p1,p2);
}

float get_ratio(float dividend, float divisor)
{
   if (divisor == 0.0)
      return (INFINITY);
   else
      return (dividend / divisor);
}

void put_ratio(float ratio)
{
      if  (ratio == INFINITY)
         printf("The ratio is undefined\n");
      else
         printf("The ratio is %f\n",ratio);
}
```

Breaking the Program Down

The first three lines of the program are the function declarations; their purpose is to declare the function type as well as the type and number of the parameters for error-checking purposes.

The next line defines a floating-point constant called INFINITY (it is a C convention to name constants in uppercase). This constant has a very high positive value—about the highest you can have with type **float**—and is used to flag a divide-by-zero. Note that since it is declared here, it is "visible" inside all of the functions (including **main**).

Next comes the function **main**, which is the main body of your program. Every C program has a function called **main**; when your program starts executing, **main** gets called, and everything proceeds from there. Once **main** is through executing, your program is finished, and you return to Turbo C (or, if you executed from a DOS prompt, to DOS).

The function **main** can be placed anywhere in the program; often it's the first function, following any prototypes or other global declarations. That makes it easy to find and helps to document the function of the entire program.

After **main** come the actual definitions of the three functions declared in the prototypes: **get_parms**, **get_ratio**, and **put_ratio**. We'll now take a look at each of these definitions.

The get_parms Function

The **get_parms** function doesn't return a value of a given type, so we've declared it to be of type **void**. However, its purpose is to read in two values and store them somewhere. Where? We have to pass two parameters to **get_parms**; these parameters are the addresses where the values should be stored. Look carefully: The two parameters are not of type **float** but are pointers to type **float**. In other words, they are supposed to be addresses of **float** variables.

That's exactly what we pass: When we call **get_parms** in **main**, the parameters are &*a*,&*b* instead of just *a*,*b*. Notice also that when **scanf** is called inside of **get_parms**, there are no address-of operators in front of *p1* and *p2*. Why? Because *p1* and *p2* are addresses already; they're the addresses of *a* and *b*.

The get_ratio Function

The **get_ratio** function does return a value (of type **float**) calculated from the two **float** values passed to it (*dividend* and *divisor*). The value returned depends upon whether or not *divisor* is 0. If it is, **get_ratio** returns INFINITY. If *divisor* is not 0, **get_ratio** returns the actual ratio. Note the format of the **return** statement.

The put_ratio Function

The **put_ratio** function doesn't return a value, so it is of type **void**. It just has a single parameter—*ratio*—which is used to determine what to print to the screen. If *ratio* equals INFINITY, then it is considered undefined; otherwise, *ratio* is printed out.

Global Declarations

Constants, data types, and variables declared outside of any function (including **main**) are considered to be *global* from that point on. This means that they can be used by any function in the entire program following their declaration. If you were to move the declaration of INFINITY to the end of the program, you would get two compiler errors, one in **get_ratio** and one in **put_ratio**, for using an undeclared identifier.

Function Declarations

You can use two different styles in declaring functions: the "classic" style and the "modern" style. The classic style, found in many C texts and programs, takes this form:

```
type   funcname();
```

This specifies the function's name (*funcname*) and the type of data value it returns (*type*). It does not give any parameter information, so no error checking or type coercion can be done. If you rewrote the function declarations in RATIO.C using this style, they would look like this:

```
void   get_parms();
float  get_ratio();
void   put_ratio();
```

The modern style uses a construct from the ANSI extensions known as a *function prototype*. This declaration adds parameter information:

```
type   funcname(pinfo,pinfo,etc.);
```

where *pinfo* takes one of the following formats:

```
type
type   pname
...
```

In other words, for each formal parameter you can specify just the data type, or you can give it a name as well. If the function takes a variable number of parameters, then you can use the ellipsis (...) for the last parameter.

This is the preferred approach, since it allows the compiler to check the numbers and types of the parameters in actual calls to the function. This approach also allows the compiler to perform proper conversions when possible. The function declarations found in the previous version of RATIO.C are function prototypes. More information about function prototypes can be found in Chapters 8 and 9.

Function Definitions

As with function declarations, there are two styles of function definitions: *classic* and *modern*.

The classic format of a function definition is like this:

```
type   funcname(pnames)
parm definitions;
{
```

```
    local declarations;
    statements;
}
```

The modern format moves the parameter definitions into the parentheses following *funcname*:

```
type   funcname(pinfo,pinfo,etc.)
```

In this example, however, the term *pinfo* represents all the information about a given parameter; its type modifiers *and* identifier name. This makes the first line of the function definition look just like the corresponding function prototype, with one important exception: There is no semicolon (;) following the definition, whereas a function prototype is always ended by a semicolon. For example, the function **get_parms** in the classic style looks like this:

```
void get_parms(p1, p2)
float *p1; float *p2;
{ ... }
```

and in the modern style it looks like this:

```
void get_parms (float * p1, float *p2)
{ ... }
```

Note that any declarations (constants, data types, variables) made within a given function (including **main**) are visible (that is, can be used and referenced) only within that function. Also note that C does not allow nested functions; you can't declare one function inside of another.

Functions can also be placed in any order in the program and are considered global throughout the entire program, including within functions declared prior to those being used. Be careful using a function before it's defined or declared: When the compiler encounters a function it hasn't seen before, it assumes the function returns an **int**. If you later define it to return something else, say a **char***, you'll get an error.

Comments

Sometimes, you want to insert notes in your program to remind you (or inform someone else) of what certain variables mean, what certain functions or statements do, and so on. These notes are known as *comments*. C, like most other programming languages, allows you to insert comments into your program.

To start a comment, you put in the slash-star character sequence (/*). From then on, the compiler will ignore everything until after it sees another */ sequence.

Comments can even extend across multiple lines, like this:

```
/* This is a long
comment, extending
over several lines. */
```

Look in the expanded version of RATIO.C for additional examples of comments.

Summary

We have started you off by creating, compiling, and running several Turbo C programs, and we have touched upon the seven basic elements of programming, showing how you use each of them in Turbo C.

There's plenty more we could say about each of the basic elements, and we will expound on them in Chapter 5.

5

More Programming in Turbo C

Glad to see you made it here. In the last chapter we gave you a taste of working with Turbo C; just enough to whet your appetite. Now you're ready to dig into some of the more subtle and esoteric issues of C programming, and we're here to serve you.

In This Chapter...

In this chapter, we cover the following:

- data structures, including pointers, arrays, and structures
- the **switch** statement
- control flow commands, including **return, break, continue, goto,** and the conditional expression operator (? :)
- programming style in C, especially with regards to some of the new C extensions
- some common pitfalls for C programmers

A Survey of Data Structures

We covered basic data types in the last chapter—things such as integers, floating-point numbers, characters, and their variants. We'll talk about how to use these elements to build data *structures*—collections of data elements. But first, we'll explore an important concept in C—*pointers*.

Pointers

Most variables you've looked at so far hold data, that is, the actual information your program is manipulating. But sometimes you want to keep track of where some data is rather than just its value. For that, you probably need pointers.

If you feel shaky about the concepts of addresses and memory, here's a quick review. Your computer holds your program and the associated data in its memory (often called **RAM**, meaning *Random Access Memory*). At its lowest level, your computer's memory is composed of *bits*, microscopic electronic circuits that can "remember" (while the computer's power is on) one of two values, which are usually interpreted as being 0 and 1.

Eight bits are grouped together into one *byte*. Large groups of bits are often given names as well; commonly, two bytes are considered a *word*; four bytes are considered a *longword*; and on the IBM PC, sixteen bytes is considered a *paragraph*.

Each byte in your computer's memory has a unique address, much as does each house on a given street. But unlike most streets, consecutive bytes have consecutive addresses; if a given byte has an address of N, then the preceding byte has an address of N-1, and the following byte has an address of N+1.

A *pointer* is a variable that holds an address of some data, rather than the data itself. Why is this useful? First, you can use a pointer to point to different data and different data structures. By changing the address the pointer contains, you can manipulate (assign, retrieve, change) information in various locations. This allows you, for example, to traverse a linked list of structures with only one pointer.

Second, using pointers allow you to create new variables while your program is executing. C lets your program ask for some amount of memory (in bytes), returning an address that you can store in a pointer. This is known as *dynamic allocation*; using it, your program can adapt to how much (or little) memory is available on a given computer.

Third, you can use a pointer to access different locations in a data structure, such as an array, a string, or a structure. A pointer really points to just one location in memory (a segment:offset); by indexing the pointer, you can access any succeeding byte(s).

You're undoubtedly convinced now that pointers are handy. So how do you use them in C? First, you have to declare them. Consider the following program:

```
main()
{
    int ivar,*iptr;

    iptr = &ivar;
    ivar = 421;
    printf("location of ivar: %p\n",&ivar);
    printf("contents of ivar: %d\n", ivar);
    printf("contents of iptr: %p\n", iptr);
    printf("value pointed to: %d\n",*iptr);
}
```

This **main** has declared two variables: *ivar* and *iptr*. The first, *ivar*, is an integer variable; that is, it holds a value of type **int**. The second, *iptr*, is a *pointer* to an integer variable; that is, it holds an *address* of a value of type **int**. You can tell that *iptr* is a pointer because it has an asterisk (*) in front of it when it is declared. In C, this * is known as the *indirection operator*.

In **main**, these assignments are as follows:

- the address of *ivar* is assigned to *iptr*
- the integer value 421 is then assigned to *ivar*

The address-of operator (&) mentioned in the previous chapter gets the address of *ivar*.

Type in and run the preceding program; you'll get output that looks like this:

```
location of ivar: 166E
contents of ivar: 421
contents of iptr: 166E
value pointed to: 421
```

The first two lines show the address and contents of *ivar*. The third shows the address that *iptr* contains. As you can see, it's the address of the variable *ivar*, that is, the location in memory where your program decided to create *ivar*. The last value printed is the data stored at that address, the same data already assigned to *ivar*.

Note that the third call to **printf** used the expression *iptr* to get its contents, the address of *ivar*. Then the last **printf** call used the expression `*iptr` to fetch the data stored at that address.

Here's a slight variation on the previous program.

```
main()
{
   int ivar,*iptr;

   iptr = &ivar;
   *iptr = 421;
   printf("location of ivar: %p\n",&ivar);
   printf("contents of ivar: %d\n", ivar);
   printf("contents of iptr: %p\n", iptr);
   printf("value pointed to: %d\n",*iptr);
}
```

This still assigns the address of *ivar* to *iptr*, but instead of assigning 421 to *ivar*, **main** assigns it to `*iptr`. The results? Exactly the same as the previous program. Why? Because the statement `*iptr = 421` is the same as the statement `ivar = 421`. And why is that so? Because *ivar* and `*iptr` refer to the same memory location—so both statements assign the value 421 to that location.

Dynamic Allocation

Here's another variation of the program:

```
#include <alloc.h>
main()
{
   int *iptr;

   iptr = (int *) malloc(sizeof(int));
   *iptr = 421;
   printf("contents of iptr: %p\n", iptr);
   printf("value pointed to: %d\n",*iptr);
}
```

This version dropped the declaration of *ivar* altogether. Instead, it's assigning to *iptr* the value returned by some function named **malloc**, which is declared in ALLOC.H (hence the `#include` directive at the start). It then assigns the value 421 to `*iptr`, which is the address *iptr* points to. If you run this program, you'll get a different value for *iptr* than you did before, but `*iptr` will still be 421.

What does the statement `iptr = (int *) malloc(sizeof(int))` do? We'll break it down one part at a time.

- The expression `sizeof(int)` returns the number of bytes that a variable of type **int** requires; using Turbo C on the IBM PC, the value it yields is 2.
- The function **malloc**(*num*) grabs *num* consecutive bytes of the available (unused) memory in your computer. It then returns the starting address of those bytes.
- The expression `(int *)` means you will consider that starting address to be a pointer to type **int**. This is known as *type casting*. In this case, Turbo C doesn't require it. But because many other C compilers do require it, if you leave it off, you will get the error message `Non-portable pointer assignment`.
- Finally, this address is stored in *iptr*. This means you have *dynamically* created an integer variable, which you can refer to as `*iptr`.

Given all this, the entire statement can be described as: "allocate from the computer's memory enough space for a variable of type **int**, then assign the starting address of that memory to *iptr*, which is a pointer to type **int**."

Was all this necessary? Yes. Why? Because without it you would have no guarantee that *iptr* was pointing to an unused area of memory. *iptr* would have some value in it, and that is the address it would use, but you wouldn't know if that section of memory was being used for other reasons. The rule for using pointers is simple: **always assign an address to a pointer before using it**. Rather, don't assign an integer value to `*iptr` without first assigning an address to *iptr*.

Pointers and Functions

Last chapter, we explained how you declare parameters for functions. Perhaps now you understand why you use pointers for formal parameters whose values you wish to change. For example, consider the following function:

```
void  swap(int *a, int *b)
{
   int  temp;
   temp = *a;  *a = *b;  *b = temp;
}
```

This function, **swap**, has declared the two formal parameters, *a* and *b*, to be pointers to **int**. This means they expect an address of an integer variable (rather than its value) to be passed. Any changes made are made to the data at the addresses passed in.

Here's a **main** function that calls **swap**:

```
main()
{
   int  i,j;

   i = 421;
   j = 53;
   printf("before: i = %4d  j = %4d\n",i,j);
   swap(&i,&j);
   printf("after: i = %4d  j = %4d\n",i,j);
}
```

You'll notice that this program does indeed swap the values of *i* and *j*. You can think of this program as being the equivalent of:

```
main()
{
   int  i,j;
   int  *a,*b,temp;

   i = 421;
   j = 53;
   printf("before: i = %4d j = %4d\n",i,j);
   a = &i;
   b = &j;
   temp = *a; *a = *b; *b = temp;
   printf("after: i = %4d  j = %4d\n",i,j);
}
```

This program, of course, produces the same results: The call `swap(&i,&j)` assigns the values of the two actual parameters (*&i* and *&j*) to the two formal parameters (*a* and *b*), then executes the statements in **swap**.

Pointer Arithmetic

What if you wanted to modify the program so that *iptr* points to three integers instead of just one?

Here's one possible solution:

```
#include <alloc.h>
main()
{
   #define NUMINTS 3
   int  *list,i;

   list = (int *) calloc(NUMINTS,sizeof(int));
   *list = 421;
   *(list+1) = 53;
   *(list+2) = 1806;
```

```
/* continued from previous page */

   printf("list of addresses: ");
   for (i = 0; i<NUMINTS; i++)
      printf("%4p ", (list+i));

   printf("\nlist of values  : ");
   for (i = 0; i<NUMINTS; i++)
      printf("%4d ",*(list+i));

   printf("\n");
}
```

Instead of using **malloc**, this routine uses **calloc**, which takes two parameters: how many items to allocate space for, and the size of each item in bytes. So now *list* points to a chunk of memory six (3 * 2) bytes long, big enough to hold three variables of type int.

Note very carefully the three statements that follow. The first statement is familiar: *list = 421. It simply says, "store 421 in the int variable located at the address in *list*."

The next one—*(list+1)=53—is important to understand. At first glance, you might interpret this as "store 53 in the int variable located one byte beyond the address in *list*." If so, you're probably concerned, since this would be right in the middle of the previous int variable (which is two bytes long). This, of course, would mess up the value that you previously stored.

Don't worry; your C compiler is more intelligent than that. It knows that *list* is a pointer to type int, and so the expression list + 1 refers to the byte address of list + (1 * sizeof(int)), so that the value 53 does not clobber the value 421 at all.

Likewise, (list+2) refers to the byte address of list + (2*sizeof(int)), and 1806 gets stored without affecting the previous two values.

In general, *ptr + i* denotes the memory address *ptr + (i * sizeof(int))*.

Type in and run the preceding program; the output will look something like this:

```
list of addresses:  06AA 06AC 06AE
list of values  :    421   53 1806
```

Note that the addresses are two bytes apart, not just one, and that the three values have been kept separate.

To sum up all of this: If you use *ptr*, a pointer to *type*, then the expression (ptr + i) denotes the memory address (ptr + (i * sizeof(type)), where `sizeof`(type) returns the number of bytes that a variable of *type* requires.

Arrays

Most high-level languages—including C—allow you to define *arrays*, that is, indexed lists of a given data type. For example, you can rewrite the last program to look like this:

```
main()
{
   #define NUMINTS 3
   int    list[NUMINTS],i;

   list[0] = 421;
   list[1] = 53;
   list[2] = 1806;
   printf("list of addresses: ");
   for (i = 0; i < NUMINTS; i++)
      printf("%p ",&list[i]);
   printf("\nlist of values  : ");
   for (i = 0; i < NUMINTS; i++)
      printf("%4d ", list[i]);
   printf("\n");
}
```

The expression `int list[NUMINTS]` declares *list* to be an array of `int`s, with space set aside for exactly three (3) `int` variables. The first variable is referred to as *list[0]*, the second as *list[1]*, and the third as *list[2]*.

The general declaration for any array is

```
type  name[size];
```

where *type* is some data type, *name* is the name you give the array, and *size* is the number of elements of *type* that *name* contains. The first element in the array is *name[0]*, while the last is *name[size-1]*; the total size of the array in bytes is *size* * (`sizeof`(*type*)).

Arrays and Pointers

You may have already figured out that there is a close relationship between arrays and pointers. In fact, if you run the previous program, your output will look very familiar:

```
list of addresses: 163A 163C 163E
list of values:     421   53 1806
```

The starting address is different, but that is the only change. The truth is, you can use the name of an array as if it were a pointer; likewise, you can index a pointer as if it were an array.

Consider the following important identities:

```
(list + i) == &(list[i])
*(list + i) == list[i]
```

In both cases, the expression on the left is equivalent to the expression on the right; you can use one in place of the other, regardless of whether you declared *list* as a pointer or as an array.

The only difference between declaring *list* as a pointer vs. as an array is in allocation. If you declare *list* as an array, your program automatically sets aside the requested amount of space. If you declare *list* as a pointer, you must explicitly create space for it using **calloc** or a similar function call, or you must assign to it the address of some space that has already been allocated.

Arrays and Strings

We talked about strings in the previous chapter and referred to declaring a string in two slightly different ways: as a pointer to characters and as an array of characters. Now you can better understand that difference.

If you declare a string as an array of **char**, the space for that string is allocated. If you declare a string as a pointer to **char**, no space is allocated; you must either allocate it yourself (using **malloc** or something similar) or assign to it the address of an existing string. An example of this is given in the section "Pitfalls in C Programming" later in this chapter.

Multi-Dimensional Arrays

Yes, you can have multi-dimensional arrays, and they are declared just as you might think:

```
type  name[size1] [size2]...[sizeN];
```

Consider the following program, which initializes a couple of two-dimensional arrays, then performs matrix multiplication on them:

```
main()
{
    int a[3][4] = { { 5,   3, -21, 42},
        { 44, 15,  0, 6},
        { 97,  6, 81, 2} };
```

```
/* continued from previous page */
    int b[4][2] = { { 22,   7},
       { 97, -53},
       { 45,   0},
       { 72,   1} };

    int c[3][2],i,j,k;

    for (i = 0; i < 3; i++) {
       for (j = 0; j < 2; j++) {
          c[i][j] = 0;
          for (k = 0; k < 4; k++)
             c[i][j] += a[i][k] * b[k][j];
       }
    }
    for (i = 0; i < 3; i++) {
       for (j=0; j<2; j++)
          printf("c[%d][%d] = %d ",i,j,c[i][j]);
       printf("\n");
    }
}
```

Take note of two things in the preceding program: The syntax for initializing a two-dimensional array consists of nested { . . . } lists separated by commas, and square brackets ([ ]) are used around each index variable.

Some languages use the syntax [i,j]; that is legal syntax in C, but is the same as saying just [j], since the comma is interpreted as the comma operator ("evaluate *i*, then evaluate *j*, then let the entire expression assume the value of *j*"). Be sure to put square brackets around each and every index variable.

Multi-dimensional arrays are stored in what is known as *row-column order*. This means that the last index varies the most rapidly. In other words, given the array *arr[3][2]*, the elements in *arr* are stored in the following order:

```
arr[0][0]
arr[0][1]
arr[1][0]
arr[1][1]
arr[2][0]
arr[2][1]
```

The same principle holds true for arrays of three, four, or more dimensions.

Arrays and Functions

What happens when you want to pass an array to a function?

Look at this function, which returns the *index* of the lowest value in an array of `int`:

```
int  lmin(int list[],int size)
{
   int  i, minindx, min;

   minindx = 0;
   min = list[minindx];

   for (i = 1; i < size; i++)
     if (list[i] < min) {
        min = list[i];
        minindx = i;
     }
   return(minindx);
}
```

Here you see one of the great strengths of C: You don't need to know how large *list[]* is at compile time. Why? Because the compiler is content to consider *list[]* to be the starting address of the array, and it doesn't really care where it ends. A call to the function **lmin** might look like this:

```
main()
{
   #define VSIZE 22
   int  i,vector[VSIZE];

   for (i = 0; i < VSIZE; i++) {
      vector[i] = rand();
      printf("vector[%2d] = %6d\n",i,vector[i]);
   }
   i = lmin(vector,VSIZE);
   printf("minimum: vector[%2d] = %6d\n",i,vector[i]);
}
```

Question: What exactly is passed to **lmin**? Answer: The starting address of *vector*. This means that if you were to make changes to *list* within *lmin*, those changes would be made to *vector* as well. For example, you could write the following function:

```
void setrand(int list[],int size);
{
   int i;
   for (i = 0; i < size; i++) list[i] = rand();
}
```

Then you could make the call `setrand(vector,VSIZE)` in **main** to initialize *vector*.

How about multi-dimensional arrays passed to functions? Do you have the same flexibility? Suppose you wanted to modify **setrand** to work on a two-dimensional array.

You'd have to do something like this:

```
void setrand(int matrix[][CSIZE],int rsize)
{
   int i,j;
   for (i = 0; i < rsize; i++) {
      for (j = 0; j < CSIZE; j++)
      matrix[i][j] = rand();
   }
}
```

CSIZE is a global constant fixing the size of the second dimension of the array. In other words, any array you passed to **setrand** would have to have a second dimension of CSIZE.

There is another solution, however. Suppose you have an array *matrix[15][7]* that you want to pass to **setrand**. If you use the original declaration of `setrand(int list[],int size)`, you can call it as follows:

```
setrand(matrix,15*7);
```

The array *matrix* will then look to **setrand** like a one-dimensional array of size 105 (which is 15*7), and everything will work just fine.

Structures

Arrays and pointers allow you to build lists of items of the same data type. What if you want to construct something out of different data types? Declare a *structure*.

A *structure* is a conglomerate data structure, a lumping together of different data types. For example, suppose you wanted to keep track of information about a star: name, spectral class, coordinates, and so on. You might declare the following:

```
typedef struct {
   char   name[25];
   char   class;
   short  subclass;
   float  decl,RA,dist;
} star ;
```

This defines the **struct** type *star*.

Having declared it—that is, having placed the previous definition at the start of your program file—you could use it as follows:

```
main()
{
    star mystar;

    strcpy(mystar.name,"Epsilon Eridani");
    mystar.class    = 'K';
    mystar.subclass = 2;
    mystar.decl     =  3.5167;
    mystar.RA       = -9.633;
    mystar.dist     =  0.303;

    /* Rest of function main() */
}
```

You refer to each *member* of a structure variable by preceding it with the variable's name followed by a period (.). The construct *varname.memname* is considered equivalent to the name of a variable of the the same type as *memname*, and you can perform all the same operations.

Structures and Pointers

You can declare pointers to structures, just as you can declare pointers to other data types. This ability is essential for creating linked lists and other dynamic data structures. In fact, pointers to structures are used so often in C that there is a special symbol for referring to the member of a structure pointed to by a pointer.

Consider the following rewrite of the previous program.

```
#include <alloc.h>
main()
{
    star *mystar;

    mystar = (star *) malloc(sizeof(star));
    strcpy(mystar -> name,"Epsilon Eridani");
    mystar -> class = 'K';
    mystar -> subclass = 2;
    mystar -> decl = 3.5167;
    mystar -> RA = -9.633;
    mystar -> dist = 0.303;

    /* Rest of function main() */
}
```

This rewrite declares *mystar* to be a *pointer* to type *star*, rather than to be a variable of type *star*. It allocates space for *mystar* via the call to **malloc**. Now when you refer to the members of *mystar*, you use *ptrname->memname*. The symbol -> means "member of the structure pointed to by"; it is a shorthand notation for *(*ptrname).memname*.

The switch Statement

You may find yourself building long `if..else if..else if..`constructs. Look at the following function:

```
#include <ctype.h>
do_main_menu(short *done)
{
   char  cmd;

   *done = 0;
   do {
      cmd = toupper(getch());
      if (cmd == 'F') do_file_menu(done);
      else if (cmd == 'R') run_program();
      else if (cmd == 'C') do_compile();
      else if (cmd == 'M') do_make();
      else if (cmd == 'P') do_project_menu();
      else if (cmd == 'O') do_option_menu();
      else if (cmd == 'E') do_error_menu();
      else handle_others(cmd, done);
   } while (!*done);
}
```

This is so common in programming that C has a special control structure for it: the **switch** statement. Here's that same function, but rewritten using the **switch** statement:

```
#include <ctype.h>
do_main_menu(short *done)
{
   char  cmd;

   *done = 0;
   do {
      cmd = toupper(getch());
      switch (cmd) {
        case 'F': do_file_menu(done); break;
        case 'R': run_program(); break;
        case 'C': do_compile(); break;
        case 'M': do_make(); break;
        case 'P': do_project_menu(); break;
        case 'O': do_option_menu(); break;
        case 'E': do_error_menu(); break;
        default : handle_others(cmd,done);
   } while (!*done);
}
```

This function enters a loop that reads in a character, converts it to uppercase, and stores it in *cmd*. It then executes the **switch** statement based on the value of *cmd*. The loop continues until the variable *done* gets assigned zero (presumably in the functions **do_file_menu** or **handle_others**).

The **switch** statement takes the value of *cmd* and compares it against each of the **case** labels. If there is a match, execution starts at that label and continues until either you encounter a **break** statement or you reach the end of the **switch** statement. If there is no match and you've included the label default label (default) in your **switch** statement, then execution starts there; if there is no default, then the entire **switch** statement is skipped.

In the **switch** statement, *value* must be *integer compatible*. In other words, it has to be easily converted to an integer; it can be a **char**, any **enum** type, and (of course) an **int** with all its variants. You cannot use reals (such as **float** and **double**), pointers, strings, or other data structures (though you can use integer-compatible elements of a data structure).

Although (*value*) can be any expression (constant, variable, function call, or any combination thereof), the case labels themselves have to be constants. What's more, you can only list one value per **case** keyword.

If **do_main_menu** hadn't used the function **toupper** to convert *cmd* to uppercase, then the **switch** statement might have looked like this:

```
switch (cmd) {
   case 'f':
   case 'F': do_file_menu(done);
      break;
   case 'r' :
   case 'R' : run_program();
      break;
   ...
```

This statement executes the function **do_file_menu** if *cmd* is either a lower- or uppercase F, and so on for the rest of the options.

Remember, you must use the **break** statement when you're finished with a given case. Otherwise, the remaining statements will be executed (until, of course, you encounter a **break** statement). If you had left off the **break** statement following the call to **do_file_menu**, typing the letter *F* would result in a call to **do_file_menu**, followed by a call to **run_program**.

There are times when you want to do that, though; consider this code:

```
typdef enum { sun, mon, tues, wed, thur, fri, sat } days;

main()
{
   days today;

   ...
   switch (today) {
      case mon:
      case tues:
      case wed:
      case thur:
      case fri: puts("go work!"); break;
      case sat: printf("clean the yard and ");
      case sun: puts("relax!");
   }
   ...
}
```

With this **switch** statement, the values *mon* through *fri* all end up executing the same **puts** statement, after which the **break** statement causes you to leave the **switch**. However, if *today* equals *sat*, then the **printf** is executed, following which the `puts("relax!")` statement is executed; if *today* equals *sun*, then only that last **puts** is executed.

Control Flow Commands

There are additional commands for use within control structures or to simulate other control structures. The **return** statement lets you exit functions early. The **break** and **continue** statements are designed to be used within loops and help you skip over statements. The **goto** statement allows you to jump around in your code. And the conditional expression (?:) lets you compress certain **if...else** statements onto just one line.

A word of advice: Think twice before using these (except, of course, for **return**). There are situations where they represent the best solution, but more often than not you can solve your problem clearly without resorting to them. Especially avoid the use of the **goto** statement; given the **return**, **break**, and **continue** statements, there shouldn't be that much need for it.

The return Statement

There are two major uses of the **return** statement. First, if a function returns a value, you *must* use it in order to pass that value back to the calling routine.

For example,

```
int    imax(int a, int b);
{
   if (a > b)
      return(a);
   else
      return(b);
}
```

Here, the routine uses the **return** statement to pass back the maximum of the two values accepted.

The second major use of the **return** statement is to exit a function at some point other than its end. For example, a function might detect a condition early on that requires that it terminate. Rather than put the rest of the function inside of an **if** statement, you can just call **return** to exit. If the function is of type **void**, you can just use **return** with no value passed back at all.

Consider this modification of the **lmin** function given earlier:

```
int lmin(int list[], int size)
{
   int i, minindx, min;

   if (size <= 0)
      return(-1);
      ...
}
```

In this case, if the parameter *size* is less than or equal to zero, then there is nothing in *list*; therefore, **return** is called right off the bat, to get out of the function. Note that an error value of –1 is returned. Since –1 is never a valid index into an array, the calling routine knows that it did something wrong.

The break Statement

Sometimes you want to quickly and easily exit a loop before you reach its end.

Consider the following program:

```
#define LIMIT 100
#define MAX   10
main()
{
    int   i,j,k,score;
    int   scores[LIMIT][MAX];

    for (i = 0; i < LIMIT; i++) {
        j = 0;
        while (j < MAX-1) {
            printf("please enter score #%d: ",j);
            scanf("%d",score);
            if (score < 0)
                break;
            scores[i][++j] = score;
        }
        scores[i][0] = j;
    }
}
```

Note the statement `if (score < 0) break;`. This says that if the user enters a negative value for the score, the **while** loop is terminated. The variable *j* is used both to index into *scores* and to keep track of the total number of scores in each row; that count is then stored in the first element of the row.

You may recall the **break** statement from its use in the **switch** statement last chapter. In that case, it caused the program to exit the **switch** statement; here, it causes the program to exit the loop and proceed with the program. The **break** statement can be used with all three loops (**for, while,** and **do...while**), as well as in the **switch** statement; however, it *cannot* be used in an **if...else** statement or just in the main body of a function.

The continue Statement

Sometimes, you don't want to get out of the loop completely; you just want to skip the rest of the loop and start at the top again. In those situations, you can use the **continue** statement, which does just that.

Look at this program:

```
#define LIMIT 100
#define MAX   10
main()
{
    int   i,j,k,score;
    int   scores[LIMIT][MAX];

    for (i = 0; i < LIMIT; i++) {
        j = 0;
        while (j < MAX-1) {
            printf("please enter score #%d: ",j);
            scanf("%d",score);
            if (score < 0)
                continue;
            scores[i][++j] = score;
        }
        scores[i][0] = j;
    }
}
```

When the **continue** statement is executed, the program skips over the rest of the loop and does the loop test again. As a result, this program works differently from the one before. Instead of exiting the inner loop when the user enters a score of –1, it assumes that an error has been made and goes to the top of the **while** loop again. Since *j* has not been incremented, it asks for the same score again.

The goto Statement

Yes, there is a **goto** statement in C. The format is simple: **goto** *label*, where *label* is some identifier, associated with a given statement. However, most intelligent uses of the **goto** statement are taken care of by the three previous statements, so consider carefully whether you really need to use it.

The Conditional Expression (?:)

You might on occasion want to select between two expressions (and the resulting values), based on some condition.

This is usually accomplished with an `if..else` statement, such as:

```
int    imin(int a, int b)
{
   if (a < b)
      return(a);
   else
      return(b);
}
```

This happens often enough that there is a special construct to perform this type of selection. Its format is

```
expr1 ? expr2 : expr3
```

This is interpreted as follows: "If *expr1* is true, then evaluate *expr2* and let the entire expression assume its value; otherwise, evaluate *expr3* and assume its value." Using this construct, you can rewrite the function **imin** as follows:

```
int  imin(int a, int b)
{
   return((a < b) ? a : b);
}
```

Better yet, you can rewrite **imin** as an in-line macro:

```
#define imin(a,b) ((a < b) ? a : b)
```

Now whenever your program sees the expression `imin(e1,e2)`, it replaces it with `((e1<e2) ? e1 : e2)` and continues compilation. This is actually a more general solution, since *a* and *b* are no longer limited to being **int**; they can be any type which allows the < relationship.

Style in C Programming: Modern vs. Classic

In C programming, there are a number of current trends to embrace certain techniques that make C easier to use. Many of these trends counteract classic traditions or methods of C programming. Most have been made possible by language extensions defined by the ANSI C Standards Committee. This section should give you a feeling for how things have been done in the past and how the new standards can help you write better C programs.

Turbo C, of course, supports both the classic programming style and the modern style.

Using Function Prototypes and Full Function Definitions

In the classic style of C programming, you declare functions merely by specifying the name and type returned.

For example, you would define the function **swap** as:

```
int  swap();
```

No parameter information is give, either as to number or type. The classic-style definition of the function looks like this:

```
int  swap(a,b)
int  *a,*b;
{
    /* Body of function */
}
```

This style results in very little error checking, which in turn can result in some very subtle and hard-to-trace bugs. Avoid it.

The modern style involves the use of function prototypes (for function declarations) and parameter lists (for function definitions).

Redeclare **swap** using a function prototype:

```
int  swap(int *a, int *b);
```

Now when your program compiles, it has all the information it needs to do complete error checking on any call to **swap**. And you can use a similar format when you define the function:

```
int  swap(int *a, int *b)
{
    /* Body of function */
}
```

The modern style increases the error checking performed even if you don't use function prototypes; if you do use prototypes, this will cause the compiler to ensure that the declarations and definitions agree.

Using enum Definitions

In classic C, lists of values are defined using the #define directive, like this:

```
#define sun    0
#define mon    1
#define tues   2
#define wed    3
#define thur   4
#define fri    5
#define sat    6
```

Nowadays, however, you can declare enumerated data types using the keyword **enum**, as shown here:

```
typedef enum {sun, mon, tues, wed, thur, fri, sat} days;
```

This has the same effect as the classic method, right down to setting *sun* = 0 and *sat* = 6; however, the modern method does more information hiding and abstraction than the long list of #define directives. And you can declare variables to be of type *days*.

Using typedef

In classic-style C, user-defined data types were seldom named, with the exception of structures and unions—and even with them you had to precede any declaration with the keyword **struct** or **union**.

In modern-style C, another level of information hiding is used when using the **typedef** directive. This allows you to associate a given data type (including **struct**s and **enum**s) with a name, then declare variables of that type.

Here are some sample type definitions with variable declarations:

```
typedef int  *intptr;
typedef char  namestr[30];
typedef enum  { male, female, unknown } sex;
typedef struct {
    namestr  last,first;
    char     ssn[9];
    sex      gender;
    short    age;
    float    gpa;
} student;
typedef student class[100];

class     hist104,ps102;
student   valedictorian;
intptr    iptr;
```

Using **typedef**s makes the program more readable; it also allows you to change a single location—where a type is actually defined—and have that change propagated through the entire program.

Declaring void functions

In the original definition of C, every function returned a value of some type; if no type was declared, the function was assumed to be of type **int**. In a similar fashion, functions that returned "generic" (untyped) pointers were usually declared to return a pointer to **char**, just because they had to return *something*.

Now there is a standard type **void**, which can be thought of as a kind of "null" type. Any function that does not explicitly return a value should be declared as being of type **void**. Note that many of the run-time memory allocation routines (such as **malloc**) are declared to be of type void *. This means they return an untyped pointer, which you can then (in Turbo C) assign to a pointer of any type without casting (though you should cast anyway, to preserve portability).

Make Use of Extensions

There are a number of minor extensions to the C language that aid program readability, replace some anachronisms, and allow you to move forward. Here's a brief listing.

String Literals

In classic C, you had to use continuation characters or some kind of concatenation in order to have large string literals in your program.

In modern-style C, you can easily spread a large literal across several lines, like this:

```
main()
{
   char  *msg;

   msg = "Four score and seven years ago, our fathers"
         " brought forth upon\nthis continent a new"
         " nation, dedicated to the ideal that all"
         " men\nare created equal";

   printf("%s",msg);
}
```

Hexadecimal Character Constants

In classic C, escape sequences specifying particular ASCII codes were all done in octal (base 8). This was because C had been originally developed on machines where binary numbers were usually represented in octal form.

Nowadays, most computers use hexadecimal (base 16) to represent binary numbers. Because of this, modern C allows you to declare character constants in hex notation. The general format is `'\xDD'`, where *DD* represents one or two hexademical digits (0..9, A..F). These escape sequences can be directly assigned to `char` variables, or they can be embedded in strings, for example, ch = `'\x20'`.

signed Types

Classic C assumed that all integer-based types were signed, and so included the type modifier `unsigned` so that you could specify otherwise. By default, variables of type `char` were considered `signed`, which meant that the underlying range of values was –128 to 127.

On microcomputers today, however, the `char` type is often thought of as being `unsigned`, and Turbo C has a compiler option to allow you to make that the default. In such a case, though, you may still want to be able to declare a `signed char`. In modern C, you can do so, since `signed` is recognized as a valid modifier.

Pitfalls in C Programming

There are a number of common errors that programmers make when they first start coding in C. Here's a list of some of them, along with suggestions how to avoid them.

Path Names with C Strings

Everyone knows that the backslash (\) in MS-DOS indicates a directory name. However, in C, the backslash is the escape character in a string. This conflict causes a bit of a problem if you give a path name with a C string.

For example, if you had the statement

```
file = fopen("c:\new\tools.dat", "r");
```

you'd expect to open the file TOOLS.DAT in the NEW directory on drive C. You won't. Instead, the \n gets you the escape sequence for the newline character (LF) and the \t gets you the tab character.

The result is your file name will have embedded in it the newline and tab characters. DOS would reject the string as an improper file name, as file names may not have newline or tab in them. The proper string is

```
"c:\\new\\tools.dat"
```

Using and Misusing Pointers

Pointers may well be the single most confusing issue to novice C programmers. When do you use pointers, and when don't you? When do you use the indirection operator (*)? When do you use the address-of operator (&)? And how can you avoid really messing up the operating system while running?

Using an Uninitialized Pointer

One serious danger is to assign a value to the address contained by a pointer without having assigned an address to that pointer.

For example,

```
main()
{
    int *iptr;

    *iptr = 421;
    printf("*iptr = %d\n",*iptr);
}
```

What makes this pitfall so dangerous is that you can often get away with it. In the previous example, the pointer *iptr* has some random address in it; that's where the value 421 is stored. This program is small enough that there is very little chance of anything being clobbered. In a larger program, though, there is an increasing chance of just that, since you may well have other information stored at the address that *iptr* happens to contain. And if you're using the tiny memory model, where the code and data segments occupy the same space, you run the risk of corrupting the machine code itself.

Strings

You may recall that you can declare strings as pointers to **char** or as arrays of **char**. You may also recall that these are the same with one very important difference: If you use a pointer to **char**, no space for the string is allocated; if you use an array, space *is* allocated, and the array variable holds the address of that space.

Failure to understand this difference can lead to two types of errors. Consider the following program:

```
main()
{
    char   *name;
    char   msg[10];

    printf("What is your name? ");
    scanf("%s",name);
    msg = "Hello, ";
    printf("%s%s",msg,name);
}
```

At first glance, this might appear to be perfectly fine; a little clumsy, but still allowable.

But this has introduced two separate errors.

The first error has to do with the statement

```
scanf("%s",name)
```

The statement itself is legal and correct. Since *name* is a pointer to **char**, you don't need to use the address-of (&) operator in front of it.

However, the program has *not* allocated any memory for *name*; the name you type in will be stored at whatever random address that *name* happens to have. You will get a warning on this (`Possible use of 'name' before definition`), but no error.

The second problem *will* cause an error. The problem lies in the statement `msg = "Hello, "`. The compiler thinks you are trying to change *msg* to the address of the constant string `"Hello, "`. You can't do that, because array names are constants that cannot be modified (just like 7 is a constant, and you can't say "7 = i"). The compiler will give you an error message `Lvalue required`.

What are the solutions to these errors? The simplest approach is to switch the ways in which *name* and *msg* have been declared:

```
main()
{
    char name[10];
    char *msg;

    printf("What is your name? ");
    scanf("%s",name);
    msg = "Hello, ";
    printf("%s%s",msg,name);
}
```

This works perfectly well. The variable *name* has space set aside to hold your name as you type it in, while *msg* lets you assign to it the address of the constant string `"Hello, "`.

If, however, you are bound and determined to keep the declarations the way they were, then you'll need to make the following changes to the code:

```
#include <alloc.h>
main()
{
    char *name;
    char msg[10];

    name = (char *) malloc(10);
    printf("What is your name? ");
    scanf("%s",name);
    strcpy(msg,"Hello, ");
    printf("%s%s",msg,name);
}
```

The call to **malloc** sets aside ten bytes of memory and assigns the address of that memory to *name*, taking care of our first problem. The function **strcpy** does a character-by-character copy from the constant string `"Hello, "` to the array *msg*.

Confusing Assignment (=) with Equality (==)

In the languages Pascal and BASIC, a comparison for equality is made with the expression `if (a = b)`. In C, that is a valid construct, but it has quite a different meaning.

Look at this code fragment:

```
if (a = b)
    puts("Equal");
else
    puts("Not equal");
```

If you're a Pascal or BASIC programmer, then you might expect this to print `Equal` if *a* and *b* have the same value, and `Not equal` otherwise. That's not what happens. In C, the expression `a = b` means "assign the value of *b* to *a*," and the entire expression takes on the value of *b*. So, the previous fragment will assign the value of *b* to *a*, then print `Equal` if *b* has a nonzero value, otherwise it will print `Not equal`.

What you *really* want is the following:

```
if (a == b)
    puts("Equal);
else
    puts("Not equal");
```

Forgetting the break in Switch Statements

You may remember that the **break** statement is used in a **switch** statement to end a particular case. Please continue to remember that. If you forget to put a **break** statement in for a given case, the case(s) after it are executed as well.

144

Array Indexing

Don't forget that arrays start at [0], not at [1]. A common error is to write code like this:

```
main()
{
   int list[100],i;

   for (i = 1; i <= 100; i++)
      list[i] = i*i;
}
```

This program leaves the first location in *list*—namely *list[0]*—uninitialized, and it stores a value in a nonexistent location of *list*—*list[100]*—possibly overwriting other data in the process.

The correct code should be written like this:

```
main()
{
   int list[100],i;

   for (i = 0; i < 100; i++)
      list[i] = i*i;
}
```

Failure to Pass-by-Address

Look at the following program and figure out what's wrong with it:

```
main()
{
   int a,b,sum;

   printf("Enter two values: ");
   scanf("%d %d",a,b);
   sum = a + b;
   printf("The sum is %d\n",sum);
}
```

Give up? The error is in the statement `scanf("%d %d",a,b)`. Remember that **scanf** requires you to pass *addresses* instead of values? The same is true of any function whose formal parameters are pointers. The previous program will compile and run, since **scanf** will take whatever random values are in *a* and *b* and use them as addresses in which to store the values you enter.

The correct statement should read `scanf("%d %d",&a,&b);` that way, the addresses of *a* and *b* are passed to **scanf**, and the values you enter are correctly stored in those variables. This same pitfall can happen with your own functions. Remember the function **swap** defined back in the section on pointers?

What would happen if you called it like this:

```
main()
{
    int i,j;

    i = 421;
    j = 53;
    printf("before: i = %4d j = %4d\n",i,j);
    swap(i,j);
    printf("after: i = %4d j = %4d\n",i,j);
}
```

The variables *i* and *j* would have the same values before and after the call to **swap**; however, the values at data addresses 421 and 53 would have their values swapped, which could cause some subtle and hard-to-trace problems.

How do you avoid this?

Use function prototypes and full function definitions.

Actually, you would have gotten a compiler error in the previous version of **main** if **swap** were defined as it was earlier in this chapter.

If, however, you defined it in the following manner, the program would compile just fine:

```
void  swap(a,b)
int   *a,*b;
{
    ...
}
```

Moving the definitions of *a* and *b* out of the parentheses disables the error checking that would go on otherwise, which is the best reason for not using the classic style of function definition.

Sailing Away

As we said at the start of the previous chapter, we can't give you a complete tutorial on C in just two chapters. But we have given it our best shot. What you should now do—what you should have been doing all along—is key in these example programs, compile them, run them, and (most importantly) modify them to see what happens when you change things around. Best of luck, and bon voyage.

C   H   A   P   T   E   R

6

Notes for Turbo Pascal Programmers

Now, before you go any farther, go back to Chapters 5 and 3 and at least skim through them. Learn how C implements the basic elements of programming. We will cover some of the same ground in this chapter, but there are many details in those two chapters that you won't find here.

In a nutshell, Pascal is a fairly disciplined and structured language, whereas C is rather free-wheeling and flexible. But C is also *caveat programmer*; it gives you plenty of rope to swing with—or hang yourself. Pascal takes care of you better than C does, and thus is more suited as a language to learn the fundamentals of programming.

Turbo C and Turbo Pascal are moving toward the center of this C-Pascal language spectrum: Turbo C adds some structure to C, and Turbo Pascal adds some flexibility to Pascal.

In This Chapter...

This chapter is not meant to be a comprehensive discussion of C and its many fine features; its goal is to help you, as a Turbo Pascal programmer, learn enough about Turbo C to start writing programs quickly. Expertise and insight will come only with time, practice, and the hundreds of lines of code that you will write.

Notes for Turbo Pascal Programmers   149

We'll show you, in this chapter, the similarities and differences between Pascal and Turbo C programming. We start off with the basics: program structure and the elements of programming. After that, we use a major example to illustrate our discussion of data structures. The end of this chapter is devoted to a discussion of programming issues that you need to be aware of, and an overview of common pitfalls that trap Pascal programmers learning C.

Throughout this chapter, we use examples of program code to illustrate the points we're making. Each example consists of a Turbo Pascal program or fragment on the left, and its equivalent in Turbo C on the right.

Program Structure

As you know, program structure in Turbo Pascal takes the following form:

```
program ProgName;
< declarations:
  const
  type                          freely mixed
  var
  procedures and functions >
begin                           { Main body of prog ProgName }
  < statements >
  end.                          { End of prog ProgName }
```

The main body of the program is executed; if it calls additional procedures and functions, they are executed as well. All identifiers—constants, types, variables, procedures, and functions—must be declared before they are used. Procedures and functions are organized in a nearly identical manner.

Program structure in C is a little more flexible:

```
< preprocessor commands >
< type definitions >
< function prototypes >           freely mixed
< variables >
< functions >
```

Functions, in turn, have the following structure:

```
<type> FuncName(<parm declarations>)
{
   <local declarations>
   <statements>
}
```

Of all the functions you declare, one must be named **main**; that is the *main body* of your program. In other words, when your Turbo C program starts execution, **main** is called, and it can in turn call other functions. A C program consists entirely of functions. However, some functions are of type **void**, meaning that they return no values; so they are like Pascal procedures. Also (unlike Pascal) you are free to ignore any values that a function returns.

An Example

Here are two programs, one written in Turbo Pascal, the other written in Turbo C, which illustrate some of the similarities and differences between the two in program structure:

Turbo Pascal	Turbo C

```
program MyProg;                         int      i,j,k;
var
  I,J,K    : Integer;

function Max(A,B : Integer) : Integer;  int  max(int a, int b)
begin                                   {
  if A > B                                 if (a > b)
    then Max := A                             return(a);
                                           else
    else Max := B                             return(b);
                                        }
end;                                     /* End of max() */
{ End of func Max }

procedure Swap(var A,B : Integer);      void swap(int *a, int *b)
var                                     {
  Temp      : Integer;                     int    temp;
begin                                      temp = *a; *a = *b; *b = temp;
  Temp := A; A := B; B := Temp          }
end;                                     /* End of swap() */
{ End of proc Swap }

begin       { Main body of MyProg }     main()
                                        {
  I := 10; J := 15;                        i = 10; j = 15;
  K := Max(I,J);                           k = max(i,j);
  Swap(I,K);                               swap(&i,&k);
  Write('I = ',I:2,' J = ',J:2);           printf("i = %2d j = %2d",i,j);
  Writeln(' K = ',K:2)                     printf(" k = %2d\n",k);
end.                                    }
{ End of program MyProg }                /* End of main */
```

If we had chosen to, we could have declared *i*, *j*, and *k* inside of **main**, instead of as global variables. In many cases, that's better programming practice, since it eliminates the chance (and temptation) of directly modifying global variables within functions, while still creating variables that exist throughout the course of the program.

If the C program on the right looks bizarre to you, just wait (you ain't seen nothin' yet!). By the time you finish this chapter, you'll be right at home with it; in fact, you'll probably be writing things that look even more bizarre.

A Comparison of the Elements of Programming

Back in Chapter 5, we talked about the seven basic elements of programming—output, data types, operations, input, conditional execution, iterative execution, and subroutines. Let's look at those again, seeing how Pascal and C both resemble and differ from each other.

Output

The main output commands in Turbo Pascal are *Write* and *Writeln*. Turbo C, on the other hand, has a variety of commands, based just exactly on what you want to do. The most commonly used, and the one that requires the most overhead, is **printf**, which takes the format:

```
printf(<format string>,<item>,<item>,...);
```

where *<format string>* is a *string* literal or a *string variable* (remember, C uses double quotes) and the *<item>*s are optional variables, expressions, etc., that match up with format commands in the format string; see Chapter 5 for more details. To get a newline (=*Writeln*) in C, insert the escape sequence \n (newline) at the end of the format string.

Here are some example routines in Turbo Pascal with equivalent (or near equivalent) C routines:

Turbo Pascal	Turbo C

```
var
  A,B,C : Integer;             int    a,b,c;
  Amt   : Real;                float  amt;
  Name  : string[20];          char   name[21]; (or *name)
  Ans   : Char;                char   ans;

Writeln('Hello, world.');      printf("Hello, world.\n");
Write('What''s your name? ');  printf("What's your name? ");
WriteLn('"Hello," said John'); printf("\"Hello,\" said John\n");

Writeln(A,' + ',B,' = ',C);    printf("%d + %d = %d\n",a,b,c);
Writeln('You owe us $',Amt:6:2);   printf("You owe us $%6.2f\n",amt);

Writeln('Your name is ',Name,'?');   printf("Your name is %s?\n",name)
Writeln('The answer is ',Ans);   printf("The answer is %c\n",ans);

Write(' A = ',A:4);            printf(" a = %4d",a);
Writeln(' A*A = ',(A*A):6);    printf(" a*a = %6d\n",a*a);
```

Two other C output routines you'll probably want to be aware of are **puts** and **putchar**. **puts** takes a single string as its argument and writes it out, automatically adding a new line. **putchar** is even simpler: It writes a single character. So, for example, the following commands are equivalent:

```
Writeln(Name);                 puts(Name);
Writeln('Hi, there!'); Writeln;    puts("Hi, there!\n");

Write(Ch);                     putchar(ch);
```

Data Types

Most Turbo Pascal data types have equivalents in Turbo C. C actually has a greater variety of data types, with different sizes of integers and floating-point values, as well as the modifiers **signed** and **unsigned**.

Here's a table giving rough equivalents between Pascal and C data types.

Turbo Pascal			**Turbo C**		
char	(1 byte)	chr(0 - 255)	char	(1 byte)	-128 - 127
byte	(1 byte)	0 - 255	unsigned char	(1 byte)	0 - 255
integer	(2 bytes)	-32768 - 32767	short	(2 bytes)	-32768 - 32767
			int	(2 bytes)	-32768 - 32767
			unsigned int	(2 bytes)	0 - 65535
			long	(4 bytes)	-2^{31} - $(2^{31}-1)$
			unsigned long	(4 bytes)	0 - $(2^{32}-1)$
real	(6 bytes)	1E-38 - 1E+38	float	(4 bytes)	$\pm$ 3.4 E $\pm$38
			double	(8 bytes)	$\pm$ 1.7 E $\pm$308
boolean	(1 byte)	false, true	0 = false, non-zero = true		

Note that there is no boolean data type in C; expressions that require a Boolean value interpret a value of zero as being *false* and any other value as being *true*.

In addition to the data types listed, Turbo C supports *enumerated* data types; however, unlike Pascal, these are effectively just pre-assigned integer constants and are completely compatible with all integral types.

Turbo Pascal	**Turbo C**

type
  Days = (Sun,Mon,Tues,Wed,
              Thurs,Fri,Sat);
	enum days { Sun,Mon,Tues,Wed,
	               Thurs,Fri,Sat };

var Today : Days;	enum days today;

Operations

Turbo C has all the operators of Turbo Pascal, and then some.

One of the more basic differences between the two languages is how *assignment* is handled. In Pascal, assignment (:=) is a statement. In C, assignment (=) is an operator that may be used in an expression.

Table 6.1 shows a side-by-side comparison of operators in Turbo Pascal and Turbo C. They are listed in order of precedence, with operations grouped together having the same precedence.

Table 6.1: Pascal and C Operators

unary minus	A := -B;	a = -b;
unary plus	A := +B;	a = +b;
logical not	not Flag	!flag
bitwise complement	A := not B;	a = ~b;
address	A := Addr(B);	a = &b;
pointer reference	A := IntPtr^;	a = *intptr;
size of	A := SizeOf(B);	a = sizeof(b);
increment	A := Succ(A);	a++ and ++a
decrement	A := Pred(A);	a - - and - - a
multiplication	A := B * C;	a = b * c;
integer division	A := B div C;	a = b / c;
floating division	X := B / C;	x = b / c;
modulus	A := B mod C;	a = b % c;
addition	A := B + C;	a = b + c;
subtraction	A := B - C;	a = b - c;
shift right	A := B shr C;	a = b >> c;
shift left	A := B shl C;	a = b << c;
greater than	A > B	a > b
greater or equal	A >= B	a >= b
less than	A < B	a < b
less or equal	A <= B	a <= b
equal	A = B	a == b
not equal	A <> B	a != b
bitwise AND	A := B and C;	a = b & c;
bitwise OR	A := B or C;	a = b	c;
bitwise XOR	A := B xor C;	a = b ^ c;
logical AND	Flag1 and Flag2	flag1 && flag2
logical OR	Flag1 or Flag2	flag1 || flag2
assignment	A := B;	a = b;
	A := A <op> B;	a <op> = b;

There are some important differences in C operators and operator precedence.

First, the *increment* (++) and *decrement* (--) operators can be placed before or after the variable name. If the operator is placed before the variable, then the variable is incremented (or decremented) before the rest of the expression is evaluated; if after, the expression is evaluated first, then the variable is incremented (or decremented).

Second, the logical operators in C (&&, | |) are *short-circuit* operators. This means that if the first item determines the truth of the expression, then the second is never evaluated. So, unlike Pascal, C lets you safely write this:

```
while (i <= limit && list[i] != 0) ... ;
```

where *limit* is the largest allowable index into the *list* array.

If the first item (`i <= limit`) is *false*, then C knows that the entire expression must be *false*, and it doesn't evaluate the second item (`list[i] != 0`), which would be an index range error.

Third, C allows you to take the general expression

```
A = A <op> B
```

where *<op>* is any binary operator (except for && and | |) and replace it with

```
A <op>= B
```

So, for example, instead of `A = A * B`, you could write `A *= B`, and so on.

Input

Again, in Turbo Pascal, you have one basic input command, *Read()*, with a few variations (*Readln()*, *Read(f,)*, etc.). In Turbo C, the main function used for keyboard input is **scanf**, which takes the format:

```
scanf(<format string>,<addr1>,<addr2>,...);
```

where *<format string>* is a string with format indicators (as in **printf**), and each *<addr>* is an address into which **scanf** stores the incoming data. This means that you will often need to use the address-of operator (&). There are other commonly used commands as well: **gets**, which reads in an entire string until you press *Enter*; and **getch**, which reads a character straight from the keyboard with no echo.

Here are some Pascal input commands with corresponding C commands:

Turbo Pascal	Turbo C
`Readln(A,B);`	`scanf("%d %d",&a,&b);`
`Readln(Name);`	`scanf("%s",name);`
	`/* or gets(name); */`
`Readln(X,A);`	`scanf("%f %d",&x,&a);`
`Readln(Ch);`	`scanf("%c",ch);`
`Read(Kbd,Ch);`	`ch = getch();`

Be aware of one important distinction between these two ways of reading in a string (**scanf** and **gets**). **scanf** reads in all characters until whitespace (blanks, tabs, newline) is encountered. By contrast, **gets** will read *everything* in (including blanks and tabs) until you press *Enter*.

Block Statement

Both Pascal and C have the concept of a *block statement* (a collection of statements that can be put in anywhere a single statement can). In Pascal, the block statement takes the form

```
begin <statement>; <statement>; ... <statement> end;
```

In C, it takes this form:

```
{ <statement>; <statement>; ... <statement>; }
```

While the form is very similar, there are two important differences:

- In Pascal you don't have to put a semicolon after the last *<statement>* in a block; in C, you do.
- In C you never put a semicolon after the closing brace (}) of a block; in Pascal, you might have to.

Conditional Execution

Both Pascal and C support two *conditional execution constructs*: the *if/then/else* statement and the *case* statement.

The if/then/else is very similar for both of them:

```
if <bool expr>           if (<expr>)
  then <statement>           <statement>;
  else <statement>       else
                             <statement>;
```

In both Pascal and C, the **else** clause is optional, and *<statement>* can be replaced with a block statement (as already described). There are a few important differences, though.

- In C, the *<expr>* doesn't have to be Boolean; it just has to somehow resolve to a zero or nonzero value, where zero is considered *false*, and nonzero is considered *true*.
- In C, the *<expr>* must be in parentheses.
- In C, there is no **then**.
- In C, semicolons are always required after the statements—unless, of course, you have a block statement there instead.

Here are a few examples in Pascal and C:

Turbo Pascal	**Turbo C**

```
if B = 0                            if (B == 0)
   then Writeln('C is undefined')       puts("c is undefined");
else begin                          else {
  C := A div B;                       c = a / b;
  Writeln('C = ',C)                   printf("c = %d\n",c);
end;                                }


C := A * B;
if C < > 0                          if ((c = a * b) != 0)
   then C := C + B;                    c += b;
   else C := A                      else
                                       c = a;
```

The **case** statement is also implemented in both Pascal and C (in which it's known as the **switch** statement), but with some important differences.

Here's the general format for Pascal and C:

Turbo Pascal	**Turbo C**

```
case <expr> of                      switch (<expr>) {
  <list>    : <statement>;              case <item>  : <statements>
  <list>    : <statement>;              case <item>  : <statements>
  ...                                   ...
  <list>    : <statement>;              case <item>  : <statements>
  else <statements>                     default      : <statements>
end;                                }
```

Besides the cosmetic changes, there are critical distinctions as well.

First, in Pascal, *<list>* can be a list of values; in Turbo Pascal, it can include ranges (*A...Z*) as well. In C, *<item>* is exactly one value. In both languages, you're limited to ordinal and constant values: integers, characters, and enumerated data types.

Second (and this is *very* important), in Pascal, *<statement>* is either a single statement or a block statement; once it is executed, the rest of the **case** statement is skipped over. In C, *<statements>* consists of zero or more statements, each ending with a semicolon. However, once they are executed, control does *not* pass to the end of the **switch** statement; instead, it continues down the list of *<statements>* until and unless it hits a **break** statement. Then, and only then, is the rest of the **switch** statement skipped. It may help to think of each **case** *<item>* : as a label, with the **switch**(<expr>) statement determining which one to jump to.

Here are a few examples:

<table>
<tr><th>Turbo Pascal</th><th>Turbo C</th></tr>
</table>

```
case Ch of                          switch (ch) {
  'C' : DoCompile;                      case 'C' : DoCompile(); break;
  'R' : begin                           case 'R' :
    if not Compiled                         if (!compiled)
    then DoCompile                              DoCompile();
    RunProgram;                             RunProgram();
  end;                                      break;
  'S' : SaveFile;                       case 'S' : SaveFile(); break;
  'E' : EditFile;                       case 'E' : EditFile(); break;
  'Q' : begin                           case 'Q' :
    if not Saved                            if (!saved)
    then SaveFile                               SaveFile();
  end;                                      break;
end;                                }


case Today of                       switch (today) {
  Mon..Fri : Writeln('go work!');       case Mon :
  Sat,Sun  : begin                      case Tue :
    if Today = Sat then begin           case Wed :
      Write('clean the yard');          case Thur:
      Write(' and ')                    case Fri : puts("go work!"); break;
    end;                                case Sat : printf("%s", "clean the"
                                                          "yard and ");
    Writeln('relax!')                   case Sun : puts("relax!");
  end
end;                                }
```

Note the second set of examples. The **case** *<item>* parts of the **switch** statement label each case you want to handle; in the case of *Mon* through *Thur*, the *<statements>* sections are empty, and control falls downward until it finds the statements labelled by case Fri :. The **break** statement then causes control to skip to the end of the **switch** statement. However, the program takes advantage of the same feature with the weekend; the label `case Sat :` causes the **printf** statement to execute, after which control falls to the following **puts** statement.

Iteration

C, like Pascal, has three types of loops: **while**, **do..while**, and **for**, which correspond closely to Pascal's three loops (**while**, **repeat..until**, and **for**). We'll present them in that order.

The while Loop

Of the three loops, the **while** loop is most similar in both languages. Here are the formats:

```
while <bool expr> do          while (<expr>)
  <statement>;                  <statement>;
```

In both languages, you use a block statement to put more than one statement in the loop. The only real difference, again, is C's greater flexibility in what it accepts for *<expr>*. For example, compare the following two loops:

```
Read(Kbd,Ch);
while Ch <> 'q' do begin       while ((ch = getch()) != 'q')
  Write(Ch); Read(Kbd,Ch)        putchar(ch);
end;
```

The do..while Loop

The **do..while** loop is similar to Pascal's **repeat..until** loop; here are the formats:

Turbo Pascal	Turbo C

`repeat`
  `<statements>`
`until <bool expr>;`
	`do`
	  `<statement>;`
	`while (<expr>);`

But, there are two important differences between these two loops:

- The **do..while** loop executes *while <expr>* is *true*, whereas the **repeat..until** executes *until <bool expr>* is *true*.

- The **repeat..until** statement doesn't require a block statement for multiple statements, while the `do..while` does.

Here's an example of each:

Turbo Pascal	Turbo C

```
repeat                                    do {
  Write('Enter a value: ');                 printf("Enter a value: ");
  Readln(A)                                 scanf("%d",&a);
until (Low <= A) and (A <= High);         } while (a < low || a > high);
```

Note another important difference between C and Pascal: In C, relational operators (>, <, etc.) have a higher precedence than logical operators (&&, | |). This means that you don't have to surround each relational expression with parentheses, as you often do in Pascal.

The for Loop

The **for** loop shows the greatest differences between Pascal and C. In Pascal, the **for** loop is rather fixed and inflexible; in C, it is almost too flexible, allowing some constructs that tend to lose all resemblance to a **for** loop.

Here are the formats of both:

Turbo Pascal	Turbo C

```
for <indx> := <start> to <finish> do      for (<expr1>; <expr2>; <expr3>)
  <statement>;                               <statement>;
```

In C (as it really is in Pascal), the **for** statement is simply a special case of the **while** statement. The given format is equivalent to

```
<expr1>;
while (<expr2>) {
   <statement>;
   <expr3>;
}
```

<expr1> is used for initialization, *<expr2>* for testing the end of the loop, and *<expr3>* to increment or otherwise modify the loop variable(s).

Here are a few examples, some of which use the **while** loop in Pascal:

Turbo Pascal	Turbo C

```
for I := 1 to 10 do begin
  Write('I = ',I:2);
  Write('  I*I = ',(I*I):4);
  Writeln('  I**3 = ',(I*I*I):6)
end;


I := 17; K := I;
while (I > -450) do begin
  K := K + I;
  Writeln('K = ',K,' I = ',I);
  I := I - 15
end;


X := D/2.0;
while (Abs(X*X-D) > 0.01) do
  X := (X + D/X)/2.0;
```

```
for (i = 1; i <= 10; i++) {
  printf("i = %2d  ",i);
  printf("i*i = %4d  ",i*i);
  printf("i**3 = %6d\n",i*i*i);
}


for (i = 17, k = i; i >- 450; i -= 15) {
  k += i,
  printf("k = %d i = %d\n",k,i);
}


for (x = d/2; fabs(x*x-d) > 0.01;
    x = (x+d/x)/2)
  ;                    /* Empty statement */
```

Notice that these loops are doing more and more inside the **for** section, until the last one actually has no statement to execute; all the work is done within the header of the loop itself.

Subroutines

Both Pascal and C have subroutines; Pascal has procedures and functions, while C has just functions. However, you can declare functions to be of type **void**, which means that they return no value at all; if you want to, you can also ignore the value that a function does return.

Here are the formats for functions in both languages:

Turbo Pascal	Turbo C

```
function FName(<parm decls>) : <type>;
  <local declarations>
begin
  <statements>
end;
```

```
<type> FName(<parm decls>)

{
    <local declarations>
    <statements>
}
```

In Pascal, *<parm decls>* takes the form *<pnames>* : *<type>*; for each set of parameters, while in C it's *<type>* *<pnames>*,.

There are other important differences as well, but they're best shown by example. Here are a few:

Turbo Pascal	Turbo C

```
function Max(A,B : Integer) : Integer;      int max(int a, int b)
begin                                       {
  if A > B                                      if (a > b)
    then Max := A                                   return(a);
    else Max := B                             else
                                                  return(b);
end;                                        }
```

Note that in C the **return** statement is used to return a value through the function, while Pascal has you assign a value to the function name.

Turbo Pascal	Turbo C

```
procedure Swap(var X,Y : Real);             void swap(float *x, float *y)
var
  Temp      : Real;
begin                                       {
                                                float temp;
  Temp := X;                                    temp = *a;
  X :- Y;                                       *a = *b;
  Y := Temp                                     *b = temp;
end;                                        }
```

In Pascal, you have two types of parameters: *var* (pass by address) and *value* (pass by value). In C, you only have pass by value. If you want a pass-by-address parameter, then that's what you have to do: Pass the address, and define the formal parameter as a pointer. That's what was done for **swap**.

Here's sample code calling these routines:

Turbo Pascal	Turbo C

```
Q := 7.5;                                   q = 7.5;
R := 9.2;                                   r = 9.2;
Writeln('Q = ',Q:5:1,' R = ',R:5:1);        printf("q = %5.1f r = %5.1f\n",q,r);
Swap(Q,R);                                  swap(&q,&r);
Writeln('Q = ',Q:5:1,' R = ',R:5:1);        printf("q = %5.1f r = %5.1f\n",q,r);
```

Note the use of the address-of operator (&) in the C code when passing *q* and *r* to **swap**.

Function Prototypes

There is an important difference between Pascal and C concerning functions: Pascal always does error checking to make sure that the number and types of parameters declared in the function match those used when the function is called.

In other words, suppose you define the Pascal function

```
function Max(I,J : Integer) : Integer;
```

and then try to call it with real values (A := Max(B,3.52);).

What will happen? You'll get a compiler error telling you that there is a type mismatch, since 3.52 is not an acceptable substitute for an integer.

Not so in C. By default, C does *no* error checking on function calls: It does not check the number of parameters, parameter types, or even the type returned by the function. This allows you a certain amount of flexibility, since you can call a function before it is ever defined. But it can also get you into deep trouble; see "Pitfall #2" later in this chapter. So, how do you avoid this?

Turbo C supports *function prototypes*. You can think of these as being somewhat analogous to **forward** declarations in Pascal. You typically place function prototypes near the start of your file, before you make any calls to those functions. The key point to remember is that the function prototype—which is a kind of declaration—must precede the actual call to the function.

A function prototype takes the format:

```
<type>  FName(<type> <pname>, <type> <pname>, etc. );
```

This is very similar to how Pascal declares functions, but with a few differences. Commas (not semicolons) are used to separate the definition of each parameter; also, you can't list multiple *<pname>*s for a single *<type>*.

Here are some sample prototypes, based on the routines already given, as well as on the routines in "A Major Example" (following):

```
int   max(int a, int b);
void  swap(float *x, float *y);
void  swapitem(listitem *i, listitem *j);
void  sortlist(list l, int c);
void  dumplist(list l, int c);
```

Unlike the Pascal **forward** statement, the C function prototype does not force you to do anything different when you actually define your function; in other words, you define your function just as you would otherwise (or you can define it using modern C style). In fact, if your function definition doesn't match the prototype, Turbo C will give you a compiler error.

Turbo C supports both the classic and modern styles, although—since C is migrating toward using the modern style—we recommend that you use function prototypes and prototype-style function definitions.

Using function prototypes can prevent a slew of problems, especially when you start compiling libraries of C routines. You should create a separate file and put in it function headers for all the routines in a given library. When you want to use any routines in that library, you include the header file into your program (with the directive #include). That way, error checking can take place at compile time, possibly saving you a fair amount of grief.

A Major Example

Now here's a long example, a complete program using most of what you've learned up until now, and then some. It defines an array *myList*, whose length is defined by the constant *LMax* and whose base type is defined as *ListItem* (which here is just *Integer*). It initializes that array to a set of numbers in descending order, displays them using the *DumpList* routine, sorts them in ascending order with *SortList*, then displays them again.

Note that the C version of this program is not necessarily the best C version. It has been written to correspond as much as possible to the Pascal version, the few places where it doesn't correspond are designed to demonstrate certain differences between C and Pascal.

Turbo Pascal	Turbo C

```pascal
program DoSort;
const
  LMax = 100;
type
  Item = Integer;
  List = array[1..LMax] of Item;
var
  myList  : List;
  Count,I : Integer;
  Ch      : Char;
procedure SortList(var L : List;
  C : Integer);
var
  Top,Min,K : Integer;

procedure SwapItem(var I,J : Item);
var
  Temp : Item;
begin

  Temp := I; I := J; J := Temp
end; { of proc SwapItem }


begin { Main body of SortList }

  for Top := 1 to C-1 do begin
    Min := Top;
    for K := Top + 1 to C do
      if L[K] < L[Min]
      then Min := K;
    SwapItem(L[Top],L[Min])
  end
end; { of proc SortList }

procedure DumpList(L : List;
                   C : Integer);
var
  I : Integer;
begin

  for I := 1 to C do
    Writeln('L[',I:3,'] = ',L[I]:4)
end; { End of proc DumpList }
```

```c
#define LMAX  100

typedef int    item;
typedef item   list[LMAX];

list   myList;
int    count, i;




void swapitem(item *i,item *j)


{
   item  temp;
   temp = *i; *i = *j; *j = temp
} /* swapitem */
void sortlist(list l, int c)
{
   int  top,min,k;
   for (top = 0; top < c-1; top++){
      min = top;
      for (k = top + 1; k <= c; k++)
         if (l[k] < l[min])
            min = k;
      swapitem(&l[top],&l[min]);
   }
} /*end of sortlist */

void dumplist(list l,int c)



{
   int   i;
   for (i = 0; i <= c; i++)
      printf("l[%3d] = %4d\n",i,l[i]);
} /* dumplist() */
```

```
begin { Main body of DoSort }            main()
  for I := 1 to LMax do                  {
    myList[I] := Random(1000);             for (i = 0; i < LMAX; i++)
  Count := LMax;                             myList[i] = rand() % 1000;
  DumpList(myList,Count);                  count = LMAX;
  Read(Kbd,Ch);                            dumplist(myList,count);
  SortList(myList,Count);                  getch();
  DumpList(myList,Count);                  sortlist(myList,count);
  Read(Kbd,Ch)                            dumplist(myList,count);
end. { of DoSort }                        getch();
                                         } /* main */
```

There are some important things to note here.

- In the Pascal version, we nested the procedure *SwapItem* inside of the procedure *SortList*; in C, you can't nest functions, so we had to move **swapitem** outside of **sortlist**.

- In C, arrays always start at location *0* and go up through *size-1*. For example, the first location in *myList* is *myList[0]*, while the last is *myList[LMAX-1]*. That's why the various **for** loops are set up the way they are.

- We didn't have to use the address-of and pointer operators when we passed *myList[]* to **sortlist**. Why? Because C always passes the address of arrays used as parameters, rather than the array itself, since it can't pass all the values in the array without causing serious problems. Likewise, when we declare the formal parameter list 1; in **dumplist** and **sortlist**, C knows to create that array at the address passed to it, so we don't have to mess with pointer operators.

- We didn't need function prototypes in this example because each function is defined before it is used. If we wanted to, we could place them in the program anywhere *after* defining the data types *item* and *list*, and they would have looked like this:

    ```
    void swapitem(item *i, item *j);
    void sortlist(list l, int c);
    void dumplist(list l, int c);
    ```

Again, note that using the function prototype does not change how you define the function.

A Survey of Data Structures

In this section we'll give you an overview of how data structures in C do (and don't) resemble Turbo Pascal data structures. The elements we'll talk about are pointers, arrays, strings, structures, and unions.

Pointers

It's possible to program for a long time in Pascal and never use pointers; not so in C. Why? Because, as mentioned before, C only uses pass-by-value parameters for its functions. If you want to modify a formal parameter and have that change the actual parameter, you have to pass the address yourself, then declare the formal parameter to be a pointer to the actual data type. Furthermore, strings are implemented in C as pointers to **char**, so any string manipulation will need pointers as well.

Here's a quick comparison of pointer declarations and use in Pascal and C, with a few examples of each:

	Turbo Pascal	Turbo C
declaration:	`<pname> : ^<type>;`	`<type>    *<pname>;`
	`IntPtr  : ^Integer;`	`int       *intptr;`
	`Buff1   : ^Intarray;`	`int       buff1[];`
	`Buff2   : array[0..N] of IntPtr;`	`int       *buff2[];`
	`PHead   : ^Node;`	`node      *phead;`
	`Head    : Node;`	`node      head;`
use:	`<pname>^ := <value>;`	`*<pname> = <value>;`
	`IntPtr^  := 22;`	`*intptr  = 22;`
	`Buffer^[152] := 0;`	`buff1[152] = 0;`
	`PHead^.Next := nil;`	`(*phead).next = NULL;`
		`/* or phead->next = NULL; */`

Note the use of parentheses for the last example (*phead*) in C, as well as the special symbol (->) in the second version for *phead*. Here are some more examples:

```
1.  Buff1^[152]  := 0;      buff1[152]   = 0;
2.  Buff2[152]^  := 0;      *buff2[152]  = 0;
3.  Head.Data^   := 0;      *head.data   = 0;
4.  Head.Next    := nil;    head.next    = NULL;
5.  PHead^.Next  := nil;    (*phead).next = NULL;
                            /*or phead -> next = NULL; */
```

The first example presumes that *buff1* points to an array of integers.

The second example indicates that *buff2* is an array of pointers to integers, so it is indexed before it is referenced.

The third assumes that *head* is a **record** (a **struct** in C) with a field *next*, which is a pointer to an integer.

The fourth assumes that *head* also has a field *next*, which is a pointer to something (it's unclear what).

The last example shows that *phead* is a *pointer* to a **record** (also a **struct**), and that record has a field *next*, which is a pointer.

The symbol -> is used as shorthand notation; that is, the expression

```
pname->fname = value;
```

says that *pname* is a pointer to some type of record, *fname* is the name of some field in that record, and that *value* is going to be assigned to the *fname* field in the record to which *pname* points.

Arrays

Arrays are fairly simple creatures in C, compared to Pascal. Arrays in C can have integer, character, or enumerated-type indices, while Pascal allows you to use *any* ordinal type. All array index ranges in C start at 0 and go to *n-1* (where *n* is the size of the array). This is very unlike Pascal, which lets you start and end the index ranges wherever you choose.

In C, array indexing is like pointer arithmetic, and the same identity holds true: The Pascal *a[i]* is equivalent to both *a[i]* and **(a + i)* in C.

The general format for arrays in the two languages follows:

Turbo Pascal	**Turbo C**
`<name> : array[<low>..<high>] of <type>;`	`<type>  <name>[<size>];`

where *<size>* is equal to (1 + *<high>* − *<low>*).

Multi-dimensional arrays in C are declared much like in Pascal: Either *<type>* is itself an array of some sort, or you add additional sizes on the end, like this:

```
<type>  <name>[<size1>][<size2>][<size3>];
```

Note that, unlike Pascal, you can not write `arr[x][y]` as `arr[x,y]` (see "Pitfall #5" following).

In C, a block of memory large enough for *<size>* instances of *<type>* is set aside, and *<name>* is a constant pointer to the beginning of that block.

This aids passing arrays to functions; more importantly, it means that (unlike Pascal) the function does not have to know how big the array is at compile time.

The result: You can pass arrays of different sizes (but the same type) to a given function.

Consider, for example, the following function, which receives an array of type **int** and returns the lowest value in the array:

```
int  amin(int a[], int n);                          /* Function declaration */
{
    int     min,i;

    min = a[0];

    for (i = 1; i < n; i++)
       if (a[i] < min)
          min = a[i];
    return(min);
}
```

You can pass an integer array of any size to this function; it will find the lowest value of the first *n* elements. Losing this flexibility is one of the biggest complaints C programmers have when using Pascal.

Strings

Standard Pascal doesn't define strings as a separate data type; Turbo Pascal does, and supplies a number of procedures and functions for working with them.

C (including Turbo C) does not define a separate string data type; instead, a string is defined as either an array of **char** or a pointer to **char**, which (as you've seen) are almost the same things.

Here are some comparative declarations:

Turbo Pascal	Turbo C
`<name> : `**`string`**`[<size>];`	`char   <name>[<size>];`
`type`	
`  BigStr  = string[255];`	`typedef char bigstr[256];`
`  StrPtr  = ^BigStr;`	`typedef char *strptr;`
`var`	
`  Line    : `**`string`**`[80];`	`char    line[81];`
`  Buffer  : BigStr;`	`bigstr  buffer;`
`  Word    : `**`string`**`[35];`	`char    word[36];`
`  Ptr     : StrPtr;`	`strptr  ptr;`

The key differences between strings in Turbo Pascal and strings in Turbo C are closely tied to the differences between arrays in the two languages.

In Turbo Pascal, the declaration

```
S : string[N]
```

is equivalent to

```
S : array of [0..N] of char
```

The string has a maximum length of N characters; the current length is stored in *S[0]*, while the actual string itself starts in location *S[1]*. You can directly assign string literals and constants to a string variable; Pascal will do the byte-by-byte transfer and correctly adjust the length.

In Turbo C, you can declare a string as

```
char strarr[N]
```

or as

```
char *strptr
```

The first declaration sets aside N memory for holding a string, then stores the address of those bytes in *strarr*. The second declaration only sets aside bytes for the pointer *strptr*, which points to **char** types.

In C, a string's length is not stored separately; instead, a *string terminator* is used to mark the end of the string. This terminator is the *null character* (ASCII 0), which requires an extra byte at the end of the string; the string itself starts in *strarr[0]*.

Because of this, the string *strarr* can only hold *N-1* "real" characters, since one byte will have to be reserved for the null-terminator. That's why the C declarations in the comparison table all have lengths one greater than their corresponding Pascal declarations.

Furthermore, since *strarr* is not the actual collection of bytes, you cannot directly assign string literals. Instead, you must use the routine **strcpy** (or one of its derivatives) to do a byte-by-byte transfer from one string to another: `strcpy(strarr,"Hello, world!");`. However, you can directly read into *strarr* using **scanf** or **gets**.

The other method of string declaration, `char *strptr`, requires you to use more care. In this case, *strptr* is just a pointer to `char`; no space for any string has been allocated, just the few bytes for the pointer itself.

You can assign string literals directly to *strptr*; since those literals are created as part of the object code itself, you merely assign their addresses to *strptr*. If you assign *strarr* to *strptr*, then both *strarr* and *strptr* now point to the same string; the same thing occurs if you assign another string pointer to *strptr*.

So, how do you get *strptr* to point to its own private string instead of somewhere else? By allocating space to it:

```
strptr = (char *) malloc(N);
```

This will set aside *N* bytes of available memory, using the **malloc** routine and assign to *strptr* the address of that string. You can then use *strcpy* to copy strings (literals and variables) into those allocated bytes.

The Pascal equivalents for this (*StrPtr, Ptr*) are only very rough equivalents. Instead of being ^*Char*, *StrPtr* is defined as ^*BigStr*. This is so that Turbo Pascal will recognize *Ptr* as being a string; it also helps to avoid any range-checking problems. Note in the following example that only the amount of space requested is actually allocated to *Ptr*.

Here is a list of roughly comparable statements; refer to the *Turbo C Reference Guide* for a complete list of Turbo C's strings (**str...**) functions. These statements presume the type declarations given in the previous comparison:

Turbo Pascal	Turbo C

```
var                             main ()
  Line,Name  : BigStr;          {
  First,Temp : string[80];          bigstr line,name;
  Ptr        : StrPtr;              char   first[81],temp[81];
  I,Len,Err  : Integer;             char *ptr;
                                    int i,len;
                                    extern char *strchr(char *s,char ch);
```

Turbo Pascal	Turbo C

```
begin
  Write('Enter name:  ');
  Readln(Name);
  I := Pos(' ',Name);
  if I = 0 then
    First := Name
  else
    First := Copy(Name,1,I-1);
  Len := Length(First);
  Writeln('Len = ',Len);
  Temp := Concat('Hi, ',Name);

  Writeln(Temp);
  if Name <> First
    then Name := First;
  I := 823; Str(I,Temp);
  Val(Temp,I,Err);
  GetMem(Ptr,81);
  Ptr^ := 'This is a test.';
  Writeln('Ptr = ',Ptr^);
  FreeMem(Ptr,81);
end.
```

```
printf("Enter name:  ");
gets(name);
ptr = strchr(name,'.');
if (ptr == NULL)
    strcpy(first,name);
else
    strncpy(first,name, ptr-name-1);
len = strlen(first);
printf("len = %d\n",len);
strcpy(temp,"Hi, ");
strcat(temp,name);
puts(temp);
if (strcmp(name,first))
   strcpy(name,first);
i = 823; sprintf(temp,"%d",i);
i = atoi(temp);
ptr = (char *) malloc(81);
strcpy(ptr,"This is a test.");
printf("ptr = %s\n",ptr);
free(ptr);
}
```

The use of *Ptr* in the Pascal source code is something of a kludge; it's included here only to give you a feeling for what the equivalent C code does.

One last point: The function prototypes for the C routines called in this example are listed in header (.H) files; so, for proper error checking, you should place the following #include statements at the start of the Turbo C program.

```
#include <stdio.h>
#include <string.h>
#include <stdlib.h>
#include <alloc.h>
```

Structures

Both Pascal and C allow you to define aggregate, heterogeneous data structures. In Pascal, they're called *records*; in C, *structures*. Here's the format for both:

| **Turbo Pascal** | **Turbo C** |

```
type                                    typedef struct  {
  <rname>   =  record                        <type> <fnames>;
  <fnames>  : <type>;                        <type> <fnames>;
  <fnames>  : <type>;                        ...
  ...                                        <type> <fnames>;
  <fnames>  : <type>                    } <rname>;
end;


var
  <vnames>   : <rname>;                 <rname> <vnames>;
```

There's also a more concise format in C for directly declaring structure variables in C, much as there is in Pascal:

| **Turbo Pascal** | **Turbo C** |

```
var                                     struct <rname> {
  <vnames> : record                          <type>  <fnames>;
  <fnames> : <type>;                         ...
  ...                                        <type>  <fnames>;
  <fnames> : <type>                     }  <vnames>;
end;
```

In this case, *<rname>* of the structure is optional; you should put it there if you plan to declare other variables to be of type *<rname>*. Beyond that, records in Pascal and structures in C are pretty much the same. Here's an example:

| **Turbo Pascal** | **Turbo C** |

```
type                                    struct student {
  Student = record                           char   last[20],first[20];
  Last,First : string[20];                    char   ssn[11];
  SSN   : string[11];                         int    age;
  Age   : Integer;                            int    tests[5];
  Tests : array[1..5] of Integer;             float  gpa;
  GPA   : Real;                          } current ;
end;

var                                     main()
  Current : Student;                     {
```

```
begin                                  strcpy(current.last = "Smith");
  Current.Last = 'Smith';                current.age = 21;
  Current.Age = 21;                      current.tests[0] = 97;
  Current.Tests[1] = 97;                 current.gpa = 3.94;
  Current.GPA = 3.94;                 }
end.
```

The only major difference between Pascal and C here is that Pascal has the **with** statement and C doesn't. We could rewrite the Pascal previous code to say **with** `Current` **do** and then refer to the fields without the `Current` in front of them. In C, you always have to have the `current.` in front. C also has the *member access* operator (->), which is used when the identifier on the left of the operator is a pointer to a structure rather a structure itself. For example, if *pstudent* is a pointer to a **struct**, then

```
pstudent -> last = "Jones";
```

assigns the string `Jones` to the last name.

Unions

Again, Pascal and C support similar concepts. In Pascal, it is called a *free union variant record*; in C, it's just called a *union*. Here are the definitions of each, along with an example:

Turbo Pascal	Turbo C

```
type                                   union <uname> {
  <uname> = record                         <type>  <fnames>;
  <fieldlist>                              <type>  <fnames>;
case <type> of                            ...
  <vlist> : (<fieldlist>);                 <type>  <fnames>;
  <vlist> : (<fieldlist>);             } ;
  ...
  <vlist> : (<fieldlist>)
end;
```

In the Pascal version, *<fieldlist>* is the usual record sequence of *<fnames>* : *<type>;*, repeated as needed.

There are two major differences between Pascal and C on this one:

First, Pascal makes you put the union at the end of a regular record, whereas C does not. However, you can declare the union first, then declare a field in a structure to be of that **union** type.

Second, Pascal allows you to have multiple types for each variant in the union. C does let you have multiple fields (hence *<fnames>*), but all must be of the same type.

Here's a sample to study, written to make the Pascal and C versions as close to each other as possible (although, admittedly, they are not fully equivalent):

Turbo Pascal	**Turbo C**

```
type                        typedef union {
  trick_word = record           int w;
case integer of                 struct {
  0 : (w : integer);                char lob;
  1 : (lob,hib: byte);              char hib;
end;                            }b;
var xp:trick_word;          } trick_word;
                            trick_word xc;
```

Note that neither the C nor the Pascal definition of *trick_word* is portable. They both depend on the byte-order of the 8086.

In C unions, as with structures, you can insert a *<vnames>* field between the closing brace and the semicolon to directly declare variables of that type. In that case, you can leave off *<uname>* if you're not going to declare any more such variables. Field references in Pascal are *xp.w*, *xp.hib*, and *xp.lob*; in C, they are *xc.w*, *xc.b.hib*, and *xc.b.lob*.

Programming Issues

As a Pascal programmer, you shouldn't have a difficult time getting up to speed with Turbo C. But there are a few areas of programming that are implemented somewhat differently in the two languages. We'll discuss each of these programming issues in this section.

Case Sensitivity

Pascal is not case sensitive; C is. This means that the identifiers *indx*, *Indx*, and *INDX* all refer to the same variable in Pascal but would refer to three different variables in C.

Note: Since function calls are not resolved until the C program is linked, differences due to case may not show up until then. For your own good, be careful with case in C.

Type Casting

Pascal, as a rule, allows only limited type casting (converting data from one type to another). The function *Ord()* will cast from any ordinal type to Integer; *Chr()* will cast from Integer (or a related type) to Char. Turbo Pascal allows some additional type casting (called *retyping*) between all ordinal types (Integer, Char, Boolean, and enumerated data type). C is much freer, allowing you to attempt to cast from any type to any type, with results that are not always favorable.

Here's the standard format for each, with a few examples:

Turbo Pascal	Turbo C
`<var> := <type>(<expr>);`	`<var> = (<type>)<expr>;`
`var Ch : Char;`	`char ch;`
`I   := Integer(Ch);`	`i = (int) ch;`
`Ch := Char(Today);`	`ch - (char) today;`
`Today := Days(3);`	`today = (days) 3;`

In addition, Turbo C will do a lot of automatic type casting, mostly between types that are *integer compatible* (types whose underlying representation is an integer value). Because of that, all three previous statements could have left out the explicit cast: You could have written

```
i = ch;     ch = today;       today = 3;
```

Constants, Variable Storage, Initialization

Turbo Pascal does not initialize variables that you declare. Neither does it preserve the value of variables declared within procedures (and functions) between calls to those subroutines. The major exception to this is that typed constants are initialized, and they will hold their values *between* calls to a subroutine in which they are defined (including any value you might assign to them during execution). In C, All global variables are initialized to 0 by default unless you explicitly initialize them to a different value.

Turbo C gives you two types of constants, allows you to pre-initialize any variables, and lets you declare variables within a function as being *static*.

Constant Types

The two types of constants take the format:

```
#define    <cname>    <value>
const      <type>     <cname> = <value>;
```

The first type (`#define`...) more closely matches Pascal's **const** definition, in that *value* is directly substituted wherever *cname* is found.

The second type (`const`...) is more like Turbo Pascal's typed constant, except that you really can't change *cname*; any attempt to modify or assign a new value to it will result in a compiler error.

Bear in mind that C allows constant expressions, for example, `char s[SIZE + 1]`. A **const** variable won't do here. A manifest constant will, but it's substituted as if by a word processor with sometimes surprising results:

```
#define MAX_SIZE   80 + 1
char   s[MAX_SIZE * 2];       /* 82, not 162! */
```

A more careful definition would be

```
#define MAX_SIZE   (80 + 1)
```

In other words, to be safe, it's always wise to parenthesize expressions in a `#define`.

Variable Initialization

Turbo C lets you initialize any variable in a manner that does match Turbo Pascal's typed constant. The format is as follows:

```
<type>    <vname>  =  <value>;
```

Items requiring more than one value (arrays, structures) should have the values enclosed in braces and separated by commas ({ *"like_this"*, *"and_this"*, *"and_this_too"* }).

```
int x = 1, y = 2;
char name[] = "Frank";
char answer = 'Y';
char key = 3;
char list[2][10] = {"First", "Second"};
```

Variable Storage

C defines several storage classes for variables; the two most important are *external* and *automatic* (local). Global variables (those declared outside of any function, including **main**) are by default external. This means that they are initialized to 0 at the start of program execution—unless, of course, you initialize them yourself.

Variables declared within functions (including within **main**) are, by default, automatic. They are not initialized to anything, unless you do it, and they lose their values between calls to that function. However, you can declare such variables to be **static**; that way, they will be initialized to 0 (once, at the start of program execution) and they will retain their values between calls to the function.

In the following example

```
init test(void)
{
    int i;
    static int count;

    ...
}
```

the variable *i* resides on the stack and must be initialized by function **test** each time the function is called. The static variable *count*, on the other hand, resides in the global data area and is initialized to zero when the program is first executed. *Count* retains its previous value each time function **test** is invoked.

Dynamic Memory Allocation

In Turbo Pascal, there are several different methods for managing the heap. Given these Turbo Pascal declarations

```
type
  ItemType = Integer;
  ItemPtr = ^ItemType;

var
  p : ItemPtr;
```

here are three different methods of allocating and deallocating dynamic memory:

```
/* New and Dispose */
```

```
New(p);                       { Automatically allocates required amount of storage }
...
Dispose(p);                   { Automatically deallocates amount of storage allocated }


/* New, Mark, and Release */

New(p);                       { Automatically allocates required amount of storage }
...
Mark(p);
Release(p);                   { Deallocates all dynamic memory from p^ to end of heap }


/* Freemem and Getmem */

GetMem(p, SizeOf(ItemType));      { Must specify amount of storage to allocate }
...
FreeMem(p, SizeOf(ItemType));   { Must specify amount of storage to deallocate }
```

In Turbo C, allocating and deallocating dynamic memory is done using routines that are quite similar to Turbo Pascal's GetMem and Dispose:

```
<type>  *<ptr>;

<ptr> = (<type>*) calloc(<num>,<size>);
/* or <ptr> = (<type>*) malloc(<total size>); */
/* or <ptr> = (<type>*) realloc(<op>,<nusz>); */
free(<ptr>);

typedef int ItemType;
ItemType *p;

p = (ItemType*) malloc(sizeof(ItemType));
...
free(p);
```

All three of the C routines (**calloc**, **malloc**, and **realloc**) return a generic pointer, which can be cast to the appropriate type. All three also return NULL if there is not enough memory available on the heap.

- The function **calloc** expects you to pass it the number of items to create and the size (in bytes) of one item; it creates the items, sets them all to 0, and returns a pointer to the entire block. This is very handy for dynamic creation of arrays.

- **malloc** is told how many bytes to allocate.

- **free** just frees up the memory pointed to by *<ptr>*.

Command-Line Arguments

When you create a .COM file using Turbo Pascal, your program can read in any arguments that you might type on the line, using the *ParamCount* and *ParamStr* functions. For example, if you were to create a program called DUMPIT.COM and execute it as follows:

```
A>dumpit myfile.txt other.txt 72
```

ParamCount would return a value of 3, and *ParamStr* would return the following values:

```
ParamStr(1)     myfile.txt
ParamStr(2)     other.txt
ParamStr(3)     72
```

Likewise, Turbo C (following standard C conventions) allows you to declare the identifiers *argc*, *argv*, and *env* as parameters to **main** as follows:

```
main(int argc, char *argv[], char *env[]);
{
    ...body of main...
}
```

where *argc* is the number of arguments, and *argv*[ ] is an array of strings holding the parameters. With the same example, *argc* would yield 4, and *argv*[ ] would point to the following:

```
argv[0]     A:\DUMPIT.EXE
argv[1]     myfile.txt
argv[2]     other.txt
argv[3]     72
argv[4]     (null)
```

In C, under 3.x versions of MS-DOS, *argv*[0] is defined (whereas *ParamStr(0)* is not) and contains the name of the program being executed. For MS-DOS 2.x, *argv*[0] points to the null string (""). Also note that *argv*[4] actually contains NULL.

The third argument, *env*[], is an array of strings, each holding a string of the form

```
envvar = value
```

where *envvar* is the name of an environment variable and *value* is the string value to which *envvar* is set.

File I/O

In standard Pascal, you have two types of files: *text* (declared as text) and *data* (declared as file of *<type>*). The sequence for opening, modifying, and closing the file is almost identical for both types. Turbo Pascal also provides a third file type (untyped files) that is quite similar to the binary file operations used in Turbo C.

C files are usually treated as streams of bytes; text vs. data distinctions are largely up to you, though the *t* (*text*) and *b* (*binary*) modifiers on **fopen** can be significant.

Here are some rough equivalencies between the two languages:

Table 6.2: File I/O Similarities

Turbo Pascal	Turbo C
var	
I : Integer;	int i;
X : Real;	float x;
Ch : Char;	char ch;
Line : **string**[80];	char line[80];
myRec : RecType;	struct rectype myrec;
buffer : **array**[1..1024] **of** char	char buffer[1024]
F1 : text;	FILE *f1;
F2 : **file of** RecType;	FILE *f2;
F3 : **file**;	FILE *f3;
Assign(<fvar>,<fname>);	<fvar> = fopen(<fname>,"r");
Reset(<fvar>);	/* or <fvar> = fopen(<fname>,"r+"); */
Reset(<untyped fvar>, <blocksize>);	/* or f1 = fopen(<fname>,"r+t"); */
	/* or f2 = fopen(<fname>,"r+b"); */
Assign(<fvar>,<fname>);	<fvar> = fopen(<fname>,"w");
Rewrite(<fvar>);	/* or <fvar> = fopen(<fname>,"w+"); */
Rewrite(<untyped fvar>, <blocksize>);	/* or f1 = fopen(<fname>,"w+t"); */
	/* or f2 = fopen(<fname>,"w+b"); */
Assign(<fvar>,<fname>);	<fvar> = fopen(<fname>,"a+");
Append(<text fvar>);	/* or <fvar> = fopen(<fname>,"a+t"); */
	/* or <fvar> = fopen(<fname>,"a+b"); */
Read(F1,Ch);	ch = getc(f1);
Readln(F1,Line);	fgets(line, 80, f1);
Readln(F1,I,X);	fgets(line, 80, f1);sscanf(line,"%d %f",&i,&x);
Read(F2,MyRec);	fread(&myrec,sizeof(myrec),1,f2);
BlockRead(F3,buffer,SizeOf(buffer));	fread(buffer,1,sizeof(buffer),f3);
Write(F1,Ch);	fputc(ch,f1);
	/* or fprintf(f1,"%c",ch); */
Write(F1,Line);	fputs(line,f1);

```
                                     /* or fprintf(f1,"%s",line); */
  Write(F1,I,X);                     fprintf(f1,"%d %f",i,x);
  Writeln(F1,I,X);                   fprintf(f1,"%d %f\n",i,x);
  Write(F2,MyRec);                   fwrite(&myrec,sizeof(myrec),1,f2);

  Seek(F2,<rec#>);                   fseek(f2,<rec#>*sizeof(rectype),0);
  Flush(<fvar>);                     fflush(<fvar>);
  Close(<fvar>);                     fclose(<fvar>);
  BlockWrite(F3,buffer,SizeOf(buffer));   fwrite(buffer,1,sizeof(buffer),f3);
```

You should refer to the *Turbo C Reference Guide* for more details on how each of these Turbo C I/O routines work.

Here's a short example of a program that dumps a text file (whose name is given on the command line) to the screen:

Turbo Pascal   **Turbo C**

```
                                #include <stdio.h>
                                main(int argc, char *argv[])
program DumpIt;                 {
var
  F  : Text;                        FILE  *f;
  Ch : Char;                        int   ch;
begin
  Assign(F,ParamStr(1));
  {$I-} Reset(F); {$I+}            f = fopen(argv[1],"r");
  if IOResult <> 0 then begin      if (f == NULL) {
    WriteLn('Cannot open ',ParamStr(1));   printf("Cannot open %s\n",argv[1]);
    Halt(1);                           return(1);
  end;                             }
  while not EOF(F) do begin
    Read(F,Ch);                    while ((ch = getc(f)) != EOF)
    Write(Ch)                          putchar(ch);
  end;
  Close(F)                         fclose(f);}
end.
                                }
```

Common Pitfalls of Pascal Programmers Using C

There are enough similarities between Pascal and C so as to make certain mistakes very common. Here are some of the pitfalls to avoid. There is a rough order to this list, based on a combination of how likely they are to occur, how difficult they would be for a Pascal programmer to see, and whether or not the compiler might catch them. (Chapter 3 also discusses some common pitfalls.)

PITFALL #1: Assignment vs. Comparison

In Pascal, A = B is the Boolean expression *A equals B* and returns *true* or *false*. In C, A = B is the assignment *A gets the value of B*; however (and this is critical to understand), this expression also returns a value, namely the value of *B* (which has just been assigned to *A*). The single most pernicious bug for Pascal programmers is the statement:

```
if (A = B) <statement>;
```

This is perfectly legal in C, and is evaluated as follows:

- the value of *B* is assigned to *A*
- the expression A = B takes on the value of *B*
- if its value is nonzero (which, in C, is *true*), *<statement>* is executed.

What you really want to write is

```
if (A == B) <statement>;
```

which does what you think it should: If *A* and *B* are equal, then *<statement>* is executed.

Remember: In C, the *is equal to* comparator is double equal signs (==), *not* a single equal sign (=). The single equal sign in C is the *assignment* operator.

PITFALL #2: Forgetting to Pass Addresses (Especially When Using scanf)

As we've explained, C only lets you pass parameters to a function by value; if you want to pass a parameter by address, you need to explicitly pass the address yourself. Suppose you've written the function **swap** as shown earlier in the chapter. You might make the mistake of calling it like this: swap(q,r);, when *q* and *r* are of type **float**. In that case, **swap** will take the values of *q* and *r*, interpret them as addresses, then cheerfully swap the values at those addresses.

How do you avoid this pitfall? The best way is to use function prototypes; that way, Turbo C can do the appropriate error checking when you compile. For **swap**, you would put the following prototype somewhere near the start of your source file:

```
void swap(float *x, float *y);
```

Now, if you compile your program with the statement swap(q,r); you'll get an error telling you that you have a type mismatch in parameter *x* in a call to **swap**.

PITFALL #3: Omitting Parentheses on Function Calls

In Pascal, a procedure that takes no parameters is called merely by using the procedure name:

```
AnyProcedure;
i := AnyFunction;
```

In C, a call to a function—even one that has no parameters—must always include a left (open) and right (close) parenthesis. It's easy to do this

```
AnyFunction;                            /* Code has no effect */
i - AnyFunction;                /* Stores the address of AnyFunction in i */
```

when you really want this

```
AnyFunction();                              /* Calls AnyFunction */
i = AnyFunction();              /* Calls AnyFunction, stores result in i */
```

PITFALL #4: Warning Messages

In addition to generating error messages, Turbo C also reports non-fatal warnings. Using the incorrect function calls from the previous example, these are the warnings that Turbo C would report:

```
Warning test.c 5: Code has no effect in function main
Warning test.c 6: Non-portable pointer assignment in function main
```

Both statements are actually legal and, since no errors occurred, an .OBJ file would be created. Beware! These types of warnings would always be fatal errors in Turbo Pascal. Don't get in the habit of taking Turbo C warning messages lightly.

PITFALL #5: Indexing Multi-Dimensional Arrays

Suppose you have a two-dimensional array named *matrix*, and you want to reference location *(i,j)*. As a Pascal programmer, you might be inclined to write something like this:

```
x = matrix[i,j];
```

That will compile perfectly well in C; however, it won't do what you think.

In C, it is legal to have a series of expressions separated by commas; in such a case, the entire expression takes on the value of the last expression, so the preceding statement is equivalent to

```
x = matrix[j];
```

It's definitely not what you wanted, but that is still a legal statement in C. All you'll get is a warning, since C thinks you are trying to assign the address of *matrix[j]*—that is, the *j*th row of *matrix[ ]*—to *x*.

In C, you must explicitly surround each array index with brackets; so what you really wanted to write was

```
x = matrix[i][j];
```

Remember: For multi-dimensional arrays, you must put each index in its own set of brackets.

PITFALL #6: Forgetting the Difference Between Character Arrays and Character Pointers

Suppose that you have the following statements:

```
char    *str1,str2[30];
str1 = "This is a test";
str2 = "This is another test";
```

The first assignment is acceptable; the second isn't. Why? *str1* is a pointer to a string; when the compiler sees that assignment statement, it creates the string `This is a test` somewhere in your object file and assigns its address to *str1*.

By contrast, *str2* is a *constant* pointer to a block of 30 bytes somewhere; you can't change the address it contains. What you want to write instead is

```
strcpy(str2,"This is another test");
```

A byte-by-byte copy is done from the constant string `This is another test` to the address pointed to by *str2*.

PITFALL #7: Forgetting That C is Case Sensitive

In Pascal, the identifiers *indx*, *Indx*, and *INDX* are all the same; uppercase and lowercase letters are treated identically. In C, they are not.

So if you declare

```
int   Indx;
```

then later try to write

```
for (indx=1; indx<10; indx++) <statement>;
```

the compiler will give you an error, saying that it doesn't recognize *indx*.

PITFALL #8: Leaving Semicolons Off the Last Statement in a Block

If you're a Pascal purist who only puts semicolons where they are required (as opposed to where they are allowed), you'll have problems with this for a while. Luckily, the compiler will catch it and flag it pretty clearly. Just remember that every C statement, with two major exceptions, must have a semicolon after it.

One major exception is the function definition

```
<type>  FuncName(<parm names>)
```

which should not have a semicolon after it.

This is not to be confused with the function prototype

```
<type>  FuncName(<type> <pname>,<type> <pname>,...);
```

which is used to declare the function but not to actually define it; somewhat like a **forward** declaration in Pascal.

The other major exception is the set of preprocessor commands (`#<cmd>`), such as

```
#include  <stdio.h>
#define   LMAX   100
```

If you forget and enter `#define LMAX 100;`, then the preprocessor will substitute *100;* every place it finds *LMAX,* semicolon and all.

Remember in C, it's *caveat* programmer. You simply have to be more careful; it's not the forgiving language Pascal is.

C H A P T E R

7

Interfacing Turbo C with Turbo Prolog

With the introduction of Turbo C, you can now merge two powerful languages currently available for a PC. By linking Turbo C modules with Turbo Prolog modules, you can incorporate artificial intelligence (AI) into your Turbo C applications. If you are an experienced C programmer, you are already aware of Turbo C's several advantages over other C implementations. If you are just learning C, now is a good time to see how Turbo C and Turbo Prolog enhance one another.

Turbo C is a procedural language, and Turbo Prolog is a language based upon logic programming. Linking your Turbo C application with Turbo Prolog can provide the following artificial intelligence (AI) advantages:

- rule-based control structure
- easy integration of natural language

Linking with Turbo Prolog also provides added AI power to your Turbo C application, so that you can solve advanced problems by simply describing the problem and letting Turbo Prolog's inference engine do the work. In many Turbo C applications, linking in Turbo Prolog programs will significantly reduce software development time, and increase code clarity and program flexibility.

In This Chapter...

In this chapter we explain the steps to compile and link Turbo C and Turbo Prolog programs, and provide four examples that demonstrate the process. The first example is a simple program that demonstrates compilation and linking. The second goes a little further and shows how to link in added C libraries. The third demonstrates allocating memory. The last example describes a practical graphics program that shows some of the power you gain by combining the two languages.

Linking Turbo C and Turbo Prolog: An Overview

Compiling and linking your Turbo C modules with Turbo Prolog modules and programs is straightforward. You only need to keep in mind the following points:

Compiling your program modules:

- Your C functions must have the _0 suffix to be called by Turbo Prolog. (See the first C example program, CSUM.C, in this chapter.)
- Your Turbo Prolog main module (the one containing a goal) replaces your C main module.
- The Turbo Prolog main module must have your C functions declared as global predicates. (See the first Prolog example program, PROSUM.PRO, in this chapter.)
- All program modules must compile to Large memory (which is the *only* memory size Turbo Prolog compiles in).
- If your program calls the Turbo Prolog library for version 1.1, you must compile your modules with register allocation turned *off* (-r-).
- Generate underbars should be set to *off* (-u-).

Linking your program modules:

- INIT.OBJ must be the first object file linked. (This is Turbo Prolog's initialization module and is found on the Turbo Prolog library disk.)
- CPINIT.OBJ must be the second object file linked and the first call in the Turbo Prolog main module. (This is a special initialization module to set memory-allocation compatibility between Turbo C and Turbo Prolog. CPINIT.OBJ can be found on your Turbo C Disks.)

- If you need Turbo C library routines, use CL.LIB, and if using real arithmetic, EMU.LIB and MATHL.LIB.

  The Link Command line must have the form

  ```
  tlink init cpinit <T_Prolog_Main> Other_files <T_Prolog_Main.sym>,
  [exename], [your_libs] prolog [emulib mathl] cl
  ```

  (This should be on a single command line.)

In addition to the preceding points, you should keep in mind the following:

- Turbo Prolog functions may call functions written in Turbo C similar to other built-in Turbo Prolog *predicates* (functions). However, Turbo C cannot currently call Turbo Prolog modules.

- All calls to Turbo C library functions must be prefixed by an underbar (_). **Note**: All Turbo C library function are prefixed by underbars. Because underbar generation is turned off, calls to library functions must have the underbars explicitly added. User-defined functions do not need the underbars.

- **malloc**, **calloc**, **free**, and other memory allocation functions are replaced by **palloc**, **malloc_heap**, and **release_heap**. **palloc**, **malloc_heap**, and **release_heap** are available in CPINIT.OBJ for memory allocation within your Turbo C functions.

  palloc allocates memory on the global stack and is called as

  ```
  char *palloc(int size)
  ```

  malloc_heap allocates memory on the Prolog heap and is called as

  ```
  char *malloc_heap(int size)
  ```

  release_heap releases memory allocated on the Prolog heap and is called by

  ```
  release_heap(char *ptr,int size)
  ```

  When **palloc** is used, the memory will automatically be freed when a fail happens, causing Turbo Prolog to backtrack across the memory allocation.

- **printf**, **putc**, and related screen output functions are not functional when linking Turbo C and Turbo Prolog. However, **wrch** can write a character to a Prolog window and **zwf** has the same functionality as **writef** in Turbo Prolog. **zwf** is similar to a limited **printf**:

  ```
  zwf(FormatString,Arg1,Arg2,...)
  ```

  FormatString is a **printf**-type format string. Refer to the *Turbo Prolog Reference Manual* to see which conversion specifications are supported.

zwf and **wrch** are in PROLOG.LIB.

C functions called by Turbo Prolog should not have return values and should be defined as **void**. The flow patterns for the arguments are specified by the Turbo Prolog global predicate declaration. For example:

```
factorial(integer,real) - (i,o) language c
```

lets Turbo Prolog know that **factorial** is a function that has two arguments—the first an integer, the second a real (floating point). The (i,o) means that the first argument (the integer) is passed in, and the second argument is a pointer to a floating point that will be assigned within **factorial**. The *c* lets Turbo Prolog know that the function uses C calling conventions. (See the third example program in this chapter DUBLIST.C and PLIST.PRO.)

Notice that values are returned by reference. For more information on flow patterns, see the discussion of alternate flow patterns in example 3.

Example 1: Adding Two Integers

The following example combines a Turbo C function (one that adds two integer numbers) with a Turbo Prolog module that writes the C function result in the current window.

Turbo C Source File: CSUM.C

```
/*
The output routine zwf works nearly like the C output
routine printf. It prints the output in the current window.
*/

extern void zwf(char *format, ...);

void sum_0(int parm1,int parm2, int *res_p)
{
  zwf("This is the sum function: parm1=%d, parm2=%d" ,parm1,parm2);
  *res_p = parm1 + parm2;
}
/* End of sum_0 */
```

Compiling CSUM.C to CSUM.OBJ

After you have edited and saved CSUM.C, you need to select the compile-time options. Turbo C provides you with two methods for doing this:

1. Select the following compile-time options from the Turbo C menus:

    O/C/Model/Large (-ml)
    O/C/Optimization/Jump Optimization ... On (-o)
    O/C/Code generation/Generate underbars ...Off (-u-)
    O/C/Optimization/Use register variables ... Off (-r-)

    Once you have selected these options, choose **Options/Store** options from the Turbo C main menu; when the setup parameters are saved, select **Compile**. Turbo C will compile CSUM.C with the selected options, producing the object module CSUM.OBJ.

2. If you prefer to compile CSUM.C with a standard DOS command line instead of using Turbo C's menus, enter the following at the DOS prompt:

    ```
    tcc -ml -O -c -u- -r- csum
    ```

Note: Turbo Prolog only compiles to the large memory model; so for Turbo C to link with Turbo Prolog, you must use the -ml (Large memory model) compile option.

Turbo Prolog Source File: PROSUM.PRO

```
global predicates
    cpinit language c    /* cpinit needs to be declared as global in your
                            Turbo Prolog Main module */
  sum(integer,integer,integer) - (i,i,o) language c
                         /* the flow pattern of sum is defined as (i,i,o)
                            specifying that the third argument is the
                            returned value and the first two are inputs. */

goal cpinit, sum(7,6,X),write("Sum=",X).
                         /* cpinit must be called before your first C
                            function is called */
```

Compiling PROSUM.PRO to PROSUM.OBJ

After you have edited and saved PROSUM.PRO, you need to compile it to an object (.OBJ) file so it will link with the Turbo C object module. To do this, select **Options/Obj** from the Turbo Prolog main menu, then select

Compile. When Turbo Prolog finishes compiling the source file to an object file, you can link and run this example.

Linking CSUM.OBJ and PROSUM.OBJ

To link Turbo Prolog modules with Turbo C modules, you can use Turbo C's Integrated Environment, Turbo Link (the stand-alone linker included with your Turbo C package), or a compatible linker (such as Microsoft linker 2.2 or later). Beyond the `tlink` or `link` command, the link command-line arguments consist of Turbo Prolog main modules, assorted other modules, output files, and libraries; except where noted, these must appear in the following order:

Turbo Prolog Initialization:

- INIT.OBJ (Turbo Prolog initialization module)

Turbo C Initialization:

- CPINIT.OBJ (Turbo C initialization; compatible with Turbo Prolog)

Turbo Prolog Main Module:

- a main Turbo Prolog module that contains a goal

Assorted Modules:

(These modules do not need to appear in any particular order.)

- assembler .OBJ modules
- Turbo C .OBJ modules
- Turbo Prolog .OBJ modules

Symbol Table Module:

- Turbo Prolog main symbol table name (this is required and must appear last in the list of modules)

Output File Names:

- the name of the executable file to be generated

Libraries:

- list all libraries containing routines needed by the assorted modules. Order is important: first, user-defined libraries; next, PROLOG.LIB; then if needed, EMU.LIB and MATHL.LIB; and last, CL.LIB.

In this example, we use Turbo Link (note the `tlink` command) and give it the following arguments:

- the Turbo Prolog programs, INIT.OBJ, CPINIT.OBJ, and PROSUM.OBJ
- the Turbo C object module CSUM.OBJ
- the symbol table PROSUM.SYM and the executable file TEST.EXE
- the libraries PROLOG.LIB and CL.LIB (use EMU.LIB and MATHL.LIB to do floating point)

Note: PROSUM.SYM is a file that contains the symbol table of the name and type of variables in the program PROSUM.OBJ.

This is the link command line for our first example:

```
tlink init cpinit prosum csum prosum.sym,test.exe,,prolog+cl
```

Example 2: Using the Math Library

The second example is similar to the first; it shows how to write two Turbo C functions and how to combine these functions with a Turbo Prolog program. We present each of the Turbo C functions in its own separate source file; CSUM1.C adds two real numbers together and returns the sum, and FACTRL.C calculates the factorial of an integer. The Turbo Prolog program, FACTSUM.PRO, writes the program results in two Prolog windows. This example uses the Turbo C large memory-model math library, MATHL.LIB.

Turbo C Source File: CSUM1.C

```
extern void zwf(char *format, ...);
void sum_0(double parm1, double parm2, double *res_p)
{
    *res_p=parm1+parm2;
    zwf("This is the sum function: parm1=%d, parm2=%d, result=%f",
            parm1,parm2,*res_p);
}
```

Turbo C Source File: FACTRL.C

```
void factorial_0(int top, double *result)       /* Product of factorial series */
{
    double x;
    int i;
    if(top<1) {
      *result = 0.0;
      return;
}
    for (x = 2.0,*result = 1.0; top>1; top--, x = x +1.0)
    *result = *result*x;
}
/* End of factorial_0 */
```

Compiling CSUM1.C and FACTRL.C to .OBJ

As in the first example, you must compile the two Turbo C modules to object (.OBJ) files before linking them with the other modules and with the Turbo Prolog main program. You can select and save compile-time options from the Turbo C main menu, then select the Compile command for each of the .C source files. Or you can opt to compile both .C source files from a standard C command line, using the tcc command. In either case, you must select at least the following compile-time options:

O/C/Model/Large   (-ml)
O/C/Optimization/Jump optimization ... On (-o)
O/C/Code generation/Generate underbars ... Off (-u-)
O/C/Optimization/Use register variables ... Off (-r-)

Turbo Prolog Source File: FACTSUM.PRO

FACTSUM.PRO is the main Turbo Prolog program, which makes two windows: one displays the output from your Turbo C modules, and the other displays the Turbo Prolog program output. This is the order in which the modules and program interact:

1. FACTSUM.PRO prompts the user to input an integer *Int*, which the Turbo Prolog program then passes to FACTRL.C.

2. The Turbo C function **factorial** in FACTRL.C returns *Result*, the factorial of *Int*, to FACTSUM.PRO.

3. FACTSUM.PRO writes *Result* in a window and again prompts the user for a number (this time, a real).

4. FACTSUM.PRO passes this second input number, *Real*, and the previously calculated factorial, *Result*, to the module CSUM1.C.

5. The Turbo C function **sum** in CSUM1.C adds *Real* and *Result*, then returns the answer, *Sum*, to FACTSUM.PRO.

6. FACTSUM.PRO writes *Sum* in a window, and the program is finished.

Here is the Turbo Prolog program FACTSUM.PRO:

```
/*
    Declaration of the Turbo C module must be located after the Turbo Prolog
    domains and database declarations (if any are present). All global modules
    are called from Turbo Prolog as global predicates, and must be followed by
    the flow pattern and language specification.
*/
global predicates
    sum(real,real,real) - (i,i,o) language c
    factorial(integer,real) - (i,o) language c
    cpinit language c                            /* calls Turbo C initialization */
/*
    This is a very simple example that has only external clauses (Turbo C
    modules), so only a goal section is needed. However, in any real application,
    a clauses section would also be needed.
*/
goal cpinit,
    makewindow(1,49,31,
               " A Turbo Prolog window to the Turbo C program ",0,0,15,80),
    makewindow(2,47,3,
               " A Turbo Prolog window to the Turbo Prolog program ",15,0,10,80),

    /* Prompt user for first input */
    write("Enter an integer; Turbo C will calculate the factorial: "),
    readint(Int),nl,
    shiftwindow(1),                  /* Change output window to Turbo C window */

    /* Call Turbo C factrl module and calculate the factorial */
    factorial(Int,Result),
    shiftwindow(2),                  /* Change output window to Turbo Prolog window */

    /* Prompt user for second input */
    write("Enter a real number to add to the factorial "),
    readreal(Real),nl,
    shiftwindow(1),                  /* Change output window to Turbo C window */

    /* Call Turbo C csum1 module and calculate the sum */
    sum(Result,Real,Sum),
    shiftwindow(2),                  /* Change output window to Turbo Prolog window */

    /* Write result of first calculation in window */
    write("The factorial of ",Int," is ",Result),nl,

    /* Write result of second calculation in window */
    write("The result: ",Result," + ",Real," = ",Sum),nl.
```

Compiling FACTSUM.PRO to FACTSUM.OBJ

As in the first example, you must compile the Turbo Prolog program source file to an object (.OBJ) file before linking it with the modules. Select **Options/Obj** from the Turbo Prolog main menu, as before, then compile the program.

Linking CSUM1.OBJ, FACTRL.OBJ and FACTSUM.OBJ

In the link command used in this example,

- the Turbo Prolog object modules are INIT.OBJ and FACTSUM.OBJ
- the Turbo C object modules are CSUM1.OBJ, FACTRL.OBJ, and CPINIT.OBJ
- the output file names are FACTSUM.SYM (symbol table) and SUM.EXE (executable file)
- the libraries needed are PROLOG.LIB, EMU.LIB, MATHL.LIB, and CL.LIB

This is the command linking the modules:

```
tlink init cpinit factsum factrl csum1 factsum.sym,sum,,prolog+emu+mathl+cl
```

Example 3: Flow Patterns and Memory Allocation

The following program presents the code for creating a Turbo Prolog *functor* and *list* in Turbo C and returning these new structures to Turbo Prolog. This example also demonstrates how memory can be allocated in Turbo Prolog's global stack. Lists are recursive structures of three elements and functors are C structures of two elements (these are described more fully after this example).

- A Turbo C module DUBLIST.C contains three functions. The first two can take an integer list and return a structure with the first integer in it, or can take a structure with an integer and return a list with that integer. The third function takes an integer n and generates a list of two integers; the first being n and the second $2n$.

- It is important to notice that there can be alternate flow patterns for each Turbo Prolog global predicate, and that each flow pattern requires an alternate Turbo C function. For the following example, **clist_0** must correspond to the first flow pattern (i,o), and **clist_1** to the second flow pattern (o,i).

```
global predicates
    clist(ilist,ifunc) - (i,o) (o,i) language c
```

- The (i,o) specifies that *ilist* is to be passed into your Turbo C function **clist_0**, and *ifunc* is a pointer to a structure that will be defined within the Turbo C function **clist_0**. The (o,i) specifies that *ifunc* is passed into **clist_1**, and *ilist* is a pointer to a list structure that will be defined within **clist_1**.

- If an additional flow pattern was specified in your Turbo Prolog global **domains**, a **clist_2** would be needed to handle the additional flow pattern.

Turbo C Source File: DUBLIST.C

```
struct ilist {
    char functor;                       /* Type of the list element */
                                        /* 1 = a list element */
                                        /* 2 = end of list */
    int val;                            /* The actual element */
    struct ilist *next;                 /* Pointer to the next node */
};
struct ifunc {
    char type;                          /* Type of functor */
    int value;                          /* Value of the functor */
};
```

```
void clist_0(struct ilist *in, struct ifunc **out)
{
   if (in->functor != 1)
      fail_cc();                                          /* Fail if empty list */
   *out = (struct ifunc *) palloc(sizeof(struct ifunc));

   (*out)->value = in->val;                          /* This sets out to f(X) */
   (*out)->type = 1;                                 /* Set the functor type */
}


void clist_1(struct ilist **out, struct ifunc *in)
{
   int temp = 0;
   struct ilist *endlist = (struct ilist *) palloc(sizeof(char));

   endlist->functor = 2;
   temp = in->value;
   temp += temp;
   *out = (struct ilist *) palloc(sizeof(struct ilist));
   (*out)->val = temp;                      /* This returns [2*X] as a list */
   (*out)->functor = 1;              /* Set the list type. If this is not */
                                     /* done, no meaningful value will be */
                                                          /* returned. */

   (*out)->next = endlist;
}


void dublist_0(int n, struct ilist **out){
/*
   This function creates the list [n,n+n]
*/
   struct ilist *temp;
   struct ilist *endlist = (struct ilist *) palloc(sizeof(char));

   endlist->functor = 2;
   temp = (struct ilist *) palloc(sizeof(struct ilist));
   temp->val = n;                       /* This sets the first element of the */
   temp->functor = 1;                                     /* list to n */
   *out = temp;

   /* Now we have to allocate a second list element */

   temp = (struct ilist *) palloc(sizeof(struct ilist));

   temp->val = n + n;                       /* This assigns the value n + n to */
   temp->functor = 1;                                /* The second element */
   temp->next = endlist;             /* Set the node after the second to an */
                                                     /* end of list node */
   (*out)->next = temp;                             /* after the first element */
}
```

Lists and Functors

Turbo Prolog lists and functors are structures in Turbo C (see DUBLIST.C).

Lists are recursive structures that have three elements. The first element is the type; the value may be 1 if it is a list element, and 2 if it is an end of the list. The second element is the actual value; it must be the same type as the element in Turbo Prolog.

For example, a list of reals would be

```
struct alist {
  char funct;
  double elem;      /* the list elements are real */
  struct alist *next;
}
```

The third element is a pointer to the next node. Each node is a structure that may be type 1 for the next element of the list or type 2 signifying the end of list or empty list.

Turbo Prolog functors are C structures that have two elements. The first element corresponds to the Turbo Prolog domain declaration. (Refer to your *Turbo Prolog Owner's Handbook* for more information on domain declarations in Turbo Prolog.) For example:

```
domains
  func = i(integer); s(string)
predicates
  call(func)
goal
  call(X)
```

The Turbo Prolog functor *func* has two types: the first is an integer and the second is a string. So in this example the type element of the Turbo C structure may be 1 or 2; 1 corresponding to the first type, and 2 to the second type.

The second element of the Turbo C structure is the actual value of this element of the functor and is defined as the *union* of the possible types of the argument.

```
union val {
    int     ival;
    char   *svar;
};
struct func {
    char type;              /* type may be 1 or 2 corresponding to
                               the Turbo Prolog domain declarations */
    union val value;    /* the value of the functor element      */
}
```

Note: The functions **palloc**, **malloc_heap**, and **release_heap** must be used for memory management (these are found in CPINIT.OBJ). These functions are needed to

1. allocate memory for Turbo C structures stored in the Turbo Prolog heap or stack, and
2. release memory in Turbo Prolog's heap.

When **palloc** is used, the memory will automatically be released when a fail occurs, causing Turbo Prolog to backtrack across the memory allocation.

Here is the Turbo C syntax for each:

```
char *palloc(size)                        /* Allocates storage in stack */

char *malloc_heap(size)                   /* Allocates storage in heap */

release_heap(ptr,size)                      /* Releases heap space */
```

Here is the Turbo Prolog main module, PLIST.PRO, that calls the functions in DUBLIST.C and prints the results.

domains
```
ilist = integer*
ifunc = f(integer)
```

global predicates
```
cpinit language c
clist(ilist,ifunc) - (i,o) (o,i) language c
dublist(integer,ilist) - (i,o) language c
```

```
goal
  clearwindow,
  clist([3],X),                    /* Binds X to f(3)      */
  write("X = ",X),nl,
  clist(Y,X),                      /* Binds Y to [6]       */
  write("Y = ",Y),nl,
  dublist(6,Z),                      /* Binds Z to [6,12] */
  write(Z),nl.
```

Compiling DUBLIST.C

As in the first two examples, you must compile the Turbo C module
DUBLIST.C to an object (.OBJ) file before linking it with the Turbo Prolog
main module PLIST.PRO.

This is the link command:

```
tlink init cpinit plist dublist plist.sym, dublist, ,prolog+emu+mathl+cl
```

Example 4: Drawing a 3-D Bar Chart

In this example, we show you how to compile and link the C and Prolog
modules to create a unified, mixed-language program that combines AI
flexibility with C graphics-handling capability. Specifically, the code
provided includes the following:

- a Turbo C module BAR.C that draws bar charts using input from
  another file
- a Turbo Prolog main module PBAR.PRO that requests input from the
  user.

Turbo C Source File: BAR.C

The source code for this program is the file BAR.C on your disk. (Refer to
Chapter 1 for a list of the files on the distribution disks.)

Compiling BAR.C

As in the first three examples, you must compile the Turbo C module
BAR.C to an object (.OBJ) file before linking it with the Turbo Prolog main
module PBAR.PRO.

Turbo Prolog Program: PBAR.PRO

The source code for this program is the file PBAR.PRO on your disk. PBAR is a Turbo Prolog program that prompts the end-user to make, save, load, or draw a bar chart.

If the end-user wishes to make a bar chart, this program will accept input specifications for the chart, position each bar in a window and call your C module to draw the bar. After each bar is drawn, it is *asserted* (a Prolog term for inserted) into the database.

The end-user may opt to save the bar chart; PBAR will save a description of the current bar chart into a file for later use.

If the end-user selects the load option, PBAR will delete the current bar chart description and load a user-specified bar chart description from a file.

Given the final option, *draw*, PBAR will use the description in the database in a recursive call to the Turbo C BAR module, which will then draw a bar chart to the specifications currently in the database.

Compiling PBAR.PRO to PBAR.OBJ

As in example 1, you must compile the Turbo Prolog main module source file to an object (.OBJ) file before linking it with the Turbo C modules.

Linking PBAR.OBJ with the Module BAR.OBJ

In the following link command, PBAR.OBJ is linked with the previously compiled Turbo C module, BAR.OBJ. The components of this link command are

- the Turbo Prolog object modules, INIT.OBJ and PBAR.OBJ
- the Turbo C object module BAR.OBJ
- the symbol table PBAR.SYM, and the output file BARCHART.EXE (executable file)
- the libraries, PROLOG.LIB and CL.LIB

This is the link command:

```
tlink init cpinit pbar bar pbar.sym,barchart,,prolog+cl
```

That's All There Is to It

With these four examples, we have shown you how to link Turbo Prolog modules with your Turbo C programs. If you are an experienced Turbo Prolog programmer but would like to know more about programming in C, we recommend reading Chapters 5 and 3 in this manual. If you are an experienced C programmer and would like to find out more about Turbo Prolog, we recommend consulting a Turbo Prolog tutorial, such as *Using Turbo Prolog* by P. Robinson (McGraw-Hill).

C H A P T E R

8

Turbo C Language Reference

The traditional reference for C is *The C Programming Language*, by Brian W. Kernighan and Dennis M. Ritchie (which we will refer to as "K&R" from now on). Their book doesn't define a complete standard for C; that task has been left to the American National Standards Institute (ANSI). Instead, K&R presents a minimum standard so that a program using only those aspects of C found in K&R can be compiled by any C implementation that supports the K&R definition.

Turbo C not only supports the K&R definition, it also implements most of the ANSI extensions. In doing so, Turbo C seeks to improve and extend the C language by adding new features and increasing the power and flexibility of old ones. We don't have space to reprint K&R or the ANSI standard here; instead we'll tell you about the additions to the K&R definition that Turbo C provides, noting which come from the ANSI standard and which are our own improvements.

In This Chapter...

To make cross-referencing easier for you, in this chapter we follow (more or less) the outline of Appendix A in K&R, which is titled "C Reference Manual." Not all sections of that appendix are referenced here; for any section we passed over, you may assume that there are no significant differences between Turbo C and the K&R definition. Also, to more easily accommodate some of the ANSI and Turbo C extensions, we have presented some information in the same order as given in the ANSI C standard rather than adhere to the K&R organization.

Comments (K&R 2.1)

The K&R definition of C does not allow comments to be nested. For example, the construct

```
/* Attempt to comment out myfunc() */

/*
   myfunc()
   {
      printf("This is my function\n");                    /* The only line */
   }
*/
```

would be interpreted as a single comment ending right after the phrase The only line; the dangling brace and end-of-comment would then trigger a syntax error. By default, Turbo C does not allow comment nesting; however, you can correctly compile a program (such as that shown) with nested comments by using the -c compiler option (Nested comments...ON in the O/C/Source menu). A more portable approach, though, is to bracket the code to be commented out with #if 0 and #endif.

Comments are replaced with a single-space character after macro expansion. In other implementations, comments are removed completely and are sometimes used for token pasting. See "Token Replacement" in this chapter.

Identifier (K&R 2.2)

An identifier is just the name you give to a variable, function, data type, or other user-defined object. In C, an identifier can contain letters (*A...Z, a...z*) and digits (0...9) as well as the underscore character (_). Turbo C also allows you to use the dollar sign character ($). However, an identifier can only start with a letter or an underscore.

Case is significant; in other words, the identifiers *indx* and *Indx* are different. In Turbo C, the first 32 characters of an identifier are significant within a program; however, you can modify this with the -i# compiler option, where # is the number of significant characters. (This is the menu option **O/S/Identifier length**.)

Likewise, the first 32 characters are significant for global identifiers imported from other modules. However, you can decide whether or not case is significant for those identifiers by using the **Case-sensitive link…On** option from the **Options/Linker** submenu or the /c option on a TLINK command line. Note, however, that identifiers of type **pascal** are never case sensitive at link time.

Keywords (K&R 2.3)

Table 8.1 shows the keywords reserved by Turbo C; these cannot be used as identifier names. Those preceded by "AN" are ANSI extensions to K&R; those preceded by "TC" are Turbo C extensions. The keywords **entry** and **fortran**, mentioned in K&R, are neither used nor reserved by Turbo C.

Table 8.1: Keywords Reserved by Turbo C

TC	asm		extern		return	TC	_cs	TC	_DH
	auto	TC	far		short	TC	_ds	TC	_DL
	break		float	AN	signed	TC	_es	TC	_DX
	case		for		sizeof	TC	_ss	TC	_BP
TC	cdecl		goto		static	TC	_AH	TC	_DI
	char	TC	huge		struct	TC	_AL	TC	_SI
AN	const		if		switch	TC	_AX	TC	_SP
	continue		int		typedef	TC	_BH		
	default	TC	interrupt		union	TC	_BL		
	do		long		unsigned	TC	_BX		
	double	TC	near	AN	void	TC	_CH		
	else	TC	pascal	AN	volatile	TC	_CL		
AN	enum		register		while	TC	_CX		

Constants (K&R 2.4)

Turbo C supports all the constant types defined by K&R with a few enhancements.

Integer Constants (K&R 2.4.1)

Constants from 0 to 4294967295 (base 10) are allowed. (Negative constants are simply unsigned constants with the unary minus operator.) Both octal (base 8) and hexadecimal (base 16) representations are accepted.

The suffix *L* (or *l*) attached to any constant forces it to be represented as a **long**. Similarly, the suffix *U* (or *u*) forces it to be **unsigned**, and it will be **unsigned long** if the value of the number itself is greater than 65535, regardless of which base is used. Note: you may use both *L* and *U* suffixes on the same constant.

Table 8.2 summaries the representations of constants in all three bases.

Table 8.2: Turbo C Integer Constants Without L or U

```
             --------Decimal Constants--------

            0 - 32767                int
        32767 - 2147483647           long
   2147483648 - 4294967295           unsigned long

     > 4294967295                    Will overflow without warning; the
                                     resulting constant will be the
                                     low-order bits of the actual value.


             --------Octal Constants--------

           00 - 077777               int
      0100000 - 0177777              unsigned int
     01000000 - 017777777777         long
0100000000000 - 0377777777777        unsigned long

   > 0377777777777                   Will overflow (as previously described)


             --------Hexadecimal Constants--------

       0x0000 - 0x7FFF               int
       0x8000 - 0xFFFF               unsigned int
      0x10000 - 0x7FFFFFFF           long
   0x80000000 - 0xFFFFFFFF           unsigned long

    > 0xFFFFFFFF                     Will overflow (as previously described)
```

Character Constants (K&R 2.4.3)

Turbo C supports two-character constants, for example, 'An', '\n\t', and '\007\007'. These constants are represented as 16-bit **int** values with the first character in the low-order byte and the second character in the high-order byte. Note that these constants are not portable to other C compilers.

One-character constants, such as 'A', '\t', and '\007', are also represented as 16-bit **int** values. In this case, the low-order byte is *sign extended* into the high byte; that is, if the value is greater than 127[base 10], the upper byte is set to −1 [=0xFF]. This can be disabled by declaring that the default **char** type is unsigned (use the −K compiler option or select **Default** char type...Unsigned in the **Options/Compiler/Source** submenu), which forces the high byte to be zero regardless of the value of the low byte.

Turbo C supports the ANSI extension of allowing hexadecimal representation of character codes, such as '\x1F', '\x82', and so on. Either x or X is allowed, and you may have one to three digits.

Turbo C also supports the other ANSI extensions to the list of allowed *escape sequences*. Escape sequences are values inserted into character and string constants, preceded by a backslash (\). Table 8.3 lists all allowed sequences; those marked with an asterisk (*) are extensions to K&R.

Table 8.3: Turbo C Escape Sequences

Sequence	Value	Char	What It Does
*\a	0x07	BEL	Audible bell
\b	0x08	BS	Backspace
\f	0x0C	FF	Formfeed
\n	0x0A	LF	Newline (linefeed)
\r	0x0D	CR	Carriage return
\t	0x09	HT	Tab (horizonal)
*\v	0x0B	VT	Vertical tab
\\	0x5c	\	Backslash
\'	0x2c	'	Single quote (apostrophe)
*\"	0x22	"	Double quote
*\?	0x3F	?	Question mark
\DDD		any	DDD = 1 to 3 digit octal value
*\xHHH	0xHHH	any	HHH = 1 to 3 digit hex value

*ANSI extensions to K&R

Note: Since Turbo C allows two-character constants, ambiguities may arise if an octal escape sequence of less than three digits is followed by a digit. In such cases, Turbo C will presume that the following character is part of the escape sequence, unless the character is not allowed for that type of number. For example, because the digits 8 and 9 in an octal value are not allowed, the constant \258 would be interpreted as a two-character constant made up of the characters \25 and 8.

Floating Constants (K&R 2.4.4)

All floating constants are by definition of type **double** as specified in K&R. However, you can coerce a floating constant to be of type **float** by adding an *F* suffix to the constant.

Strings (K&R 2.5)

According to K&R, a string constant consists of exactly one string unit, containing double quotes, text, double quotes ("like this"). You must use the backslash (\ ) as a continuation character in order to extend a string constant across line boundaries.

Turbo C allows you to use multiple string unitsin a string constant; it will then do the concatenation for you. For example, you could do the following:

```
main()
{
   char    *p;

   p = "This is an example of how Turbo C"
       " will automatically\ndo the concatenation for"
       " you on very long strings,\nresulting in nicer"
       " looking programs.";
   printf(p);
}
```

The output of the program is:

```
This is an example of how Turbo C will automatically
do the concatenation for you on very long strings,
resulting in nicer looking programs.
```

Hardware Specifics (K&R 2.6)

K&R recognizes that the size and numeric range of the basic data types (and their various permutations) are very implementation specific and usually derive from the architecture of the host computer. This is true for Turbo C, just as it is for all other C compilers. Table 8.4 lists the sizes and resulting ranges of the different data types for Turbo C. Note that the type **long double** is accepted but is treated the same as **double**.

Table 8.4: Turbo C Data Types, Sizes, and Ranges

Type	Size (bits)	Range
unsigned char	8	0 – 255
char	8	–128 – 127
enum	16	–32768 – 32767
unsigned short	16	0 – 65535
short	16	–32768 – 32767
unsigned int	16	0 – 65535
int	16	–32768 – 32767
unsigned long	32	0 – 4294967295
long	32	–2147483648 – 2147483647
float	32	3.4E-38 – 3.4E+38
double	64	1.7E-308 – 1.7E+308
long double	64	1.7E-308 – 1.7E+308
pointer	16	(near, _cs, _ds, _es, _ss pointers)
pointer	32	(far, huge pointers)

Conversions (K&R 6)

Turbo C supports the standard mechanisms for automatically converting from one data type to another. The following sections indicate additions to K&R or implementation-specific information.

char, int, and enum (K&R 6.1)

Assigning a character constant to an integer object results in a full 16-bit assignment, since both one- and two-character constants are represented as 16-bit values (see K&R 2.4.3). Assigning a character object (such as a variable) to an integral object will result in automatic sign extension, unless you've made the default **char** type unsigned (with the –K compiler option). Objects of type **signed char** always use sign extension; objects of type **unsigned char** always set the high byte to zero when converted to **int**.

Values of type **enum** convert straight to **int** with no modifications; likewise, **int** values can be converted straight to an enumerated type. **enum** values and characters convert exactly as do **int** values and characters.

Pointers (K&R 6.4)

In Turbo C, different pointers in your program may be of different sizes, depending upon the memory model or pointer type modifers you use. For example, when you compile your program in a particular memory model, the addressing modifiers (**near**, **far**, **huge**, **_cs**, **_ds**, **_es**, **_ss**) in your source code can override the pointer size given by that memory model.

A pointer must be declared as pointing to some particular type, even if that type is **void** (which really means pointer to anything). However, having been declared, that pointer can point to an object of any other type. Turbo C allows you to reassign pointers like this, but the compiler will warn you when pointer reassignment happens—unless the pointer was originally declared to be of type pointer to **void**. However, pointers to data types cannot be converted to pointers to functions, and vice versa.

Arithmetic Conversions (K&R 6.6)

K&R refers to the *usual arithmetic conversions*, which specify what happens when any values are used in an arithmetic expression (operand, operator, operand). Here are the steps used by Turbo C to convert the operands in an arithmetic expression:

1. Any noninteger or nondouble types are converted as shown in Table 8.5. After this, any two values associated with an operator are either **int** (including the **long** and **unsigned** modifiers) or **double**.

2. If either operand is of type **double**, the other operand is converted to **double**.

3. Otherwise, if either operand is of type **unsigned long**, the other operand is converted to **unsigned long**.

4. Otherwise, if either operand is of type **long**, then the other operand is converted to **long**.

5. Otherwise, if either operand is of type **unsigned**, then the other operand is converted to **unsigned**.

6. Otherwise, both operands are of type **int**.

The result of the expression is the same type as that of the two operands.

Table 8.5: Methods Used in Usual Arithmetic Conversions

Type	Converts to	Method
char	int	sign-extended
unsigned char	int	zero-filled high byte (always)
signed char	int	sign-extended (always)
short	int	if unsigned, then unsigned int
enum	int	same value
float	double	pads mantissa with 0's

Operators (K&R Section 7.2)

Turbo C supports the unary + operator, while K&R does not. Normally, Turbo C will regroup expressions, rearranging commutative operators (such as * and binary +) in an effort to create an efficiently compiled expression. However, Turbo C will not reorganize expressions around a unary +. This means that you can control a floating-point expression that is sensitive to precision errors or overflow by means of a unary + operator, without having to split it up into separate expressions involving assignments to temporaries. For example, if *a*, *b*, *c*, and *f* are all of type **float**, then the expression

```
f = a + +(b + c);
```

forces the expression *(b + c)* to be evaluated before adding the result to *a*.

Type Specifiers and Modifiers (K&R 8.2)

Turbo C supports the following basic types not found in K&R:

- unsigned char
- unsigned short

- unsigned long
- long double
- enumeration
- void

The first three basic types in this list are self-explanatory; the fourth is equivalent to the type **double**. The types **int** and **short** are equivalent in Turbo C, both being 16 bits. See "Hardware Specifics" for more details on how different types are implemented.

The enum Type

Turbo C implements enumerated types as found in the ANSI standard. An enumerated data type is used to describe a discrete set of integer values. For example, you could declare the following:

```
enum days { sun, mon, tues, wed, thur, fri, sat };
```

The names listed in *days* are integer constants with the first (*sun*) being automatically set to zero and each succeeding name being one more than the preceding one (*mon* = 1, *tues* = 2, and so on). However, you can set a name to a specific value; following names without specified values will then increase by one, as before. For example,

```
enum coins { penny = 1, nickle = 5, dime = 10, quarter = 25};
```

A variable of an enumerated type can be assigned any value of type **int**—no type checking beyond that is enforced.

The void Type

In K&R, every function returns a value; if no type is declared, then the function is of type **int**. Turbo C supports the type **void** as defined in the ANSI standard. This is used to explicitly document a function that does not return a value. Likewise, an empty parameter list can be documented with the reserved word **void**. For example,

```
void putmsg(void)
{
    printf("Hello, world\n");
}

main()
{
    putmsg();
}
```

As a special construct, you may cast an expression to **void** in order to explicitly indicate that you're ignoring the value returned by a function. For example, if you want to pause until the user presses a key but ignore what is typed, you might write this:

```
(void) getch();
```

Finally, you can declare a pointer to **void**. This doesn't create a pointer to nothing; it creates a pointer to any kind of data object, the type of which is not necessarily known. You can assign any pointer to a **void** pointer (and vice versa) without a cast. However, you cannot use the indirection operator (*) with a **void** pointer, since the underlying type is undefined.

The signed Modifier

In addition to the three type adjectives defined by K&R—**long**, **short**, and **unsigned**—Turbo C supports three more: **signed**, **const**, and **volatile** (all of which are defined in the ANSI standard).

The signed modifier is the opposite of **unsigned** and explicitly says that the value is stored as a signed (two's complement) value. This is done primarily for documentation and completeness. However, if you compile with the default **char** type unsigned (instead of signed), you must use the **signed** modifier in order to define a variable or function of type **signed char**. The modifier **signed** used by itself signifies **signed int**, just as **unsigned** by itself means **unsigned int**.

The const Modifier

The **const** modifier, as defined in the ANSI standard, prevents any assignments to the object or any other side effects, such as increment or decrement. A **const** pointer cannot be modified, though the object to which it points can be. Note: The modifier **const** used by itself is equivalent to **const int**. Consider the following examples:

```
const float  pi     = 3.1415926;
const        maxint = 32767;
char *const  str    = "Hello, world";           /* A constant pointer */
char const   *str2  = "Hello, world";       /* A pointer to a constant string */
```

Given these, the following statements are illegal:

```
pi  = 3.0;                              /* Assigns a value to a const */
i   = maxint--;                              /* Increments a const */
str = "Hi, there!";                    /* Points str to something else */
```

Note, however, that the function call strcpy(str,"Hi, there!") is legal, since it does a character-by-character copy from the string literal "Hi, there!" into the memory locations pointed to by *str*.

The volatile Modifier

The **volatile** modifier, also defined by the ANSI standard, is almost the opposite of **const**. It indicates that the object may be modified; not only by you, but also by something outside of your program, such as an interrupt routine or an I/O port. Declaring an object to be **volatile** warns the compiler not to make assumptions concerning the value of the object while evaluating expressions containing it, since the value could (in theory) change at any moment. It also prevents the compiler from making the variable a register variable.

```
volatile  int  ticks;
interrupt   timer()
{
   ticks++;
}

wait(int interval)
{
   ticks = 0;
   while (ticks < interval);
                                            /* Do nothing */
}
```

These routines (assuming **timer** has been properly associated with a hardware clock interrupt) will implement a timed wait of ticks specified by the argument *interval*. Note that a highly optimizing compiler might not load the value of *ticks* inside the **while** loop, since the loop doesn't change the value of *ticks*.

The cdecl and pascal Modifiers

Turbo C allows your programs to easily call routines written in other languages, and vice versa. When you mix languages like this, you have to deal with two important issues: *identifiers* and *parameter passing*.

When you compile a program in Turbo C, all the global identifiers in the program—that is, the names of functions and global variables—are saved in the resulting object code file for linking purposes. By default, those identifiers are saved in their original case (lower, upper, or mixed). Also, an underscore (_) is prepended to the front of the identifer, unless you have selected the -u- (Generate underbars...Off) option.

Likewise, any external identifiers you declare in your program are presumed to have the same format. Linking is (by default) case sensitive, so identifiers used in different source files must match exactly in both spelling and case.

pascal

In certain situations, such as referencing code written in other languages, this default method of saving names can be a problem.

So Turbo C gives you a way around the problem. You can declare any identifier to be of type `pascal`. This means that the identifier is converted to uppercase and that no underscore is stuck on the front. (If the identifier is a function, this also affects the parameter-passing sequence used, see "Function Type Modifiers" for more details.) It no longer matters what case is used in the source code; for linking purposes, it's considered uppercase only.

cdecl

You can make all the global identifiers in a source file of type `pascal` by compiling with the -p (Calling convention...Pascal) option. However, you may then want to ensure that certain identifiers have their case preserved and keep the underscore on the front, especially if they're C identifiers from another file.

You can do so by declaring those identifiers to be `cdecl` (which also has an effect on parameter passing for functions).

You'll notice, for example, that all the functions in the header files (STDIO.H, etc.) are of type **cdecl**. This ensures that you can link with the library routines, even if you compile using -p.

See K&R Section 10.1.1 in this chapter, as well as Chapter 9, for more details.

The near, far, and huge Modifiers

Turbo C has three modifiers that affect the indirection operator (*); that is, they modify pointers to data. These are **near**, **far**, and **huge**. The meaning of these keywords is explained in greater detail in Chapter 9, but here's a brief overview.

Turbo C allows you to compile using one of several memory models. The model you use determines (among other things) the internal format of pointers to data. If you use a small data model (tiny, small, medium), all data pointers are only 16 bits long and give the offset from the Data Segment (DS) register. If you use a large data model (compact, large, huge), all pointers to data are 32 bits long and give both a segment address and an offset.

Sometimes, when using one size of data model, you want to declare a pointer to be of a different size or format than the current default. You do so using the modifiers **near**, **far**, and **huge**.

A **near** pointer is only 16 bits long; it uses the current contents of the Data Segment (DS) register for its segment address. This is the default for small data models. Using **near** pointers limits your data to the current 64K data segment.

A **far** pointer is 32 bits long, and contains both a segment address and an offset. This is the default for large data models. Using **far** pointers allows you to refer to data anywhere in the 1-MB address space of the Intel 8088/8086 processors.

A **huge** pointer is also 32 bits long, again containing both a segment address and an offset. However, unlike **far** pointers, a **huge** pointer is always kept *normalized*. The details of this are given in Chapter 9, but here are the implications:

■ Relational operators (==, !=, <, >, <=, >=) all work correctly and predictably with **huge** pointers; they do not with **far** pointers.

- Any arithmetic operations on a **huge** pointer affect both the segment address and the offset because of normalization; on a **far** pointer, only the offset is affected.
- A given **huge** pointer can be incremented through the entire 1 MB address space; a **far** pointer will eventually wrap around to the start of its 64 K segment.
- Using **huge** pointers requires additional time because the normalization routines have to be called after any arithmetic operations on the pointers.

Structures and Unions (K&R Section 8.5)

Turbo C follows the K&R implementation of structures and unions and provides the following additional features.

Word Alignment

If you use the –a compiler option (Alignment…Word), Turbo C will pad the structure (or union) with bytes as needed for word alignment. This ensures three things:

- The structure will start on a word boundary (even address).
- Any non-**char** member will have an even offset from the beginning of the structure.
- A byte will be added (if necessary) at the end to ensure that the entire structure contains an even number of bytes.

Bitfields

In Turbo C, a bitfield may be either a **signed** or **unsigned int** and may occupy from 1 to 16 bits. Bitfields are allocated from low-order to high-order bits within a word.

For example,

```
struct mystruct {
    int         i : 2;
    unsigned    j : 5;
    int           : 4;
    int         k : 1;
    unsigned    m : 4;
} a,b,c;
```

produces the following layout:

15	14	13	12	11	10	9	8	7	6	5	4	3	2	1	0
x	x	x	x	x	x	x	x	x	x	x	x	x	x	x	x

m	k	(unused)	j	i

Integer fields are stored in two's complement form with the left-most bit being the sign bit. For example, a **signed int** bitfield 1 bit wide (such as *a.k*) can only hold the values –1 and 0, since any non-zero value will be interpreted as –1.

Statements (K&R 9)

Turbo C implements all the statements described in K&R without exception and without modification.

External Function Definitions (K&R 10.1)

In Turbo C, **extern** declarations given inside a function obey proper block scope; they will not be recognized beyond the scope of the block in which they are defined. However, Turbo C will remember the declarations in order to compare them with later declarations of the same object.

Turbo C implements most of the ANSI enhancements to the K&R definition of functions. This includes additional function modifers, as well as function prototypes. Turbo C also has a few enhancements of its own, such as functions of type **interrupt**.

Function Type Modifiers (K&R 10.1.1)

In addition to **extern** and **static**, Turbo C has a number of type modifiers specific to function definitions: **pascal**, **cdecl**, **interrupt**, **near**, **far**, and **huge**.

The pascal Function Modifier

The **pascal** modifier is specific to Turbo C and is intended for functions (and pointers to functions) that use the Pascal parameter passing sequence. This allows you to write C functions that can be called from programs written in other languages; likewise, it will allow your C programs to call external routines written in languages other than C. The function name is converted to all uppercase for linking purposes.

Note: Using the -p compiler option (Calling convention...Pascal) will cause all functions (and pointers to those functions) to be treated as if they were of type **pascal**. Also, functions declared to be of type **pascal** can still be called from C routines, so long as the C routine sees that the function is of type **pascal**. For example, if you have declared and compiled the following function:

```
pascal putnums(int i, int j, int k)
{
    printf("And the answers are:  %d, %d, and %d\n",i,j,k);
}
```

another C program could then link it in and call it, given the following declarations:

```
pascal putnums(int i, int j, int k);

main()
{
    putnums(1,4,9);
}
```

Functions of type **pascal** cannot take a variable number of arguments, unlike functions such as **printf**. For this reason, you cannot use an ellipsis (...) in a **pascal** function definition. (See "Function Prototypes" for an explanation of using the ellipsis to define a function with a variable number of arguments.)

The cdecl Function Modifier

The **cdecl** modifier is also specific to Turbo C. Like the **pascal** modifier, it is used with functions and pointers to functions. Its purpose is to override the -p compiler directive and allow a function to be called as a regular C function. For example, if you were to compile the previous program with the -p option set, but wanted to use **printf**, you might do something like this:

```
extern cdecl printf();
putnums(int i, int j, int k);

cdecl main()
{
    putnums(1,4,9);
}

putnums(int i, int j, int k)
{
    printf("And the answers are:  %d, %d, and %d\n",i,j,k);
}
```

If a program is compiled with the -p option, all functions used from the run-time library will need to have **cdecl** declarations. If you'll look at the header files (such as STDIO.H), you'll see that every function is explicitly defined as **cdecl** in anticipation of this. Note that **main** must also be declared as **cdecl**; this is because the C start-up code always tries to call **main** with the C calling convention.

The interrupt Function Modifier

The **interrupt** modifier is another one specific to Turbo C. **interrupt** functions are designed to be used with the 8086/8088 interrupt vectors. Turbo C will compile an **interrupt** function with extra function entry and exit code so that registers AX, BX, CX, DX, SI, DI, ES, and DS are preserved. The other registers of BP, SP, SS, CS, and IP are preserved as part of the C-calling sequence or as part of the interrupt handling itself. Here is an example of a typical **interrupt** definition:

```
void interrupt myhandler()
{
    ...
}
```

You should declare interrupt functions to be of type **void**. Interrupt functions may be declared in any memory model. For all memory models except huge, DS is set to the program data segment. For the huge model, DS is set to the module's data segment.

Function Prototypes (K&R 10.1.2)

When you are declaring a function, K&R only allows a function declarator consisting of the function name, its type, and an empty set of parentheses. The parameters (if any) are declared only when you actually define the function itself.

The ANSI standard—and Turbo C—allow you to use function prototypes to declare a function. These are declarators that include information about the function parameters. The compiler uses that information to check function calls for validity. The compiler also uses that information to coerce arguments to the proper type. Suppose you have the following code fragment:

```
long  lmax(long v1, long v2);

main()
{
   int    limit = 32;
   char   ch    = 'A';
   long   mval;

   mval = lmax(limit,ch);
}
```

Given the function prototype for **lmax**, this program will convert *limit* and *ch* to **long** using the standard rules of assignment before they are placed on the stack for the call to **lmax**. Without the function prototype, *limit* and *ch* would have been placed on the stack as an integer and a character, respectively; in that case, the stack passed to **lmax** would not match in size or content what **lmax** was expecting, leading to problems. Since K&R C does not do any checking of parameter type or number, using function prototypes aids greatly in tracking down bugs and other programming errors.

Function prototypes also aid in documenting code. For example, the function **strcpy** takes two parameters: a source string and a destination string. The question is, which is which? The function prototype

```
char  *strcpy(char *dest, char *source);
```

makes it clear. If a header file contains function prototypes, then you can print that file to get most of the information you need for writing programs that call those functions.

A function declarator with parentheses containing the single word **void** indicates a function that takes no arguments at all:

```
f(void)
```

Otherwise, the parentheses contain a list of declarators separated by commas. The declarator may be in the form of a cast, as in

```
func(int *, long);
```

or it may include an identifier, as in

```
func(int * count, long total);
```

In the two lists of declarators just mentioned, the function **func** accepts two parameters: a pointer to **int** named *count* and a **long** (integer) named *total*. If an identifier is included, it has no effect except to be used in the diagnostic message, if and when a parameter-type mismatch occurs.

A function prototype normally defines a function as accepting a fixed number of parameters. For C functions that accept a variable number of parameters (such as **printf**), a function prototype may end with an ellipsis (...), like this:

```
f(int *count, long total,...)
```

With this form of prototype, the fixed parameters are checked at compile time, and the variable parameters are passed as if no prototype were present.

Here are some more examples of function declarators and prototypes.

```
int  f();
```
/* A function returning an int with no information about parameters. This is the K&R "classic style." */

```
int  f(void);
```
/* A function returning an int that takes no parameters. */

```
int  p(int,long);
```
/* A function returning an int that accepts two parameters, the first an int and the second a long. */

```
int  pascal q(void);
```
/* A pascal function returning an int that takes no parameters at all. */

```
char far * s(char *source, int kind);
```
/* A function returning a far pointer to a char and accepting two parameters: the first, a pointer to a char; the second, an int. */

```
int  printf(char *format,...);
```
/* A function returning an int and accepting a pointer to a char fixed parameter and any number of additional parameters of unknown type. */

```
int  (*fp)(int);
```
/* A pointer to a function returning an int and accepting a single int parameter. */

Here is a summary of the rules governing how Turbo C deals with language modifiers and formal parameters in function calls, both with and without prototypes.

Rule #1: The language modifiers for a function definition must match the modifiers used in the declaration of the function at all calls to the function.

Rule #2: A function may modify the values of its formal parameters, but this has no effect on the actual arguments in the calling routine, except for interrupt functions. See "Interrupt Functions" in Chapter 9 for more information.

When a function prototype has not been previously declared, Turbo C converts integral arguments to a function call according to the integral widening (expansion) rules described in "Arithmetic Conversions." When a function prototype is in scope, Turbo C converts the given argument to the type of the declared parameter as if by assignment.

When a function prototype includes an ellipsis (...), Turbo C converts all given function arguments as in any other prototype (up to the ellipsis). The compiler will widen any arguments given beyond the fixed parameters, according to the normal rules for function arguments without prototypes.

If a prototype is present, the number of arguments must match (unless an ellipsis is present in the prototype). The types must be compatible only to the extent that an assignment can legally convert them. You can always use an explicit cast to convert an argument to a type that is acceptable to a function prototype.

The following example should clarify these points.

```
int    strcmp(char *s1, char *s2);           /* Full prototype */
char   *strcpy();                              /* No prototype */
int    samp1(float, int, ...);                /* Full prototype */

samp2()
{
    char   *sx, *cp;
    double z;
    long   a;
    float  q;

    if (strcmp(sx, cp))                                    /* 1. Correct */
        strcpy(sx, cp, 44);            /* 2. OK in Turbo C but not portable */

    samp1(3, a, q);                                        /* 3. Correct */
    strcpy(cp);                                       /* 4. Run-time error */
    samp1(2);                                          /* 5. Compile error */

}
```

The five calls (numbered by comment) in this example illustrate different points about function calls and prototypes.

In call #1, the use of **strcmp** exactly matches the prototype and everything is proper.

In call #2, the call to **strcpy** has an extra argument (**strcpy** is defined for two arguments, not three). In this case, Turbo C will waste a little time and code pushing an extra argument. However, there is no syntax error because the compiler has not been told about the arguments to **strcpy**. This call is not portable.

In call #3, the prototype directs that the first argument to **samp1** be converted to **float** and the second argument to **int**. The compiler will warn about possible loss of significant digits because a conversion from **long** to **int** chops the upper bits. (You can eliminate this warning with an explicit cast to **int**). The third argument, q, lines up with the ellipsis in the prototype, so it is converted to **double** according to the usual arithmetic conversions; the whole call is correct.

In call #4, **strcpy** is again called, but now with too few arguments. This will cause an execution error and it may crash the program. The compiler will say nothing (even though the number of parameters differs from that in a previous call to the same function!), since there is no function prototype for **strcpy**.

In call #5, **samp1** is called with too few arguments. Since **samp1** requires a minimum of two arguments, this statement is an error. The compiler will give a message about too few arguments in a call.

Important Note: If your function prototype does not match the actual function definition, Turbo C will detect this *if and only if* that definition is in the same file as the prototype. If you create a library of routines with a corresponding header file of prototypes, you might consider including that header file when you compile the library, so that any discrepancies between the prototypes and the actual definitions will be caught.

Scope Rules (K&R 11)

Turbo C is more liberal in allowing non-unique identifiers than K&R specifies a compiler need be. There are four distinct classes of identifiers in this implementation:

Variables, typedefs, and **enumeration members** must be unique within the block in which they are defined. Externally declared identifiers must be unique among externally declared variables.

Structure, union, and **enumeration tags** must be unique within the block in which they are defined. Tags declared outside of any function must be unique within all tags defined externally.

Structure and **union member** names must be unique within the structure or union in which they are defined. There is no restriction on the type or offset of members with the same member name in different structures.

Goto labels must be unique within the function in which they are declared.

Compiler Control Lines (K&R 12)

Turbo C supports all the control commands found in K&R. These preprocessor directives are source lines with an initial #, which may be preceded or followed by whitespace.

Token Replacement (K&R 12.1)

Turbo C implements the K&R definition of #define and #undef with the following additions.

■ The following identifiers may not appear in a #define or #undef directive:

    __STDC__
    __FILE__
    __LINE__
    __DATE__
    __TIME__

■ Two tokens may be pasted together in a macro definition by separating them with ## (plus optional whitespace on either side). The preprocessor removes the whitespace and the ##, combining the separate tokens. This can be used to construct identifiers; for example, given the construct

    #define VAR(i,j)   (i ## j)

then VAR(x,6) would expand to *x6*. This replaces the sometimes-used (but non-portable) method of using (i/**/j).

- Nested macros mentioned in a macro definition string are expanded only when the macro itself is expanded, not when the macro is defined. This mostly affects the interaction of `#undef` with nested macros.

- The # symbol can be placed in front of a macro argument in order to *stringize* the argument, (convert it to a string). When the macro is expanded, #*<formal arg>* is replace with "*<actual arg>*". So, given the following macro definition:

  ```
  #define TRACE(flag) printf(#flag "=%d\n", flag)
  ```

  then the code fragment

  ```
  highval = 1024;
  TRACE(highval);
  ```

  becomes

  ```
  highval = 1024;
    printf("highval" "= %d\n", highval);
  ```

  which, in turn, becomes

  ```
  highval = 1024;
    printf("highval=%d\n", highval);
  ```

- Unlike other implementations, Turbo C does *not* expand macro arguments inside strings and character constants.

File Inclusion (K&R 12.2)

Turbo C implements the `#include` directive as found in K&R but has the following additional feature: If the preprocessor can't find the include file in the default directory, assuming that you used the form

```
#include "filename"
```

then it searches the directories specified with the compiler option `-I`.

If you used the form `#include <filename>`, then only those directories specified with `-I` are searched. (Directories listed under the menu option **O/Environment/Include** directories are equivalent to those given with the `-Ipathname` command-line option.)

You may construct the `#include` path name, including delimiters, using macro expansion. If the next line after the keyword begins with an identifier, the preprocessor scans the text for macros. However, if a string is enclosed in quotes or angle brackets, Turbo C will not examine it for embedded macros.

So, if you have the following:

```
#define    myinclude    "c:\tc\include\mystuff.h"
#include myinclude
#include "myinclude.h"
```

then the first `#include` statement will cause the preprocessor to look for C:\TC\INCLUDE\MSTUFF.H, while the second will cause it to look for MYINCLUDE.H in the default directory.

Also, you may not use string literal concatenation and token pasting in macros that are used in an `#include` statement. The macro expansion must produce text that reads like a normal `#include` directive.

Conditional Compilation (K&R 12.3)

Turbo C supports the K&R definition of conditional compilation by replacing the appropriate lines with a line containing only whitespace. The lines thus ignored are those beginning with `#if`, `#ifdef`, `#ifndef`, `#else`, `#elif`, and `#endif` directives as well as any lines that are not to be compiled as a result of the directives. All conditional compilation directives must be completed in the source or include file in which they are begun.

Turbo C also supports the ANSI operator `defined(symbol)`. This will evaluate to 1 (*true*) if the symbol has been previously defined (using `#define`) and has not been subsequently undefined (using `#undef`); otherwise, it evaluates to 0 (*false*). So the directive

```
#if defined(mysym)
```

is the same as

```
#ifdef mysym
```

The advantage is that you can use `defined` repeatedly in a complex expression following the `#if` directive, such as

```
#if defined(mysym) || defined(yoursym)
```

Finally, Turbo C (unlike ANSI) allows you to use the **sizeof** operator in a preprocessor expression. Thus, you can write the following

```
#if (sizeof(void *) == 2)
#define SDATA
#else
#define LDATA
#endif
```

Line Control (K&R 12.4)

Turbo C supports the K&R definition of `#line`. Macros are expanded in `#line` as they are in the `#include` directive.

Error Directive (ANSI C 3.8.5)

Turbo C supports the `#error` directive, which is mentioned (but not explicitly defined) in the ANSI standard. The format is:

```
#error errmsg
```

and the message issued is

```
Fatal: filename line# Error directive: errmsg
```

Typically, programmers include this directive in a preprocessor conditional that catches some undesired compile-time condition. In the normal case, that condition won't be true. In the event that the condition is true, you want the compiler to print an error message and stop the compile. You do this by putting an `#error` directive within a conditional that is true for the indesired case.

For example, suppose you `#define` *MYVAL*, which must be either 0 or 1. You could then include the following conditional in your source code to test for an incorrect value of *MYVAL*:

```
#if (MYVAL != 0 && MYVAL != 1)
#error MYVAL must de defined to either 0 or 1
#endif
```

The preprocessor scans the text to remove comments but displays any remaining text without looking for embedded macros.

Pragma Directive (ANSI C 3.8.6)

Turbo C supports the `#pragma` directive, which (like `#error`) is vaguely defined in the ANSI standard. Its purpose is to permit implementation-specific directives of the form:

```
#pragma <directive name>
```

With `#pragma`, Turbo C can define whatever directives it desires without interfering with other compilers that support `#pragma`. Why? Because, by definition, if the compiler doesn't recognize the directive name, it ignores the `#pragma` directive.

#pragma inline

Turbo C recognizes two `#pragma` directives. The first is

```
#pragma inline
```

This directive is equivalent to the -B compiler option. It tells the compiler that there is in-line assembly language code in your program (see Chapter 9). This is best placed at the top of the file, since the compiler restarts itself with the -B option when `#pragma inline` is encountered. Actually, you can leave off both the -B option and the `#pragma inline` directive, and the compiler will restart itself anyway as soon as it encounters **asm** statements; the purpose of the option and the directive is to save some compile time.

#pragma warn

The other `#pragma` directive is

```
#pragma warn
```

This directive allows you to override specific -w*xxx* command-line options (or specific Display warnings...On options).

For example, if your source code contains the directives

```
#pragma warn +xxx
#pragma warn -yyy
#pragma warn .zzz
```

the *xxx* warning will be turned *on* (even if on the **O/C/Errors** submenu it was toggled to *off*), the *yyy* warning will be turned *off*, and the *zzz* warning will be restored to the value it had when compilation of the file began.

A complete list of the three-letter abbreviations and the warnings to which they apply is given in Appendix C in the *Turbo C Reference Guide*.

Null Directive (ANSI C 3.7)

For the sake of completeness, the ANSI standard and Turbo C recognize the null directive, which simply consists of a line containing the character #. This directive is always ignored.

Predefined Macro Names (ANSI C 3.8.8)

The ANSI standard requires five predefined macros to be made available by the implementation. Turbo C implements all five. Note that each of these starts and ends with two underscore characters (_ _).

__LINE__   The number of the current source-file line being processed—a decimal constant. The first line of a source file is defined to be 1.

__FILE__   The name of the current source file being processed—a string literal.

This macro changes whenever the compiler processes an `#include` directive or a `#line` directive, or when the include file is complete.

__DATE__   The date the preprocessor began processing the current source file—a string literal.

Each inclusion of __DATE__ in a given file is guaranteed to contain the same value, regardless of how long the processing takes. The date appears in the format *mmm dd yyyy*, where *mmm* equals the month (Jan, Feb, etc.), *dd* equals the day (1...31, with the first character of *dd* a blank if the value is less than 10), and *yyyy* equals the year (1986, 1987, etc.).

__TIME__   The time the preprocessor began processing the current source file—a string literal.

Each inclusion of __TIME__ is guaranteed to contain the same value, regardless of how long the processing takes. It takes the format *hh:mm:ss*, where *hh* equals the hour (00...23), *mm* equals minutes (00...59), and *ss* equals seconds (00...59).

__STDC__	The constant 1, if you compile with the ANSI compatibility (-A) flag (**ANSI** keywords only...ON); otherwise, the macro is undefined.

Turbo C Predefined Macros

The Turbo C preprocessor defines several additional macros for your use. As with the ANSI-prescribed macros, each starts and ends with two underscore characters.

__TURBOC__	Gives the current Turbo C version number—a hexadecimal constant. Version 1.0 is 0x0100; version 1.2 is 0x0102; and so on.
__PASCAL__	Signals -p flag; set to the integer constant 1 if -p flag is used; undefined otherwise.
__MSDOS__	The integer constant 1 for all compiles.
__CDECL__	Signals that the -p flag was not used (**C**alling convention...C): set to the integer constant 1 if -p was not used; undefined otherwise.

The following six symbols are defined based on the memory model chosen at compile time. Only one is defined for any given compilation; the others, by definition, are undefined. For example, if you compile with the small model, __SMALL__ is defined and the rest are not, so that the directive #if defined(__SMALL__) will be *true*, while #if defined(__HUGE__) (or any of the others) will be *false*. The actual value for any of these defined macros is 1.

__TINY__	The tiny memory model selection options
__SMALL__	The small memory model selection options
__MEDIUM__	The medium memory model selection options
__COMPACT__	The compact memory model selection options
__LARGE__	The large memory model selection options
__HUGE__	The huge memory model selection options

Anachronisms (K&R 17)

None of the anachronisms mentioned in K&R exist in Turbo C.

9

Advanced Programming in Turbo C

We knew you'd get around to this chapter sooner or later. You've undoubtedly worked through the earlier chapters at an alarming rate, absorbing knowledge like a sponge absorbs water. And now you want to explore new and more rarified realms. Glad to have you here.

We'll cover three major topics in this chapter. First, we'll talk about memory models, from tiny to huge. We'll tell you what they are, how to choose one, and why you would (or would not) want to use a particular memory model. Next, we'll discuss the issues in mixed language programming. You've seen that some already in Chapter 7, which talked about mixing Turbo C and Turbo Prolog. Here, we'll be talking about how to mix with other languages, including Pascal and assembly language. After that, we'll look at three aspects of low-level programming in Turbo C: in-line assembly code, pseudo-variables, and interrupt-handling. Finally, we'll look at floating-point issues. So let's get started.

Memory Models

What are memory models, and why do you have to worry about them? To answer that question, we have to take a look at the computer system you're working on. Its central processing unit (CPU) is a microprocessor belonging to the Intel iAPx86 family; probably an 8088, though possibly an 8086, an 80186, or a 80286. For now, we'll just refer to it as an 8086.

The 8086 Registers

General Purpose Registers

AX	AH	AL	accumulator (math operations)
BX	BH	BL	base (indexing)
CX	CH	CL	count (loops, etc.)
DX	DH	DL	data (holding data)

Segment Address Registers

CS		code segment pointer
DS		data segment pointer
SS		stack segment pointer
ES		extra segment pointer

Special Purpose Registers

SP		stack pointer
BP		base pointer
SI		source index
DI		destination index

Figure 9.1: 8086 Registers

Figure 9.1 shows the registers found in the 8086 processor, with a brief description of what each is used for. There are two more registers—IP (instruction pointer) and the flag register—but Turbo C can't access them, so they aren't shown here.

General Purpose Registers

The general purpose registers are the ones used most often to hold and manipulate data. Each has some special functions that only it can do. For example,

- Many math operations can only be done using AX.
- BX can be used to hold the offset portion of a far pointer.
- CX is used by some of the 8086's LOOP instructions.
- DX is used by certain instructions to hold data.

But there are many operations that all these registers can do; in many cases, you can freely exchange one for another.

Segment Registers

The segment registers hold the starting address of each of the four segments. As described in the next section, the 16-bit value in a segment register is shifted left 4 bits (multiplied by 16) to get the true 20-bit address of that segment.

Special Purpose Registers

The 8086 also has some special purpose registers.

- The SI and DI registers can do many of the things the general purpose registers can, plus they are used as index registers. They're also used by Turbo C for register variables.
- The SP register points to the current top-of-stack and is an offset into the stack segment.
- The BP register is a secondary stack pointer, usually used to index into the stack in order to retrieve parameters.

The base pointer (BP) register is used in C functions as a base address for arguments and automatic variables. Parameters have positive offsets from BP, which vary depending on the memory model and the number of registers saved on function entry. BP always points to the saved previous

BP value. Functions that have no parameters and declare no arguments will not use or save BP at all.

Automatic variables are given negative offsets from BP, with the first automatic variables having the largest magnitude negative offset.

Memory Segmentation

The Intel 8086 microprocessor has a *segmented memory architecture*. It has a total address space of 1 megabyte, but it is designed to directly address only 64K of memory at a time. A 64K chunk of memory is known as a segment; hence the phrase, "segmented memory architecture."

Now, how many different segments are there, where are they located, and how does the 8086 know where they're located?

- The 8086 keeps track of four different segments: *code*, *data*, *stack*, and *extra*. The code segment is where the machine instructions are; the data segment, where information is; the stack is, of course, the stack; and the extra segment is used (usually) for extra data.

- The 8086 has four 16-bit segment registers (one for each segment) named CS, DS, SS, and ES; these point to the code, data, stack, and extra segments, respectively.

- A segment can be located anywhere in memory—at least, almost anywhere. For reasons that will become clear as you read on, a segment must start on an address that's evenly divisible by 16 (in base 10).

Address Calculation

Okay, so how does the 8086 use these segment registers to calculate an address? A complete address on the 8086 is composed from two 16-bit values: the segment address and the offset. Suppose the data segment address—the value in the DS register—is 2F84 (base 16), and you want to calculate the actual address of some data that has an offset of 0532 (base 16) from the start of the data segment; how is that done?

Address calculation is done as follows: shift the value of the segment register four (4) bits to the left (equivalent to one hex digit), then add in the offset.

The resulting 20-bit value is the actual address of the data, as illustrated here:

```
DS register (shifted):   0010 1111 1000 0100 0000  =  2F840
Offset:                            0000 0101 0011 0010  =  00532
```

```
Address:                 0010 1111 1101 0111 0010  =  2FD72
```

The starting address of a segment is always a 20-bit number, but a segment register only holds 16 bits—so the bottom four bits are always assumed to be all zeros. This means—as we said—that segments can only start every 16 bytes through memory, at an address where the last 4 bits (or last hex digit) are zero.

So, if the DS register is holding a value of 2F84, then the data segment actually starts at address 2F840. By the way, a chunk of 16 bytes is known as a *paragraph*, so you could say that a segment always starts on a paragraph boundary.

The standard notation for an address takes the form *segment:offset*; for example, the previous address would be written as 2F84:0532. Note that since offsets can overlap, a given segment:offset pair is not unique; the following addresses all refer to the same memory location:

```
0000:0123
0002:0103
0008:00A3
0010:0023
0012:0003
```

One last note: Segments can (but do not have to) overlap. For example, all four segments could start at the same address, which means that your entire program would take up no more than 64K—but that's all the space you would have for your code, your data, and your stack.

Near, Far, and Huge Pointers

What do pointers have to do with memory models and Turbo C? A lot. The type of memory model you choose will determine the default type of pointers used for code and data. However, you can explicitly declare a pointer (or a function) to be of a specific type, regardless of the model being used. Pointers come in three flavors: *near* (16 bits), *far* (32 bits) and *huge* (also 32 bits); let's look at each.

Near Pointers

A 16-bit (near) pointer relies upon one of the segment registers to finish calculating its address; for example, a pointer to a function would add its 16-bit value to the left-shifted contents of the code segment (CS) register. In a similar fashion, a near data pointer contains an offset to the data segment (DS) register. Near pointers are easy to manipulate, since any arithmetic (such as addition) can be done without worrying about the segment.

Far Pointers

A far (32-bit) pointer contains not only the offset within the segment, but also (as another 16-bit value) the segment address, which is then left-shifted and added to the offset. By using far pointers, you can have multiple code segments; that, in turn, allows you to have programs larger than 64K. Likewise, with far data pointers you can address more than 64K worth of data.

When you use far pointers for data, you need to be aware of some potential problems in pointer manipulation. As explained in the section on address calculation, you can have many different segment:offset pairs refer to the same address. For example, the far pointers 0000:0120, 0010:0020, and 0012:0000 all resolve to the same 20-bit address. However, if you had three different far pointer variables—a, b, and c—containing those three values respectively, then all the following expressions would be *false*:

```
if (a == b) ...
if (b == c) ...
if (a == c) ...
```

A related problem occurs when you want to compare far pointers using the >, >=, <, and <= operators. In those cases, only the offset (as an **unsigned**) is used for comparison purposes; given that a, b, and c still have the values previously listed, the following expressions would all be *true*:

```
if (a > b) ...
if (b > c) ...
if (a > c) ...
```

The equals (==) and not-equals (!=) operators use the 32-bit value as an **unsigned long** (not as the full memory address). The comparison operators (<=, >=, <, and >) use just the offset.

The == and != operators need all 32 bits, so the computer can compare to the NULL pointer (0000:0000). If you used only the offset value for equality checking, any pointer with 0000 offset would be equal to the NULL pointer, which is not what you want.

One more thing you should be aware of: If you add values to a far pointer, only the offset is changed. If you add enough to cause the offset to exceed FFFF (its maximum possible value), the pointer just wraps around back to the beginning of the segment. For example, if you add 1 to 5031:FFFF, the result would be 5031:0000 (not 6031:0000). Likewise, if you subtract 1 from 5031:0000, you would get 5031:FFFF (not 5030:000F).

If you want to do pointer comparisons, then it's safest to use either near pointers—which all use the same segment address—or huge pointers, described next.

Huge Pointers

Huge pointers are also 32 bits long and, like far pointers, contain both a segment address and an offset. Unlike far pointers, however, they are *normalized*, to avoid the problems described in "Far Pointers."

What is a normalized pointer? It is a 32-bit pointer which has as much of its value in the segment address as possible. Since a segment can start every 16 (10 in base 16) bytes, this means that the offset will only have a value from 0 to 15 (0 to F in base 16).

How do you normalize a pointer? Simple: convert it to its 20-bit address, then use the right 4 bits for your offset and the left 16 bits for your segment address. For example, given the pointer 2F84:0532, we convert that to the absolute address 2FD72, which we then normalize to 2FD7:0002. Here are a few more pointers with their normalized equivalents:

```
0000:0123    0012:0003
0040:0050    0045.0006
500D:9407    594D:0007
7418:D03F    811B:000F
```

Now you know that huge pointers are always kept normalized. Why is this important? Because it means that for any given memory address, there is only one possible huge address—segment:offset pair—for it. And that means that the == and != operators return correct answers for any huge pointers.

In addition to that, the >, >=, <, and <= operators are all used on the full 32-bit value for huge pointers. Normalization guarantees that the results there will be correct also.

Finally, because of normalization, the offset in a huge pointer automatically wraps around every 16 values, but—unlike far pointers—the segment is adjusted as well. For example, if you were to increment 811B:000F, the result would be 811C:0000; likewise, if you decrement 811C:0000, you get

811B:000F. It is this aspect of huge pointers that allows you to manipulate data structures greater than 64K in size.

There is a price for using huge pointers: additional overhead. Huge pointer arithmetic is done with calls to special subroutines. Because of this, huge pointer arithmetic is significantly slower than that of far or near pointers.

Turbo C's Six Memory Models

Avoiding overhead—except when you want it—is just what Turbo C allows you to do. There are six different memory models you can choose from: tiny, small, medium, compact, large, and huge. Which one you pick depends upon what your requirements are. Here's a brief summary of each:

Tiny: As you might guess, this is the smallest of the memory models. All four segment registers (CS, DS, SS, ES) are set to the same address, so you have a total of 64K for all of your code, data, and arrays. Near pointers are always used. Use this when memory is an absolute premium. Tiny model programs can be converted to .COM format.

Small: The code and data segments are different and don't overlap, so you have 64K of code and 64K of static data. The stack and extra segments start at the same address as the data segment. Near pointers are always used. This is a good size for average applications.

Medium: Far pointers are used for code, but not for data. As a result, static data is limited to 64K, but code can occupy up to 1 MB. Best for large programs that don't keep much data in memory.

Compact: The inverse of medium: far pointers are used for data, but not for code. Code is then limited to 64K, while data has a 1-MB range. Best if your code is small but you need to address a lot of data.

Large: Far pointers are used for both code and data, giving both a 1-MB range. Only needed for very large applications.

Huge: Far pointers are used for both code and data. Turbo C normally limits the size of all static data to 64K; the huge memory model sets aside that limit, allowing static data to occupy more than 64K.

The following illustrations (Figures 9.2 through 9.7) show how memory in the 8086 is apportioned for the six Turbo C memory models.

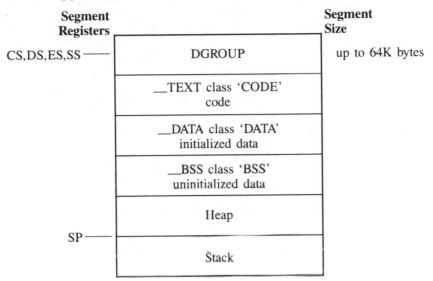

Figure 9.2: Tiny Model Memory Segmentation

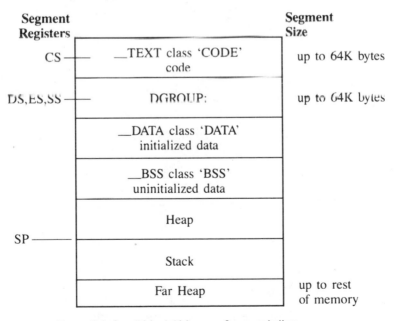

Figure 9.3: Small Model Memory Segmentation

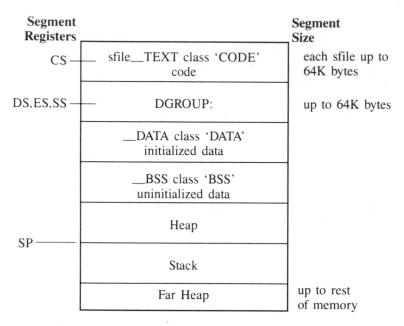

Figure 9.4: Medium Model Memory Segmentation

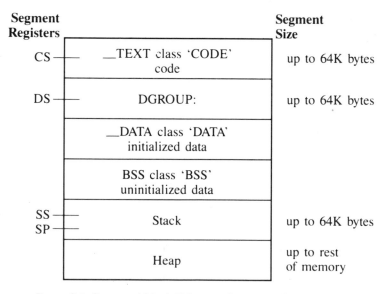

Figure 9.5: Compact Model Memory Segmentation

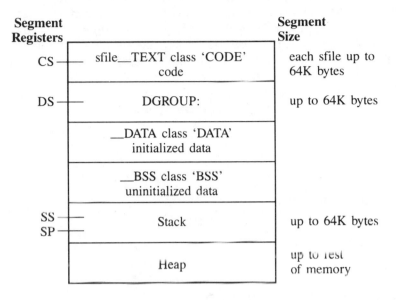

Figure 9.6: Large Model Memory Segmentation

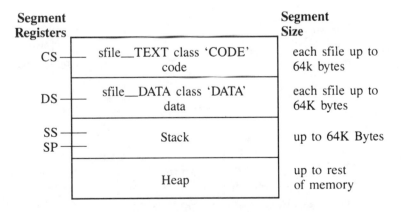

Figure 9.7: Huge Model Memory Segmentation

Table 9.1 summarizes the different models and how they compare to one another. The models are often grouped according to whether their code or data models are *small* (64K) or *large* (1 MB); these groups correspond to the rows and columns in Table 9.1. So, for example, the models tiny, small, and compact are known as *small code models* because, by default, code pointers are near; likewise, compact, large, and huge are known as *large data models* because, by default, data pointers are far. Note that this is also true for the huge model—the default data pointers are far, not huge. If you want huge data pointers, you must declare them explicitly as huge.

Table 9.1: Memory Models

Data Size	Code Size	
	64K	1 MB
64K	Tiny (data, code overlap; total size = 64K)	
	Small (no overlap; total size = 128K)	Medium (small data, big code)
1 MB	Compact (big data, small code)	Large (big data, code)
		Huge (same as large but static data > 64K)

Important Note: When you compile a module (a given source file with some number of routines in it), the resulting code for that module cannot be greater than 64K, since it must all fit inside of one code segment. This is true even if you're using a large code model (medium, large, huge). If your module is too big to fit into one (64K) code segment, you must break it up into different source code files, compile each file separately, then link them

Turbo C User's Guide

together. Similarly, even though the huge model permits static data to total more than 64K, in *each module* it still must be less than 64K.

Mixed-Model Programming: Addressing Modifiers

Turbo C introduces seven new keywords not found in standard (Kernighan and Ritchie or ANSI) C: **near, far, huge, _cs, _ds, _es, _ss**. These can be used as modifiers to pointers (and in some cases, to functions), with certain limitations and warnings.

In Turbo C, you can modify functions and pointers with the keywords **near, far,** or **huge**. We explained **near, far,** and **huge** data pointers earlier in this chapter. **near** functions are invoked with near calls and exit with near returns. Similarly, **far** functions are called far and do far returns. **huge** functions are like **far** functions, except that **huge** functions can set DS to a new value, while **far** functions cannot.

There are also four special **near** data pointers: **_cs, _ds, _ss,** and **_es**. These are 16-bit pointers that are specifically associated with the corresponding segment register. For example, if you were to declare a pointer to be

```
char _ss *p;
```

then *p* would contain a 16-bit offset into the *stack segment*.

Functions and pointers within a given program will default to near or far, depending on the memory model you select. If the function or pointer is near, then it is automatically associated with either the CS or the DS register.

Table 9.2 shows just how this works. Note that the size of the pointer corresponds to whether it is working within a 64K memory limit (near, within a segment) or inside the general 1 MB memory space (far, has its own segment address).

Table 9.2: Pointer Results

Memory Model	Function Pointers	Data Pointers
Tiny	near, _cs	near, _ds
Small	near, _cs	near, _ds
Medium	far	near, _ds
Compact	near, _cs	far
Large	far	far
Huge	far	far

Declaring Functions to Be Near or Far

On occasion, you'll want (or need) to override the default function type of your memory model shown in Table 9.1.

For example, suppose you're using the large memory model, but you've got a recursive (self-calling) function in your program, like this:

```
double  power(double x,int exp)
{
   if (exp <= 0)
      return(0);
   else
      return(x*power(x,exp-1));
}
```

Every time **power** calls itself, it has to do a far call, which uses more stack space and clock cycles. By declaring power as **near**, you eliminate some of the overhead by forcing all calls to that function to be near:

```
double  near power(double x,int exp)
```

This guarantees that **power** is callable only within the code segment in which it was compiled, and that all calls to it are near calls.

This means that if you are using a large code model (medium, large, or huge), you can only call **power** from within the module it is defined. Other modules have their own code segment and thus cannot call **near** functions in different modules. Furthermore, a near function must be either defined or declared before the first time it is used or the compiler won't know it needs to generate a near call.

Conversely, declaring a function to be far means that a far return is generated. In the small code models, the far function must be declared or defined before its first use to ensure it is invoked with a far call.

Look back at the **power** example. It is wise to also declare **power** as static, since it should only be called from within the current module. That way, being a static, its name will not be available to any functions outside the module. Since **power** always takes a fixed number of arguments, you could optimize further by declaring it **pascal**, like this:

```
static double near pascal power(double x, int exp)
```

Declaring Pointers to Be Near, Far, or Huge

You've seen why you might want to declare functions to be of a different model than the rest of the program. Why might you want to do the same thing for pointers? For the same reasons given in the preceding section : either to avoid unnecessary overhead (declaring **near** when the default would be **far**) or to reference something outside of the default segment (declaring **far** or **huge** when the default would be **near**).

There are, of course, potential pitfalls in declaring functions and pointers to be of non-default types. For example, say you have the following small model program:

```
void myputs(s)
char *s;
{
   int  i;
   for (i=0; s[i] != 0; i++) putc(s[i]);
}

main()
{
   char  near *mystr;

   mystr = "Hello, world\n";
   myputs(mystr);
}
```

This program works fine, and, in fact, the **near** declaration on *mystr* is redundant, since all pointers, both code and data, will be near.

But what if you recompile this program using the compact (or large or huge) memory model? The pointer *mystr* in **main** is still near (it's still a 16-bit pointer). However, the pointer *s* in **myputs** is now far, since that's the default. This means that **myputs** will pull two words out of the stack in an effort to create a far pointer, and the address it ends up with will certainly not be that of *mystr*.

How do you avoid this problem? The solution is to define **myputs** in modern C style, like this:

```
void  myputs(char *s);
{
    /*body of myputs*/

}
```

Now when Turbo C compiles your program, it knows that **myputs** expects a pointer to `char`; and since you're compiling under the large model, it knows that the pointer must be `far`. Because of that, Turbo C will push the data segment (DS) register onto the stack along with the 16-bit value of *mystr*, forming a far pointer.

How about the reverse case: parameters to **myputs** declared as `far` and compiling with a small data model? Again, without the function prototype, you will have problems, since **main** will push both the offset and the segment address onto the stack, but **myputs** will only expect the offset. With the prototype-style function definitions, though, **main** will only push the offset onto the stack.

Moral: If you're going to explicitly declare pointers to be of type `far` or `near`, then be sure to use function prototypes for any functions that might use them.

Pointing to a Given Segment:Offset Address

How do you make a far pointer point to a given memory location (a specific segment:offset address)? You can use the built-in library routine **MK_FP**, which takes a segment and an offset and returns a far pointer. For example:

```
MK_FP(segment_value, offset_value)
```

Given a far pointer, *fp*, you can get the segment component with **FP_SEG(*fp*)** and the offset component with **FP_OFF(*fp*)**. For more information about these three Turbo C library routines, refer to the *Turbo C Reference Guide*.

Building Proper Declarators

A declarator is a statement in C that you use to declare functions, variables, pointers, and data types. And C allows you to build very complex declarators. This section gives you some examples of declarators so that you can get some practice at designing (and reading) them; it'll also show you some pitfalls to avoid.

Traditional C programming has you build your complete declarator in place, nesting definitions as needed. Unfortunately, this can make for programs that are difficult to read (and write).

Consider, for example, the following declarators, assuming that you are compiling under the small memory model (small code, small data).

Table 9.3: Declarators without Typedefs

`int f1();`	function returning int
`int *p1;`	pointer to int
`int *f2();`	function returning pointer to int
`int far *p2;`	far pointer to int
`int far *f3();`	near function returning far pointer to int
`int * far f4();`	far function returning near pointer to int
`int (*fp1)(int);`	pointer to function returning int and accepting int parameter
`int (*fp2)(int *ip);`	pointer to function returning int and accepting pointer to int
`int (far *fp3)(int far *ip)`	far pointer to function returning int and accepting far pointer to int
`int (far *list[5])(int far *ip);`	array of five far pointers to functions returning int and accepting far pointers to int
`int (far *gopher(int (far * fp[5])(int far *ip)))(int far *ip);`	near function accepting array of five far pointers to functions returning int and accepting far pointers to int, and returning one such pointer

These are all valid declarators; they just get increasingly hard to understand. However, with judicious use of **typedef**, you can improve the legibility of these declarators.

Here are the same declarators, rewritten with the help of **typedef** statements:

Table 9.4: Declarators with Typedefs

`int     f1();`	function returning int
`typedef int *intptr;`	
`intptr  p1;`	pointer to int
`intptr  f2();`	function returning pointer to int
`typedef int far *farptr;`	
`farptr  p2;`	far pointer to int
`farptr  f3();`	near function returning far pointer to int
`intptr  far f4();`	far function returning near pointer to int
`typedef int (*fncptr1)(int);`	
`fncptr1 fp1;`	pointer to function returning int and accepting int parameter
`typedef int (*fncptr2)(intptr);`	
`fncptr2 fp2;`	pointer to function returning int and accepting pointer to int
`typedef int (far *ffptr)(farptr);`	
`ffptr   fp3;`	far pointer to function returning int and accepting far pointer to int
`typedef ffptr    ffplist[5];`	
`ffplist list;`	array of five far pointers to functions returning int and accepting far pointers to int
`ffptr   gopher(ffplist);`	near function accepting array of five far pointers to functions returning int and accepting far pointers to int, and returning one such pointer

As you can see, there's a big difference in legibility and clarity between this **typedef** declaration of *gopher* and the previous one. If you'll use **typedef** statements and function prototypes wisely, you'll find your programs easier to write, debug, and maintain.

Using Library Files

Turbo C offers a version of the standard library routines for each of the six memory models. Running in the Integrated Environment (TC), Turbo C is smart enough to link in the appropriate libraries in the proper order, depending upon which model you've selected. Likewise, running as a stand-alone compiler (TCC), Turbo C is smart enough when you tell it to automatically link.

If, however, you're using TLINK (the Turbo C linker) directly (as a stand-alone linker), you need to specify which libraries to use. If you're not going to use all six memory models, then you only need to copy (to your working disk or your hard disk) the files for the model(s) you are using. Here's a list of the library files needed for each memory model:

Tiny	C0T.OBJ, MATHS.LIB, CS.LIB
Small	C0S.OBJ, MATHS.LIB, CS.LIB
Compact	C0C.OBJ, MATHC.LIB, CC.LIB
Medium	C0M.OBJ, MATHM.LIB, CM.LIB
Large	C0L.OBJ, MATHL.LIB, CL.LIB
Huge	C0H.OBJ, MATHH.LIB, CH.LIB

Note that the tiny and small models use the same libraries, but have different startup files (C0T.OBJ vs. C0S.OBJ). Also, if your system has an 8087 math coprocessor, then you'll need the file FP87.LIB; if instead you want to emulate the 8087, you'll need the file EMU.LIB.

Here are some example TLINK command lines:

```
tlink c0m a b c, prog, mprog, fp87 mathm cm
tlink c0c d e f, plan, mplan, emu mathc cc
```

The first will produce an executable program called PROG.EXE, with the medium-model libraries and the 8087 support library linked in. The second command line will yield PLAN.EXE, compiled as a compact-model program that emulates the 8087 floating-point routines if a coprocessor is not available at run time.

Note: The order of objects and libraries is very important. You must always put the C start-up module (C0x.OBJ) first in the list of objects. The library list should contain, in this specific order:

- your own libraries (if any)
- FP87.LIB or EMU.LIB, followed by MATHx.LIB (only necessary if you are using floating point)
- Cx.LIB (standard Turbo C run-time library file)

(The x in C0x, MATHx, and Cx refers to the letter specifying the memory model: $t, s, m, c, l,$ or h.)

Linking Mixed Modules

What if you compiled one module using the small memory model, and another module using the large model, then wanted to link them together? What would happen?

The files would link together fine, but the problems you would encounter would be similar to those described in "Declaring Functions to Be Near or Far." If a function in the small module called a function in the large module, it would do so with a near call, which would probably be disastrous. Furthermore, you could face the same problems with pointers as described in "Declaring Pointers to Be Near, Far, or Huge," since a function in the small module would expect to pass and receive **near** pointers, while a function in the large module would expect **far** pointers.

The solution, again, is to use function prototypes. Suppose that you put **myputs** into its own module and compile it with the large memory model. You should then create a header file called MYPUTS.H (or some other name with an .H extension), which would have the following function prototype in it:

```
void far myputs(char far *s);
```

Now, if you put **main** into its own module (called MYMAIN.C), you should set things up like this:

```
#include <stdio.h>
#include "myputs.h"
main()
{
    char  near *mystr;

    mystr = "Hello, world\n";
    myputs(mystr);
}
```

When you compile this program, Turbo C reads in the function prototype from MYPUTS.H and sees that it is a **far** function that expects a **far** pointer. Because of that, it will generate the proper calling code, even if it's compiled using the small memory model.

What if, on top of all this, you need to link in library routines? Your best bet is to use one of the large model libraries and declare everything to be **far**. To do this, make a copy of each header file you would normally include (such as STDIO.H), and rename the copy to something appropriate (such as FSTDIO.H).

Turbo C User's Guide

Then edit each function prototype in the copy so that it is explicitly **far**, like this:

```
int far cdecl printf(char far * format, ...);
```

That way, not only will **far** calls be made to the routines, but the pointers passed will be **far** pointers as well. Modify your program so that it includes the new header file:

```
#include <fstdio.h>
main()
{
   char  near *mystr;
   mystr = "Hello, world\n";
   printf(mystr);
}
```

Compile your program with TCC, then link it with TLINK, specifying a large model library, such as CL.LIB. Mixing models is tricky, but it can be done; just be prepared for some difficult bugs if you do things wrong.

Mixed-Language Programming

Turbo C eases the way for your C programs to call routines written in other languages and, in return, for programs written in other languages to call your C routines. In this section, we make it clear how easy interfacing Turbo C to other languages can be; we also provide support information for such interface.

We will talk first about the two major sequences for passing parameters, and then get on with showing you how to write your own assembly-language module.

Parameter-Passing Sequences: C and Pascal

Turbo C supports two methods of passing parameters to a function. One is the standard C method, which we will explain first; the other is the Pascal method.

C Parameter-Passing Sequence

Suppose you have declared the following function prototype:

```
void funca(int p1, int p2, int p3);
```

By default, Turbo C uses the C parameter-passing sequence, also called the C calling convention. When this function (**funca**) is called, the parameters are pushed on the stack in right-to-left order (*p3, p2, p1*), following which the return address is pushed on the stack. So, if you make the call

```
main()
{
    int   i,j;
    long  k;
    ...
    i = 5; j = 7; k = 0x1407AA;
    funca(i,j,k);
    ...
}
```

the stack will look like this (just before the return address is pushed):

```
SP + 06:     0014
SP + 04:     07AA     k = p3
SP + 02:     0007     j = p2
SP:          0005     i = p1
```

(Remember that, on the 8086, the stack grows from high memory to low memory, so that *i* is currently at the *top* of the stack.) The routine being called doesn't need to know (and, for that matter, can't know) exactly how many parameters have been pushed onto the stack. All it assumes is that the parameters it expects are there.

Also—and this is very important—the routine being called should not pop parameters off the stack. Why? Because the calling routine will. For example, the assembly language that the compiler produces from the C source code for this main function looks something like this:

```
mov    word ptr [bp-8],5                         ; Set i = 5
mov    word ptr [bp-6],7                          ; Set j = 7
mov    word ptr [bp-2],0014h                ; Set k = 0x1407AA
mov    word ptr [bp-4],07AAh
push   word ptr [bp-2]                 ; Push high word of k
push   word ptr [bp-4]                  ; Push low word of k
push   word ptr [bp-6]                            ; Push j
push   word ptr [bp-8]                            ; Push i
call   near ptr funca                  ; Call funca (push addr)
add    sp,8                                  ; Adjust stack
```

Note carefully that last instruction: `add sp,8`. The compiler knows at that point exactly how many parameters have been pushed onto the stack; it also knows that the return address was pushed by the call to **funca** and was already popped off by the `ret` instruction at the end of **funca**.

Pascal Parameter-Passing Sequence

The other approach is the standard Pascal method for passing parameters (also known as the Pascal calling convention). Note that this does *not* mean you can call Turbo Pascal functions from Turbo C: you can't. This sequence pushes the parameters on left-to-right, so that if **funca** is declared as

```
void pascal funca(int p1, int p2, int p3);
```

then, when this function is called, the parameters are pushed on the stack in left-to-right order (*p1, p2, p3*), following which the return address is pushed on the stack. So, if you make the call

```
main()
{
    int   i,j;
    long  k;
    ...
    i = 5; j = 7; k = 0x1407AA;
    funca(i,j,k);
    ...
}
```

the stack will look like this (just before the return address is pushed):

```
SP + 06:     0005     i = p1
SP + 04:     0007     j = p2
SP + 02:     0014
SP:          07AA     k = p3
```

So, what's the big difference? Well, besides switching the order in which the parameters are pushed, the Pascal parameter-passing sequence assumes that the routine being called (**funca**) knows how many parameters are being passed to it and adjusts the stack accordingly. In other words, the assembly language for the call to **funca** now looks like this:

```
push  word ptr [bp-8]                    ; Push i
push  word ptr [bp-6]                    ; Push j
push  word ptr [bp-2]          ; Push high word of k
push  word ptr [bp-4]          ; Push low word of k
call  near ptr funca          ; Call funca (push addr)
```

Note that there is no add sp, 8 instruction after the call. Instead, **funca** uses the instruction ret 8 at termination to clean up the stack before returning to **main**.

By default, all functions you write in Turbo C use the C method of parameter passing. The only exception is when you use the -p compiler option (Calling convention...Pascal), in which case all functions use the Pascal method. In that situation, you can force a given function to use the C method of parameter passing by using the modifier **cdecl**, as in

```
void  cdecl funca(int p1, int p2, int p3);
```

That overrides the -p compiler directive.

Now, why would you want to use the Pascal calling convention at all? There are three major reasons.

- You may be calling existing assembly-language routines that use that calling convention.
- You may be calling routines written in another language.
- The calling code produced is slightly smaller, since it doesn't have to clean up the stack afterwards.

What problems might arise from using the Pascal calling convention?

First, it's not as robust as the C calling convention. You cannot pass a variable number of parameters (as you can with the C convention), since the routine being called has to know how many parameters are being passed and clean up the stack accordingly. Passing either too few or too many parameters will almost certainly lead to serious problems, whereas doing so to a C-convention routine usually has no ill effects (beyond, possibly, wrong answers).

Second, if you use the -p compiler option, then you must be sure to include any header files for standard C functions that you call. Why? Because if you don't, Turbo C will use the Pascal calling convention to call each of those functions—and your program will surely crash because (1) the parameters will be in the wrong order, and (2) nobody will clean up the stack.

The header files declare each of those functions as **cdecl**, so if you #include them, the compiler will see that and use the C calling convention instead. However, because **cdecl** identifiers are underscored while **pascal** identifiers are not, you will get lots of link errors—unless you selected Generate underbars...Off and linked with no case-sensitivity. Then you're in big trouble.

The upshot is this: If you're going to use the Pascal calling convention in a Turbo C program, be sure to use function prototypes as much as possible, with each function explicitly declared as **cdecl** or **pascal**. It's useful in this case to enable the "prototype required" warning option to ensure that every function called has a prototype.

Assembly-Language Interface

Now you know how each of the calling conventions work, which tells you what the Turbo C compiler does. What do you do in the routine being called? Take a look now at how to write assembly-language routines that you can call from Turbo C.

Note: In this section, we assume that you know how to write 8086 assembly-language routines and how to define segments, data constants, etc. If you are unfamiliar with these concepts, read the Microsoft *Macro Assembler Reference Manual* for more information.

Setting Up to Call .ASM from Turbo C

You should write assembly-language routines as modules to be linked into your C programs. However, there are certain conventions that you must follow to (1) ensure that the linker can get the necessary information, and (2) ensure that the file format jibes with the memory model used for your C program. The general layout is as follows:

Identifier	Name	File Name
< text >	SEGMENT	BYTE PUBLIC 'CODE'
	ASSUME	CS: < text >, DS: < dseg >
	<................. code segment ....>	
< text >	ENDS	
< dseg >	GROUP	_DATA, _BSS
< data >	SEGMENT	WORD PUBLIC 'DATA'
	<.......... initialized data segment ....>	
< data >	ENDS	
_BSS	SEGMENT	WORD PUBLIC 'BSS'
	<......... uninitialized data segment ....>	
_BSS	ENDS	
	END	

The identifiers *<text>*, *<data>*, and *<dseg>* in this layout have specific replacements, depending upon the memory model being used; Table 9.5 shows what you should use for each model. *filename* in Table 9.5 is the name of the module; it should be used consistently in the NAME directive and in the identifier replacements (following).

Note that with the huge memory model, there is no _BSS segment, and the GROUP definition is dropped completely. In general, _BSS is optional; you only define it if you will be using it.

The best way to create an assembly-language template is to compile an empty program to .ASM (using the TCC option -s) and look at the generated assembly code.

Table 9.5: Identifier Replacements and Memory Models

Model	Identifier Replacements	Code and Data Pointers
Tiny, Small	<code> = _TEXT <data> = _DATA <dseg> = DGROUP	Code: DW _TEXT:xxx Data: DW DGROUP:xxx
Compact	<code> = _TEXT <data> = _DATA <dseg> = DGROUP	Code: DW _TEXT:xxx Data: DD DGROUP:xxx
Medium	<code> = filename_TEXT <data> = _DATA <dseg> = DGROUP	Code: DD xxx Data: DW DGROUP:xxx
Large	<code> = filename_TEXT <data> = _DATA <dseg> = DGROUP	Code: DD xxx Data: DD DGROUP:xxx
Huge	<code> = filename_TEXT <data> = filename_DATA <dseg> = filename_DATA	Code: DD xxx Data: DD xxx

Defining Data Constants and Variables

Memory models also affect how you define any data constants that are pointers to code, data, or both. Table 9.5 shows what those pointers should look like, where *xxx* is the address being pointed to.

Note carefully that some definitions use DW (Define Word), while others use DD (Define Doubleword), indicating the size of the resulting pointer. Numeric and text constants are defined normally.

Variables are, of course, defined just the same as constants. If you want variables that are not initialized to specific values you can declare them in the _BSS segment, entering a question mark (?) where you would normally put a value.

Defining Global and External Identifiers

Now you have created a module, but that isn't going to do you much good unless your Turbo C program knows what functions it can call and what variables it can reference. Likewise, you may want to be able to call your Turbo C functions from within your assembly-language routines, or you may want to be able to reference variables declared within your Turbo C program.

When making these calls, you need to understand something about the Turbo C compiler and linker. When you declare an external identifier, the compiler automatically sticks an underscore (_) on the front before saving that identifier in the object module. This means that you should put an underscore on the front of any identifiers in your assembly language module that you want to reference from your C program. Pascal identifiers are treated differently than C identifiers—they are uppercased and are *not* prefixed with an underscore character.

Underscores (_) for C identifiers are optional, but *on* by default. They can be turned *off* with the –u– command-line option. However, if you are using the standard Turbo C libraries, you will encounter problems unless you rebuild the libraries. (To do this, you will need another Turbo C product—the source code to the run-time libraries; contact Borland International for more information.)

If any **asm** code in your source file references any C identifiers (data or functions), those identifiers must begin with underscore characters.

The Microsoft Assembler (MASM) is not case sensitive; in other words, when you assemble a program, all identifiers are saved as uppercase only. The /mx switch to MASM makes it case sensitive for externals. The Turbo C linker does the same thing with **extern** identifiers, so things should match up fine. You'll notice that in our examples, we put keywords and directives in uppercase, and all other identifiers and op codes in lowercase; this matches the style found in the MASM reference manual. You are free to use all uppercase (or all lowercase), or any mixture thereof, as you please.

To make the identifiers (names of routines and variables) visible outside of your assembly-language module, you need to declare them as being PUBLIC.

So, for example, if you were to write a module that had the integer functions *max* and *min*, and the integer variables MAXINT, *lastmax* and *lastmin*, you would put the statement

```
PUBLIC  _max,_min
```

in your code segment, and the statements

```
 PUBLIC   _MAXINT,_lastmax,_lastmin
_MAXINT  DW  32767
_lastmin DW  0
_lastmax DW  0
```

in your data segment.

Setting Up to Call Turbo C from .ASM

In a fashion similar to what we mentioned in the previous section, you use the EXTRN statement to let your assembly-language module reference functions and variables that are declared in your Turbo C program.

Referencing Functions

To be able to call a C function from an assembly-language routine, you must declare it in your module with the statement

```
EXTRN <fname> : <fdist>
```

where *<fname>* is the name of the function and *<fdist>* is either near or far, depending upon whether the C function is near or far. If *<fdist>* is near, then the EXTRN statement must appear within the code segment of your module; if it's far, then the EXTRN statement should appear outside of any segment. So you could have the following in your code segment:

```
EXTRN  _myCfunc1:near, _myCfunc2:far
```

allowing you to call **myCfunc1** and **myCfunc2** from within your assembly-language routines.

Referencing Data

To reference variables, you should place the appropriate EXTRN statement(s) inside of your data segment, using the format

```
EXTRN  <vname> : <size>
```

where *<vname>* is the name of the variable and *<size>* indicates the size of the variable.

The possible values for <size> are as follows:

- BYTE (1 byte)
- WORD (2 bytes)
- DWORD (4 bytes)
- QWORD (8 bytes)
- TBYTE (10 bytes)

Arrays must use the size of the array elements for <size>. Structures should be declared with the most frequently used size in the structure substituted for <size>.

So, if your C program had the following global variables:

```
int    i,jarray[10];
char   ch;
long   result;
```

you could make them visible within your module with the following statement:

```
EXTRN _i:WORD, _jarray:WORD, _ch:BYTE, _result:DWORD
```

Last Important Note: If you're using the huge memory model, the EXTRN statements must appear outside of any segments. This applies to both procedures and variables.

Defining Assembly-Language Routines

Now that you know how to set everything up, it's a good time to look at how to actually write a function in assembly language. There are some important things to consider: parameter passing, returning values, and register conventions.

Suppose you want to write the function **min**, which you can assume has the following function prototype in C:

```
int  extern min(int v1, int v2);
```

You want **min** to return the minimum of the two values passed to it. The overall format of **min** is going to be

```
      PUBLIC  _min
_min  PROC    near
         .
         .
         .
_min  ENDP
```

This assumes, of course, that **min** is going to be a near function; if it were a far function, you would substitute **far** for **near**. Note that we've added the underscore to the start of **min**, so that the Turbo C linker can correctly resolve the references.

Passing Parameters

Your first decision is which parameter-passing convention to use; barring an adequate reason to use it, you'll avoid the Pascal convention and go with the C method instead. This means that when **min** gets called, the stack is going to look like this:

```
SP + 04:  v2
SP + 02:  v1
SP:       return addr
```

You want to get to the parameters without popping anything off the stack, so you'll save the base pointer (BP), move the stack pointer (SP) into the base pointer, then use that to index directly into the stack to get your values. Note that when you push BP onto the stack, the relative offsets of the parameters will increase by two, since there will now be two more bytes on the stack.

Handling Return Values

Your function returns an integer value; where do you put that? For 16-bit (2 byte) values (**char**, **short**, **int**, **enum**, and **near** pointers), you use the AX register; for 32-bit (4 byte) values (including **far** and **huge** pointers), you use the DX register as well, with the high-order word (segment address for pointers) in DX and the low-order word in AX.

float and **double** values are returned in the 8087 top-of-stack (TOS) register, ST(0); if the 8087 emulator is being used, then the value is returned in the emulator TOS register.

Structure values are returned by placing the value in a static data location, then returning a pointer to that location (AX in the small data models, DX:AX in the large data models).

The calling function must then copy that value to wherever it's needed. Structures that are 1 or 2 bytes long are returned in AX (like any normal **int**), while 4-byte structures are returned in AX and DX.

For the **min** example, all you're dealing with is a 16-bit value, so you can just place the answer in AX.

Here's what your code looks like now:

```
        PUBLIC  _min
_min    PROC    near
        push    bp              ; Save bp on stack
        mov     bp,sp           ; Copy sp into bp
        mov     ax,[bp+4]       ; Move v1 into ax
        cmp     ax,[bp+6]       ; Compare with v2
        jle     exit            ; If v1 > v2
        mov     ax,[bp+6]       ; Then load ax with v2
exit:   pop     bp              ; Restore bp
        ret                     ; And return to C
_min    ENDP
```

What if you declare **min** as a **far** function—how will that change things? The major difference is that the stack on entry will now look like this:

```
SP + 06:  v2
SP + 04:  v1
SP + 02:  return segment
SP:       return offset
```

This means that the offsets into the stack have increased by two, since two extra bytes (for the return segment) had to be pushed onto the stack. Your far version of **min** would look like this:

```
        PUBLIC  _min
_min    PROC    far
        push    bp              ; Save bp on stack
        mov     bp,sp           ; Copy sp into bp
        mov     ax,[bp+6]       ; Move v1 into ax
        cmp     ax,[bp+8]       ; Compare with v2
        jle     exit            ; If v1 > v2
        mov     ax,[bp+6]       ; Then load ax with v2
exit:   pop     bp              ; Restore bp
        ret                     ; And return to C
_min    ENDP
```

Note that all the offsets for *v1* and *v2* increased by two, to reflect the additional bytes on the stack.

Now, what if (for whatever reason) you declare **min** as a **pascal** function; that is, you decide to use the Pascal parameter-passing sequences.

Your stack on entry will now look like this (assuming **min** is back to being a **near** function):

```
SP + 04:  v1
SP + 02:  v2
SP:       return addr
```

In addition, you will need to follow pascal conventions for the identifier **min**: uppercase and no underscore.

Besides having swapped the locations of *v1* and *v2*, this convention also requires **min** to clean up the stack when it leaves, by specifying in the RET instruction how many bytes to pop off the stack. In this case, you have to pop off four additional bytes for *v1* and *v2* (the return address is popped off automatically by RET).

Here's what the modified routine looks like:

```
        PUBLIC  MIN
MIN     PROC    near                            ; Pascal version
        push    bp                              ; Save bp on stack
        mov     bp,sp                           ; Copy sp into bp
        mov     ax,[bp+6]                       ; Move v1 into ax
        cmp     ax,[bp+4]                       ; Compare with v2
        jle     exit                            ; If v1 > v2
        mov     ax,[bp+4]               ; Then load ax with v2
exit:   pop     bp                              ; Restore bp
        ret     4                    ; Clear stack and return
MIN     ENDP
```

Here's one last example to show you why you might want to use the C parameter-passing sequence. Suppose you redefined **min** as follows:

```
int  extern min(int count, int v1, int v2,...);
```

min can now accept any number of integers and will return the minimum value of them all. However, since **min** has no way of automatically knowing how many values are being passed, make the first parameter a *count value*, indicating how many values follow it.

For example, you might use it as follows:

```
i = min(5, j, limit, indx, lcount, 0);
```

assuming *i, j, limit, indx,* and *lcount* are all of type **int** (or a compatible type). The stack upon entry will look like this:

```
SP + 08:  (etc.)
SP + 06:  v2
SP + 04:  v1
SP + 02:  count
SP:       return addr
```

The modified version of **min** now looks like this:

```
        PUBLIC  _min
_min    PROC    near
        push    bp              ; Save bp on stack
        mov     bp,sp           ; Copy sp into bp
        mov     ax,0            ; Set ax = 0
        mov     cx,[bp+4]       ; Move count into cx
        cmp     cx,ax           ; Compare with 0
        jle     exit            ; If <= 0, then exit
        mov     ax,[bp+4]       ; Move first value into ax
        jmp     ltest           ; And test loop
compare: cmp    ax,[bp+6]       ; Compare with next value
        jle     ltest           ; If next value is lower
        mov     ax,[bp+6]       ; Then load ax with next value
ltest:  add     bp,2            ; Move to new value
        loop    compare         ; Then loop back
exit:   pop     bp              ; Restore bp
        ret                     ; And return to C
_min    ENDP
```

Note that this version correctly handles all possible values of *count*.

- If *count* <= 0, **min** returns 0.
- If *count* = 1, **min** returns the first value in the list.
- If *count* >= 2, **min** makes successive comparisions to find the lowest value in the parameter list.

Register Conventions

You used several registers (BP, SP, AX, BX, CX) in **min**; were you able to do so safely? What about any registers that your Turbo C program might be using?

As it turns out, you wrote this function correctly. Of those you used, the only register that you had to worry about was BP, and you saved that on the stack on entry, then restored it from the stack on exit.

The other two registers that you have to worry about are SI and DI; these are the registers Turbo C uses for any register variables. If you use them at all within an assembly-language routine, then you should save them (probably on the stack) on entering the routine, and restore them on leaving. However, if you compile your Turbo C program with the -r- option (**Use register variables...Off**), then you don't have to worry about saving SI and DI.

Note: You must use caution if you use the -r- option. Refer to Appendix C in the *Turbo C Reference Guide* for details about this register variables option.

The registers CS, DS, SS, and ES may have corresponding values depending upon the memory model being used. Here are the relationships:

Tiny	CS = DS = SS; ES = scratch
Small, Medium	CS != DS, DS = SS; ES = scratch
Compact, Large	CS != DS != SS; ES = scratch (one CS per module)
Huge	CS != DS != SS; ES = scratch (one CS and one DS per module)

Calling C Functions from .ASM Routines

Yes, you can go the other way: You can call your C routines from within your assembly-language modules. First, though, you have to make the C function visible to your assembly-language module. We've already discussed briefly how to do this: Declare it as EXTRN, with either a **near** or a **far** modifier. For example, say you've written the following C function:

```
long docalc(int *fact1, int fact2, int fact3);
```

For simplicity, assume **docalc** is a C function (as opposed to Pascal). Assuming you're using the tiny, small, or compact memory model, you'd declare it as this in your assembly module:

```
EXTRN   _docalc:near
```

Likewise, if you were using the medium, large, or huge memory models, you'd declare it as _docalc:far.

docalc is to be called with three parameters:

- the address of a location named *xval*
- the value stored in a location named *imax*
- a third constant value of 421 (base 10)

You should also assume that you want to save the result in a 32-bit location named *ans*. The equivalent call in C would then be

```
ans = docalc(&xval,imax,421);
```

You'll need to push 421 on the stack first, then *imax*, then the address of *xval*, and then call **docalc**. When it returns, you'll need to clean up the stack, which will have six extra bytes on it, and then move the answer into *ans* and *ans+2*.

Here's what your code will look like:

```
mov    ax,421                              ; Get 421, push onto stack
push   ax
push   imax                          ; Get imax, push onto stack
lea    ax,xval                       ; Get &xval, push onto stack
push   ax
call   _docalc                                    ; Call docalc
add    sp,6                                 ; Clean up stack
mov    ans,ax                     ; Move 32-bit result into ans
mov    ans+2,dx                     ; Including high-order word
```

What if **docalc** used the Pascal parameter-passing sequence instead? Then you would have to reverse the order of the parameters, and you wouldn't have to worry about cleaning up the stack upon return, since the routine would (should) have done that for you. Also, you would need to spell **docalc** in the assembly source using Pascal conventions (uppercase and no underscore).

The EXTRN statement is then

```
EXTRN  DOCALC:near
```

and the code to call **docalc** is

```
lea    ax,xval                       ; Get &xval, push onto stack
push   ax
push   imax                       ; Get imax, push onto stack
mov    ax,421                         ; Get 421, push onto stack
push   ax
call   DOCALC                                      ; Call docalc
mov    ans,ax                     ; Move 32-bit result into ans
mov    ans+2,dx                    ; Including high-order word
```

That's all you need to know to get started interfacing other languages with Turbo C.

Low-Level Programming: Pseudo-Variables, In-Line Assembly, and Interrupt Functions

What if you want to do some low-level work, but don't want to go to all the trouble of setting up a separate assembly-language module? Turbo C still has the answer for you—three answers, in fact: pseudo-variables, in-line assembly, and interrupt functions. Take a look at the rest of this chapter to see how each of these can help you get the job done.

Pseudo-Variables

The CPU in your system (the 8088/8086/80186/80286 processor) has a number of registers, or special storage areas, which it uses to manipulate values. Each register is 16 bits (2 bytes) long; most of them have some special purpose, though several can be used for general purposes as well. See "Memory Models" at the beginning of this chapter for specific details on these CPU registers.

Sometimes in low-level programming, you may want to directly access these registers from your C program.

- You might want to load values into them before calling a system routine.
- You might want to see what values they currently hold.

Turbo C makes it very easy for you to access these registers through *pseudo-variables*. A pseudo-variable is simply an identifier that corresponds to a given register: You can use it as if it were a variable of type **unsigned int** or **unsigned char**.

Table 9.6 shows a complete list of the pseudo-variables you can use, their types, the registers they correspond to, and what those registers are usually used for.

Table 9.6: Turbo C Pseudo-Variables

Pseudo-variable	Type	Register	Usual Purpose
_AX	unsigned int	AX	General/accumulator
_AL	unsigned char	AL	Lower byte of AX
_AH	unsigned char	AH	Upper byte of AX
_BX	unsigned int	BX	General/indexing
_BL	unsigned char	BL	Lower byte of BX
_BH	unsigned char	BH	Upper byte of BX
_CX	unsigned int	CX	General/counting and loops
_CL	unsigned char	CL	Lower byte of CX
_CH	unsigned char	CH	Upper byte of CX
_DX	unsigned int	DX	General/holding data
_DL	unsigned char	DL	Lower byte of DX
_DH	unsigned char	DH	Upper byte of DX
_CS	unsigned int	CS	Code segment address
_DS	unsigned int	DS	Data segment address
_SS	unsigned int	SS	Stack segment address
_ES	unsigned int	ES	Extra segment address
_SP	unsigned int	SP	Stack pointer (offset to SS)
_BP	unsigned int	BP	Base pointer (offset to SS)
_DI	unsigned int	DI	Used for register variables
_SI	unsigned int	SI	Used for register variables

Why would you even want to directly access these variables from Turbo C?

You might need to set registers to certain values before calling low-level system routines. For example, you can call certain routines in your computer's ROM by executing the INT (interrupt) instruction, but first you have to put the necessary information into certain registers, like this:

```
void readchar(unsigned char page, unsigned char *ch, unsigned char *attr);
{
    _AH = 8;                     /* Service code: read char, attribute */
    _BH = page;                  /* Specify which display page */
    geninterrupt(0x10)           /* Call INT 10h services */
    *ch = _AL;                   /* Get ASCII code of character read */
    *attr = _AH;                 /* Get attribute of character read */
}
```

As you can see, the service code and the display page number are both being passed to the INT 10h routine; the values returned are copied over into *ch* and *attr*.

The pseudo-variables can be treated just as if they were regular global variables of the appropriate type (**unsigned int, unsigned char**).

However, since they refer to the CPU's registers, rather than some arbitrary location in memory, there are some restrictions and concerns you must be aware of.

- You cannot use the address-of operator (&) with a pseudo-variable, since a pseudo-variable has no address.

- Since the compiler is constantly generating code that uses the registers (after all, that's what most of the 8086's instructions do), you have absolutely no guarantee that values you place in pseudo-variables will be preserved for any length of time.

  This means you must assign values right before using them and read values right after obtaining them, as in **readchar** (previous example). This is especially true of the general purpose registers (AX, AH, AL, etc.), since the compiler freely uses these for temporary storage. On top of that, the CPU changes them in ways you might not expect, using (for example) CX when it sets up a loop or does a shift operation, or using DX to hold the upper word of a 16-bit multiply.

- You can't rely on their values remaining the same across a function call. As an example of this, take the following code fragment:

```
_CX = 18;
myFunc();
i = _CX;
```

  Not all registers are saved during a function call, so you have no guarantee that *i* will get assigned a value of 18. The only registers that you can count on having the same values before and after a function call are _CS, _BP, _SI, and _DI.

- You need to be very careful modifying certain registers, since this could have unexpected and untoward effects. For example, directly storing values to _CS, _SS, _SP, or _BP can (and almost certainly will) cause your program to behave erratically, since the machine code produced by the Turbo C compiler uses those registers in various ways.

Using In-Line Assembly Language

You've already seen how to write separate assembly-language routines and link them in to your Turbo C program. But Turbo C also lets you write assembly-language code right inside your C program. This is known as *in-line assembly*.

To use in-line assembly in your C program, you can use the -B compiler option. If you don't, and the compiler encounters in-line assembly, it (the compiler) will issue a warning and restart itself with the -B option. You can avoid this with the #pragma inline statement in your source, which in effect enables the -B option for you when the compiler encounters it.

You must have a copy of the Microsoft Macro Assembler (MASM), version 4.0 or later. The compiler first generates an assembly file, and then invokes MASM on that file to produce the .OBJ file.

Of course, you also need to be familiar with the 8086 instruction set and architecture. While you're not writing complete assembly-language routines, you still need to know how the instructions you're using work, how to use them, and how not to use them.

Having done all that, you need only use the keyword **asm** to introduce an in-line assembly-language instruction. The format is

```
asm <opcode> <operands> <; or newline>
```

where

- *<opcode>* is a valid 8086 instruction (several tables of allowable opcodes will follow).
- *<operands>* contains the operand(s) acceptable to the *<opcode>*, and can reference C constants, variables, and labels.
- < ; or *newline>* is a semicolon or a newline, either of which signals the end of the **asm** statement.

A new **asm** statement may be placed on the same line, following a semicolon, but no **asm** statement can continue to the next line.

Semicolons may not be used to start comments (as they may in MASM). When commenting **asm** statements, use C style comments, like this:

```
asm mov ax,ds;                          /* This comment is OK */
asm pop ax; asm pop ds; asm iret;       /* This is legal too */
asm push ds                             ;THIS COMMENT IS INVALID!!
```

Note that the last line will generate an error, since (as it declares) the comment there is invalid.

The *<opcode>* *<operand>* pair is copied straight to the output, embedded in the assembly language that Turbo C is generating from your C instructions. Any C symbols are replaced with appropriate assembly-language equivalents.

The in-line assembly facility is not a complete assembler, so many errors will not be immediately detected. MASM (the Microsoft assembler) will catch whatever errors there might be. However, MASM might not identify the location of errors, particularly since the original C source line number is lost.

Each **asm** statement counts as a C statement. For example,

```
myfunc()
{
   int  i;
   int x;

   if  (i > 0)
      asm  mov  x,4
   else
      i = 7;
}
```

This construct is a valid C **if** statement. Note that no semicolon was needed after the `mov x,4` instruction. **asm** statements are the only statements in C which depend upon the occurrence of a newline. OK, so this is not in keeping with the rest of the C language, but this is the convention adopted by several UNIX-based compilers.

An assembly statement may be used as an executable statement inside a function, or as an external declaration outside of a function. Assembly statements located outside any function are placed in the DATA segment, and assembly statements located inside functions are placed in the CODE segment.

Here is an in-line assembly version of the function **min** (introduced in "Handling Return Values" earlier in this chapter).

```
int min (int V1, int V2)
{
   asm  mov  ax,V1
   asm  cmp  ax,V2
   asm  jle  minexit
   asm  mov  ax,V2
   minexit:
   return (_AX);
}
```

This example demonstrates why using in-line assembly with Turbo C is more versatile and powerful than calling .ASM routines. This one in-line assembly example works for modules compiled with large code, small code, Pascal calling convention, or C calling convention.

The .ASM equivalent always must be changed, depending on the memory model and the calling convention (C or Pascal). In the .ASM equivalent of *min*, you must always account for parameter offsets and the spelling of the identifier (*_min* or *MIN*); not so with this in-line assembly version.

Any of the 8086 instruction opcodes may be included as in-line assembly statements. There are four classes of instructions allowed by the Turbo C Compiler:

- normal instructions—the regular 8086 opcode set
- string instructions—special string-handling codes
- jump instructions—various jump opcodes
- assembly directives—data allocation and definition

Note that all operands are allowed by the compiler, even if they are erroneous or disallowed by the assembler. The exact format of the operands is not enforced by the compiler.

Opcodes

The following is a summary list of the opcode mnemonics that may be used as normal instructions:

Table 9.7: Opcode Mnemonics

aaa	fcom	fldl2t	fsub	or
aad	fcomp	fldlg2	fsubp	out
aam	fcompp	fldln2	fsubr	pop
aas	fdecstp**	fldpi	fsubrp	popa
adc	fdisi	fldz	ftst	popf
add	fdiv	fmul	fwait	push
and	fdivp	fmulp	fxam	pusha
bound	fdivr	fnclex	fxch	pushf
call	fdivrp	fndisi	fxtract	rcl
cbw	feni	fneni	fyl2x	rcr
clc	ffree**	fninit	fyl2xp1	ret
cld	fiadd	fnop	hlt	rol
cli	ficom	fnsave	idiv	ror
cmc	ficomp	fnstcw	imul	sahf
cmp	fidiv	fnstenv	in	sal
cwd	fidivr	fnstsw	inc	sar
daa	fild	fpatan	int	sbb
das	fimul	fprem	into	shl
dec	fincstp**	fptan	iret	shr
div	finit	frndint	lahf	stc
enter	fist	frstor	lds	std
f2xm1	fistp	fsave	lea	sti
fabs	fisub	fscale	leave	sub
fadd	fisubr	fsqrt	les	test
faddp	fld	fst	mov	wait
fbld	fld1	fstcw	mul	xchg
fbstp	fldcw	fstenv	neg	xlat
fchs	fldenv	fstp	not	xor
fclex	fldl2e	fstsw		

Note: When using 80186 instruction mnemonics in your in-line assembly statements, you must include the -1 command-line option. This forces appropriate statements into the assembly-language compiler output so that the Microsoft 4.0 Assembler will expect the mnemonics. Also, if you are using an older assembler, these mnemonics may not be supported at all.

Another Note: If you are using in-line assembly in routines that use floating point emulation (the TCC option -f), the opcodes marked with "**" are not supported.

String Instructions

In addition to the listed opcodes, string instructions given in the following table may be used alone or with repeat prefixes.

Table 9.8: String Instructions

cmps	insw	movsb	outsb	scasw
cmpsb	lods	movsw	outsw	stos
cmpsw	lodsb	msb	scas	stosb
ins	lodsw	outs	scasb	stosw
insb	movs			

Repeat Prefixes

The following repeat prefixes may be used:

rep	repe	repne	repnz	repz

Jump Instructions

Jump instructions are treated specially. Since a label cannot be included on the instruction itself, jumps must go to C labels (discussed in "Using Jump Instructions and Labels"). The allowed jump instructions are given here:

Table 9.9: Jump Instructions

ja	jge	jnc	jnp	js
jae	jl	jne	jns	jz
jb	jle	jng	jnz	loop
jbe	jmp	jnge	jo	loope
jc	jna	jnl	jp	loopne
jcxz	jnae	jnle	jpe	loopnz
je	jnb	jno	jpo	loopz
jg	jnbe			

Assembly Directives

The following assembly directives are allowed in Turbo C in-line assembly statements:

```
db          dd          dw          extrn
```

In-Line Assembly References to Data and Functions

You can use C symbols in your **asm** statements; Turbo C will automatically convert them to appropriate assembly-language operands and will tack underscores onto identifier names. Any symbol can be used, including automatic (local) variables, register variables, and function parameters.

In general, a C symbol can be used in any position where an address operand would be legal. Of course, a register variable can be used wherever a register would be a legal operand.

If the assembler encounters an identifier while parsing the operands of an in-line assembly instruction, it searches for the identifier in the C symbol table. The names of the 8086 registers are excluded from this search. Either uppercase or lowercase forms of the register names may be used.

In-Line Assembly and Register Variables

The two most frequently used register declarations in a function are treated as register variables, and all other register declarations are treated as automatic (local) variables. If the keyword **register** occurs in a declaration which cannot be a register, the keyword is ignored.

Only **short**, **int** (or the corresponding **unsigned** types), or 2-byte pointer variables may be placed in a register. SI and DI are the 8086 registers used for register variables. In-line assembly code may freely use SI or DI as scratch registers if no register declarations are given in the function. The C function entry and exit code automatically saves and restores the caller's SI and DI.

If there is a register declaration in a function, in-line assembly may use or change the value of the register variable by using SI or DI, but the preferred method is to use the C symbol in case the internal implementation of register variables ever changes.

In-Line Assembly, Offsets, and Size Overrides

When programming, you don't need to be concerned with the exact offsets of local variables. Simply using the name will include the correct offsets.

However, it may be necessary to include appropriate WORD PTR, BYTE PTR, or other size overrides on assembly instruction. A DWORD PTR override is needed on LES or indirect far call instructions.

Using C Structure Members

You can, of course, reference structure members in an in-line assembly statement in the usual fashion, that is, *<variable>.<member>*. In such a case, you are dealing with a variable, and you can store or retrieve values. However, you can also directly reference the member name (without the variable name) as a form of numeric constant. In this situation, the constant equals the offset (in bytes) from the start of the structure containing that member. Consider the following program fragment:

```
struct myStruct {
    int     a_a;
    int     a_b;
    int     a_c;
} myA ;

myfunc()
{
    ...
    asm  mov  ax,myA.a_b
    asm  mov  bx,[di].a_c
    ...
}
```

We've declared a structure type named **myStruct** with three members, *a_a*, *a_b*, and *a_c*; we've also declared a variable *myA* of type **myStruct**. The first in-line assembly statement moves the value contained in *myA.a_b* into the register AX. The second moves the value at the address [DI]+offset(a_c) into the register BX (it takes the address stored in DI and adds to it the offset of *a_c* from the start of **myStruct**). In this sequence, these assembler statements produce the following code:

```
mov  ax ,DGROUP:myA+2
mov  bx ,[di+4]
```

Why would you even want to do this? If you load a register (such as DI) with the address of a structure of type **myStruct**, then you can use the member names to directly reference the members. The member name actually may be used in any position where a numeric constant is allowed in an assembly statement operand.

The structure member must be preceded by a dot (.) to signal that a member name, rather than a normal C symbol, is being used. Member names are replaced in the assembly output by the numeric offset of the structure member (the numeric offset of a_c is 4), but no type information is retained. Thus members may be used as compile-time constants in assembly statements.

However, there is one restriction. No two structures that you are using in in-line assembly can have the same member name—each member name must be unique. This restriction will be resolved in a later version of Turbo C.

Using Jump Instructions and Labels

You may use any of the conditional and unconditional jump instructions, plus the loop instructions, in in-line assembly. They are only valid inside a function. Since no labels can be given in the **asm** statements, jump instructions must use C goto labels as the object of the jump. Direct far jumps cannot be generated.

Indirect jumps are also allowed. To use an indirect jump, you can use a register name as the operand of the jump instruction. In the following code, the jump goes to the C **goto** label *a*.

```
int     x()
{
a:                                      /* This is the goto label "a" */
   ...
   asm  jmp  a                          /* Goes to label "a" */
   ...
}
```

Interrupt Functions

The 8086 reserves the first 1024 bytes of memory for a set of 256 far pointers—known as interrupt vectors—to special system routines known as *interrupt handlers*. These routines are called by executing the 8086 instruction

```
int  <int#>
```

where *<int#>* goes from 0h to FFh. When this happens, the computer saves the code segment (CS), instruction pointer (IP), and status flags, disables the interrupts, then does a far jump to the location pointed to by the corresponding interrupt vector. For example, one interrupt call you're likely to see is

```
int  21h
```

which calls most DOS routines. But many of the interrupt vectors are unused, which means, of course, that you can write your own interrupt handler and stick a **far** pointer to it into one of the unused interrupt vectors.

To write an interrupt handler in Turbo C requires that you define the function to be of type **interrupt**; more specifically, it should look like this:

```
void  interrupt myhandler(bp, di, si, ds, es, dx,
                          cx, bx, ax, ip, cs, flags, ... );
```

As you can see, all the registers are passed as parameters, so you can use and modify them in your code without using the pseudo-variables discussed earlier in this chapter. Also note that you can have additional parameters (*flags*, ...) passed to the handler; those should be defined appropriately.

A function of type **interrupt** will automatically save (in addition to SI, DI, and BP) the registers AX through DX, ES, and DS. These same registers are restored on exit from the interrupt handler.

Interrupt handlers may use floating-point arithmetic in all memory models. Any interrupt handler code that uses an 8087 must save the state of the chip and restore it on exit from the handler.

An interrupt function may modify its parameters. Changing the declared parameters will modify the corresponding register when the interrupt handler returns. This may be useful when you are using an interrupt handler to act as a user service, much like the DOS INT 21 services. Also, note that an interrupt function exits with a IRET (return from interrupt) instruction.

So, why would you want to write your own interrupt handler? For one thing, that's how most memory-resident routines work. They install themselves as interrupt handlers. That way, whenever some special or periodic action takes place (clock tick, keyboard press, and so on), these routines can intercept the call to that routine handling the interrupt and see what action needs to take place. Having done that, they can then pass control on to the routine that was there.

Using Low-Level Practices

You've already seen a few examples of how to use these different low-level practices in your code; now's the time to look at a few more. For starters, you will write an actual interrupt handler that does something harmless yet visible (or, in this case, audible): It will beep whenever it's called.

First, you need to write the function itself. Here's what it would look like:

```
#include        <dos.h>

void  interrupt  mybeep(unsigned bp, unsigned di, unsigned si,
                        unsigned ds, unsigned es, unsigned dx,
                        unsigned cx, unsigned bx, unsigned ax)
{
    int     i, j;
    char    originalbits, bits;
    unsigned char    bcount = ax >> 8;

    /* Get the current control port setting */
    bits = originalbits = inportb(0x61);

    for (i = 0; i <= bcount; i++){

        /* Turn off the speaker for awhile */
        outportb(0x61, bits & 0xfc);
        for     (j = 0; j <= 100; j++)
          ; /* empty statement */

        /* Now turn it on for some more time */
        outportb(0x61, bits | 2);
        for     (j = 0; j <= 100; j++)
          ; /* another empty statement */
        }

    /* Restore the control port setting */
    outportb(0x61, originalbits);
}
```

Next, you need to write a function to install your interrupt handler. You will pass it the address of the function and its interrupt number (0…255 or 0x00…0xFF). The function must do three things:

- disable interrupts so that nothing funny happens while it is updating the vector table
- store the function address passed into the appropriate location
- enable interrupts so that everything is working fine again

Here's what your installation routine looks like:

```
void  install(void interrupt (*faddr)(), int inum)
{
    setvect(inum, faddr);
}
```

Finally, you will want to call your beep routine to test it out. Here's a function to do just that:

```
void  testbeep(unsigned char bcount, int inum)
{
    _AH = bcount;
    geninterrupt(inum);
}
```

Having written all these, your **main** function looks like this:

```
main()
{
    char  ch;

    install(mybeep,10);
    testbeep(3,10);
    ch = getch();
}
```

Using Floating-Point Libraries

There are two types of numbers you work with in C: integer (**int, short, long,** etc.) and floating point (**float, double**). Your computer's processor is set up to easily handle integer values, but it takes more time and effort to handle floating point values.

However, the iAPx86 family of processors has a corresponding family of math *co*processors, the 8087 and the 80287.

The 8087 and 80287 (both of which we refer to here as "the 8087" or "the coprocessor") are special hardware numeric processors that can be installed in your PC. They execute floating-point instructions very quickly. If you use floating point a lot, you'll probably want a coprocessor. The CPU in your computer interfaces to the 8087 via special interrupts.

Turbo C is designed to help you adapt your program to your computer and to your needs.

- If you don't need to use floating-point values at all, you can tell the compiler that.
- If you do need to use floating-point values but your computer doesn't have a math coprocessor (8087/80287), you can tell Turbo C to link in special routines to make it look as though you do have one. In that case, if your program is run on a system with a coprocessor, the chip is automatically used (and your program runs much faster).
- If you're writing programs only for systems that have a math coprocessor, you can instruct the Turbo C compiler to produce code that always uses the 8087/80287 chip.

The following examples assume you've set up your working disks according to the instructions in Chapter 1; in particular, the TCC and TLINK examples assume that the file TURBOC.CFG exists, with the correct -L and -I paths set, and that the library and start-up object files are stored in a subdirectory named \LIB.

Emulating the 8087/80287 Chip

What if you want to use floating point, but your computer doesn't have a math coprocessor? Or what if you have to write a program for computers that might or might not have one? Relax; Turbo C handles that situation well.

With the emulation option, the compiler will generate code as if the 8087 were present but will link in the emulation library (EMU.LIB). When the program runs, it will use the 8087 if it is present; if no coprocessor is present at run time, the program will use special software that *emulates* the 8087.

The emulation library works like this:

- When your program starts to run, the C start-up code will determine if an 8087 is present or not.
- If the coprocessor is there, the program will allow the special interrupts for the 8087 to be passed straight through to the 8087 chip.
- If the coprocessor is not there, the program causes the interrupts to be intercepted and diverted to the emulation routines.

Suppose you modify RATIO.C to look like this:

```
main()
{
    float   a,b,ratio;

    printf("Enter two values:   ");
    scanf("%f %f",&a,&b);
    ratio = a/b;
    printf("The ratio is %0.2f\n",ratio);
}
```

If you are using TC (the user-interface version), you need to go to the **Options** menu, select **Compiler**, select **Code generation**, then select the **Floating-point** item until the field following it reads **Emulation**. When you compile and link your program, Turbo C will automatically select the proper options and libraries for you.

If you're using TCC (the stand-alone compiler), your command line should look like this:

```
tcc -mX ratio
```

If you link the resulting code manually, you must specify both the appropriate math library (depending on the model size) and the EMU.LIB file. The emulation option (-f) is on by default, so you don't need to give it unless your TURBOC.CFG file contains one of the other floating-point switches (-f- or -f87).

Your invocation of TLINK should look like this:

```
tlink lib\c0X ratio, ratio, ratio, lib\emu.lib
      lib\mathX.lib lib\cX.lib
```

where *X* is a letter indicating the proper model library.

Note: The `tlink` command is given all on one line.

Also remember that **the order of the libraries is very important**.

Using the 8087/80287 Math Coprocessor Chip

If you are absolutely sure your program will be run only on systems that have an 8087 or 80287 chip, you can create programs that will take advantage of that chip. At the same time, your resulting .EXE files will be smaller, since Turbo C won't have to include the 8087 emulation routines (EMU.LIB).

If you are using TC (the user-interface version), you need to go to the Options menu, select Compiler, select Code generation, then select the Floating point item until the field following it says 8087/80287. When you compile and link your program, Turbo C will automatically select the proper options and libraries for you.

If you're using TCC (the stand-alone compiler), you need to use the -f87 option on your command line, like this:

```
tcc -f87 -mX ratio
```

This tells Turbo C to generate in-line calls to the 8087/80287 chip. When TLINK is invoked, the files FP87.LIB and MATHx.LIB are linked in.

If you manually link the resulting code, you must specify both the appropriate math library (depending on the model size) and the FP87 library, like this:

```
tlink lib\c0X ratio, ratio, ratio, lib\fp87.lib
      lib\mathX.lib lib\cX.lib
```

where, as always, X is a letter indicating the proper model library.

If You Don't Use Floating Point...

If your program doesn't use any floating-point routines, the linker will not link in any of the floating-point libraries (EMU.LIB or FP87.LIB, along with MATHx.LIB) at link time, even if you listed them on the command line. You can optimize the link step by omitting these libraries from the linker command line (if, as we said, your program uses no floating point).

Suppose you want to compile and link the following program (saved as RATIO.C):

```
main()
{
    int     a,b,ratio;

    printf("Enter two values:  ");
    scanf("%d %d",&a,&b);
    ratio = a/b;
    printf("The ratio is %d\n",ratio);
}
```

Since this program uses no floating-point routines, you can choose to compile it with floating-point emulation on, or with no floating point at all.

If you are using TC (the user-interface version) and choose to compile with emulation on, just select Compile to OBJ from the Compile menu.

(Emulation *On* is the default.) The linker will include the floating-point libraries at the link step, but none will actually be linked.

If you want to speed up the linking process, you can specify "no floating point." Go to the **Options** menu, select **Compiler**, select **Code generation**, then select the Floating point item.

Repeatedly pressing *Enter* at this command cycles you through three options: None, Emulation, and 8087/80287. You want the None option. You can then press *Esc* three times to get back to the menu bar (or just press *F10*).

When you compile and link this program with Floating point set to None, Turbo C does not attempt to link in any floating-point math routines.

If you're using TCC (the stand-alone compiler), you need to use the $-f-$ option on your command line, like this:

```
tcc -f- -mX ratio.c
```

This tells Turbo C that you have no floating-point instructions in your program at all. It also says that you used the x memory model, where x is a letter indicating the desired model (t = tiny, s = small, c = compact, m = medium, l = large, h = huge).

Since RATIO.C is a stand-alone program, TCC will automatically invoke TLINK, linking in C0x.OBJ and Cx.LIB, and producing RATIO.EXE.

If you used the "compile only" ($-c$) option on the TCC command line, you need to manually link the resulting code.

In that case, you don't need to (and shouldn't) specify any math library; your invocation of TLINK should look like this:

```
tlink lib\c0x ratio, ratio, ratio, lib\cx.lib
```

This links together C0x.OBJ and RATIO.OBJ, uses the library Cx.LIB, and produces the files RATIO.EXE and RATIO.MAP.

The 87 Environment Variable

If you build your program with 8087 emulation (in other words, you select Floating point...Emulation from the menus or you include the $-f$ option on the TCC command line), the C0x.OBJ start-up module will use 8087 auto-detection logic when you run the program. This means that the start-up code will automatically check to see if an 8087 is available.

If the 8087 is available, then the program will use it; if it is not there, the program will use the emulation routines.

288   *Turbo C User's Guide*

There are some instances in which you might want to override this default auto-detection behavior. For example, your own run-time system might have an 8087, but you need to verify that your program will work as intended on systems without a coprocessor. Or your program may need to run on a PC-compatible system, but that particular system returns incorrect information to the auto-detection logic (saying that a non-existent 8087 is available, or vice versa).

Turbo C provides an option for overriding the start-up code's default auto-detection logic; this option is the 87 environment variable.

You set the 87 environment variable at the DOS prompt with the SET command, like this:

```
C> SET 87=N
```

or

```
C> SET 87=Y
```

Setting the 87 environment variable to N (for No) tells the start-up code that you do not want to use the 8087 (even though it might be present in the system).

Conversely, setting the 87 environment variable to Y (for Yes) means that the coprocessor is there, and you want the program to use it. Caveat Programmer!! If you set 87 = Y when, in fact, there is no 8087 available on that system, your program will crash and burn in a logical inferno.

The 87 environment variable is able to override the default auto-detection logic because, when you start to run your program, the start-up code first checks to see if the 87 variable has been defined.

- If the 87 variable has been defined, the start-up code looks no further, and your program runs in the prescribed mode.
- If the 87 variable has not been defined, the start-up code goes through its auto-detection logic to see if an 8087 chip is available, and the program runs accordingly.

If the 87 environment variable has been defined (to any value) but you want to undefine it, enter the following at the DOS prompt:

```
C> SET 87=
```

(This means press *Enter* immediately after typing the equal sign.)

Registers and the 8087

There are a couple of points relating to registers that you should be aware of when using floating point.

First, in 8087 emulation mode, register wrap-around is not supported.

Second, if you are mixing floating point with in-line assembly, you may need to take special care when using registers. This is because the 8087 register set is emptied before Turbo C calls a function. You might need to pop and save the 8087 registers before calling functions which use the coprocessor, unless you are sure that enough free registers exist.

Using matherr with Floating Point

When an error is detected in one of the floating-point routines during execution of a program, that routine automatically calls **_matherr** with several arguments. **_matherr** then stuffs an exception structure (defined in math.h) with its arguments and calls **matherr** with a pointer to that structure.

The **matherr** routine is a hook that you can use to write your own error-resolution routine. By default, **matherr** does nothing but return 0. However, you can modify **matherr** to deal with floating-point routine errors in any way you desire. Such a modified **matherr** then returns non-zero if the error was resolved, or 0 if it was not.

For more information about **matherr** and **_matherr** refer to the **matherr** description in the lookup section of the *Turbo C Programmer's Reference Guide*.

Caveats and Tips

Turbo C's Use of RAM

Turbo C does not generate any intermediate data structures to disk when it is compiling (Turbo C writes only .obj files to disk); instead it uses RAM for intermediate data structures between passes. Because of this, you might encounter the message OUT OF MEMORY... if there is not enough memory available for the compiler.

The solution to this problem is to make your functions smaller or to split up the file that has large functions. You might also delete any RAM-resident programs you have installed to free up more memory for Turbo C to use.

Should You Use Pascal Conventions?

No—not unless you have read and really understood this chapter. Remember, if you are compiling your main file with pascal calling conventions, make sure to declare **main** as a C function:

```
cdecl main(int argc, char * argv[], char * envp[])
```

Summary

You've seen how to use all three aspects of low-level programming in Turbo C (pseudo-variables, in-line assembly, interrupt functions); you've learned about interfacing with other languages, including assembly; you've been introduced to some of the details of using floating-point routines; and you've discovered how the different memory models on the 8086 interact. Now it's up to you to use these techniques to gain complete control of your computer; best of luck.

Index

F

False 103
far (keyword) 220, 241
Far pointers 242
FCNTL.H 11
Field
  references 176
  width 92
  –width specifiers 99
File
  dependencies 81
  executable 78
  inclusion 231
  I/O 182
  main menu 32
  names on command line 78
FILECOMP.C 13
Flag register 239
float (keyword) 93, 112, 212
FLOAT.H 11
Floating-point
  arithmetic 282
  constant 112, 212
  emulation 285
  error handling 290
  expression 215
  libraries 284
  numbers 93
  option toggle 50
Flow
  control 132
  patterns 198
fopen 182
for (keyword) 109, 161
For loop 109, 161
Format
  commands 91, 152
  specifications 91
  string 91, 152
Forward declarations 164
FP87.LIB 11, 255, 287
Frame standard stack 50
free 191
Free union variant record 175
Function

allocation 144, 191
arrays and 126
cdecl type 224
C vs. Pascal 162
declaration 111, 114, 137, 162
declarator 225
definitions 113, 114, 137, 188
entry and exit code 279
input 101, 113
interrupt type 224
main 112
output 91, 152
pascal type 223
pointers and 121
prototypes 114, 137, 164, 188, 225,
  252, 256
recursive 250
referencing from .ASM 264
return values 163, 266
type modifiers 223
user-written 113

G

General purpose registers 239, 274
Generate underbars 51, 190, 219, 260
Generation code 49
getch 102, 156
GETOPT.C 13
gets 102, 156
Global
  declarations 114
  definition 263
  identifier 263
  stack 198
  variables 152, 179
goto (keyword) 132, 135, 281
Goto statement 135

H

Hardware specifics 213
Header files 11, 165, 173, 256, 260
Hello world 64, 84
HELLO.C 10, 64, 84

Help
  getting 24, 34
  hot key 34
Hexadecimal character constants 140
Hot keys 26, 69
huge (keyword) 220, 241
Huge pointers 243

I

Identifier
  case 208, 219
  global 219
  length 208
  length setting 53
  naming restrictions 97
  non-unique 229
  Pascal-type vs. C-type 219
if (keyword) 106, 158
If statement 104, 106
Illustration menu system 30
In-line assembly 271, 274
Include directories setting 58
Include Files 11, 173
Increment operator 98, 155
Index
  range error 156
  registers 239
  variable 109
Indirection operator 100, 119, 220
Indirect jumps 281
Infinite loop 110
Initialization
  module 190
  of variables 178
Initialize segments toggle 57
Input
  C vs. Pascal 156
  functions 101
Installation
  floppy disk 15
  hard disk 17
Instruction
  pointer 239
  set toggle 49
Instructions

jump 278, 281
  string 278
int (keyword) 94, 213
Integer
  compatible value 131, 177
  constants 210
Integers 93
Integrated Environment 10, 16, 17, 23
Interactive input 101
Interfacing
  to other languages 257
  with assembly 261
Intermediate data structures 290
interrupt (keyword) 222, 224, 282
Interrupt
  functions 271, 281
  handlers 281, 283
  routines 273
  vectors 224, 281
IO.H 11
Iterative execution 107, 160

J

Jump
  instructions 278, 281
  optimization toggle 52

K

Keep messages command 62
Kernighan and Ritchie 2, 4, 84, 207
Keyboard input 156
Keywords, ANSI only 53

L

Labels, goto 281
Large data models 248
Legends 110
Less common errors 55
Libraries
  default 57
  files 254

Q

R

T

U

V

VALUES.H 12
Variables
  automatic (local) 279
  definition 262
  global 152
  index 109
  initialization 178
  referencing 264
  storage 179
  string 152
Violations, ANSI 55
void (keyword) 111, 139, 162, 216, 226
volatile (keyword) 218

W

Warn duplicate symbols toggle 58
Warnings
  definition of 87
  Display 55
  Portability 55

Stack 58
  stop after setting 55
while (keyword) 107, 110, 160
While loop 107, 160
Whitespace 101
Window
  active 33
  Edit 25, 33
  Message 25, 34, 68
  switching 34
  zoomed 59, 68
Word 118
Working environment 65
wrch 191
Write to command 40
Writing
  programs 88
  to disk 40, 89

Z

Zoom 34, 68
Zoomed windows toggle 59
zwf 191

Borland
Software

BORLAND
INTERNATIONAL

4585 Scotts Valley Drive, Scotts Valley, CA 95066

SIDEKICK:® THE DESKTOP ORGANIZER

Whether you're running WordStar,® Lotus,® dBASE,® or any other program, SideKick puts all these desktop accessories at your fingertips—Instantly!

A full-screen WordStar-like Editor to jot down notes and edit files up to 25 pages long.

A Phone Directory for names, addresses, and telephone numbers. Finding a name or a number is a snap.

An Autodialer for all your phone calls. It will look up and dial telephone numbers for you. (A modem is required to use this function.)

A Monthly Calendar from 1901 through 2099.

Appointment Calendar to remind you of important meetings and appointments.

A full-featured Calculator ideal for business use. It also performs decimal to hexadecimal to binary conversions.

An ASCII Table for easy reference.

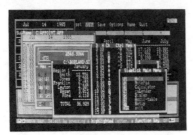

All the SideKick windows stacked up over Lotus 1-2-3.® From bottom to top: SideKick's "Menu Window," ASCII Table, Notepad, Calculator, Appointment Calendar, Monthly Calendar, and Phone Dialer.

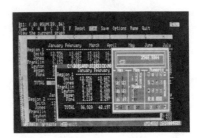

Here's SideKick running over Lotus 1-2-3. In the SideKick Notepad you'll notice data that's been imported directly from the Lotus screen. In the upper right you can see the Calculator.

The Critics' Choice

"In a simple, beautiful implementation of WordStar's block copy commands, SideKick can transport all or any part of the display screen (even an area overlaid by the notepad display) to the notepad."
—Charles Petzold, PC MAGAZINE

"SideKick deserves a place in every PC."
—Gary Ray, PC WEEK

"SideKick is by far the best we've seen. It is also the least expensive."
—Ron Mansfield, ENTREPRENEUR

"If you use a PC, get SideKick. You'll soon become dependent on it."
—Jerry Pournelle, BYTE

Suggested Retail Price: $84.95 (not copy protected)

Minimum system configuration: IBM PC, XT, AT, PCjr and true compatibles. PC-DOS (MS-DOS) 2.0 or greater. 128K RAM. One disk drive. A Hayes-compatible modem, IBM PCjr internal modem, or AT&T Modem 4000 is required for the autodialer function.

SideKick is a registered trademark of Borland International, Inc. dBASE is a registered trademark of Ashton-Tate. IBM, XT, AT, and PCjr are registered trademarks of International Business Machines Corp. AT&T is a registered trademark of American Telephone & Telegraph Company. Lotus and 1-2-3 are registered trademarks of Lotus Development Corp. WordStar is a registered trademark of MicroPro International Corp. Hayes is a trademark of Hayes Microcomputer Products, Inc.
Copyright 1987 Borland International

BOR0060C

Traveling SIDEKICK®

The Organizer For The Computer Age!

Traveling SideKick is *BinderWare,*® both a binder you take with you when you travel and a software program—which includes a Report Generator—that *generates* and *prints out* all the information you'll need to take with you.

Information like your phone list, your client list, your address book, your calendar, and your appointments. The appointment or calendar files you're already using in your SideKick® can automatically be used by your Traveling SideKick. You don't waste time and effort reentering information that's already there.

One keystroke prints out a form like your address book. No need to change printer paper;

you simply punch three holes, fold and clip the form into your Traveling SideKick binder, and you're on your way. Because Traveling SideKick is CAD (Computer-Age Designed), you don't fool around with low-tech tools like scissors, tape, or staples. And because Traveling SideKick is electronic, it works this year, next year, and all the "next years" after that. Old-fashioned daytime organizers are history in 365 days.

What's inside Traveling SideKick

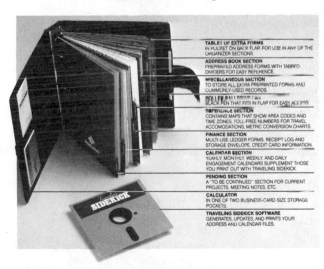

TABLET OF EXTRA FORMS
IN POCKET ON BACK FLAP, FOR USE IN ANY OF THE ORGANIZER SECTIONS.

ADDRESS BOOK SECTION
PREPRINTED ADDRESS FORMS WITH TABBED DIVIDERS FOR EASY REFERENCE.

MISCELLANEOUS SECTION
TO STORE ALL EXTRA PREPRINTED FORMS AND COMMONLY-USED RECORDS.

ROLLER BALL PEN THAT FITS IN FLAP FOR EASY ACCESS.

REFERENCE SECTION
CONTAINS MAPS THAT SHOW AREA CODES AND TIME ZONES, TOLL-FREE NUMBERS FOR TRAVEL ACCOMODATIONS, METRIC CONVERSION CHARTS.

FINANCE SECTION
MULTI-USE LEDGER FORMS, RECEIPT LOG AND STORAGE ENVELOPE, CREDIT CARD INFORMATION.

CALENDAR SECTION
YEARLY, MONTHLY, WEEKLY, AND DAILY ENGAGEMENT CALENDARS SUPPLEMENT THOSE YOU PRINT OUT WITH TRAVELING SIDEKICK.

PENDING SECTION
A "TO BE CONTINUED" SECTION FOR CURRENT PROJECTS, MEETING NOTES, ETC.

CALCULATOR
IN ONE OF TWO BUSINESS-CARD-SIZE STORAGE POCKETS.

TRAVELING SIDEKICK SOFTWARE
GENERATES, UPDATES, AND PRINTS YOUR ADDRESS AND CALENDAR FILES.

What the software program and its Report Generator do for you before you go—and when you get back

Before you go:
- Prints out your calendar, appointments, addresses, phone directory, and whatever other information you need from your data files

When you return:
- Lets you quickly and easily enter all the new names you obtained while you were away into your SideKick data files

It can also:
- Sort your address book by contact, zip code or company name
- Print mailing labels
- Print information selectively
- Search files for existing addresses or calendar engagements

Suggested Retail Price: $69.95 (not copy protected)

Minimum system configuration: IBM PC, XT, AT, Portable, PCjr, 3270 and true compatibles. PC-DOS (MS-DOS) 2.0 or later. 256K RAM mimimum.

BORLAND *INTERNATIONAL*

SideKick, BinderWare and Traveling SideKick are registered trademarks of Borland International, Inc. IBM, AT, XT, and PCjr are registered trademarks of International Business Machines Corp. MS-DOS is a registered trademark of Microsoft Corp. Copyright 1987 Borland International

BOR 0083A

SUPERKEY® THE PRODUCTIVITY BOOSTER

RAM-resident
Increased productivity for IBM®PCs or compatibles

SuperKey's simple macros are electronic shortcuts to success. By letting you reduce a lengthy paragraph into a single keystroke of your choice, SuperKey eliminates repetition.

SuperKey turns 1,000 keystrokes into 1!

SuperKey can record lengthy keystroke sequences and play them back at the touch of a single key. Instantly. Like magic.

In fact, with SuperKey's simple macros, you can turn "Dear Customer: Thank you for your inquiry. We are pleased to let you know that shipment will be made within 24 hours. Sincerely," into the one keystroke of your choice!

SuperKey keeps your confidential files—confidential!

Without encryption, your files are open secrets. Anyone can walk up to your PC and read your confidential files (tax returns, business plans, customer lists, personal letters, etc.).

With SuperKey you can encrypt any file, *even* while running another program. As long as you keep the password secret, only *you* can decode your file correctly. SuperKey also implements the U.S. government Data Encryption Standard (DES).

- ☑ RAM resident—accepts new macro files even while running other programs
- ☑ Pull-down menus
- ☑ Superfast file encryption
- ☑ Choice of two encryption schemes
- ☑ On-line context-sensitive help
- ☑ One-finger mode reduces key commands to single keystroke
- ☑ Screen OFF/ON blanks out and restores screen to protect against "burn in"
- ☑ Partial or complete reorganization of keyboard

- ☑ Keyboard buffer increases 16 character keyboard "type-ahead" buffer to 128 characters
- ☑ Real-time delay causes macro playback to pause for specified interval
- ☑ Transparent display macros allow creation of menus on top of application programs
- ☑ Data entry and format control using "fixed" or "variable" fields
- ☑ Command stack recalls last 256 characters entered

Suggested Retail Price: $99.95 (not copy protected)

Minimum system configuration: IBM PC, XT, AT, PCjr, and true compatibles. PC-DOS (MS-DOS) 2.0 or greater. 128K RAM. One disk drive.

 **BORLAND** *INTERNATIONAL*

SuperKey is a registered trademark of Borland International, Inc. IBM, XT, AT, and PCjr are registered trademarks of International Business Machines Corp. MS-DOS is a registered trademark of Microsoft Corp.

BOR 0062C

REFLEX: THE WORKSHOP™

Includes 22 "instant templates" covering a broad range of business applications (listed below). Also shows you how to customize databases, graphs, crosstabs, and reports. It's an invaluable analytical tool and an important addition to another one of our best sellers, Reflex: The Database Manager.

Fast-start tutorial examples:

Learn Reflex® as you work with practical business applications. The Reflex Workshop Disk supplies databases and reports large enough to illustrate the power and variety of Reflex features. Instructions in each Reflex Workshop chapter take you through a step-by-step analysis of sample data. You then follow simple steps to adapt the files to your own needs.

22 practical business applications:

Workshop's 22 "instant templates" give you a wide range of analytical tools:

Administration
- Scheduling Appointments
- Planning Conference Facilities
- Managing a Project
- Creating a Mailing System
- Managing Employment Applications

Sales and Marketing
- Researching Store Check Inventory
- Tracking Sales Leads
- Summarizing Sales Trends
- Analyzing Trends

Production and Operations
- Summarizing Repair Turnaround

- Tracking Manufacturing Quality Assurance
- Analyzing Product Costs

Accounting and Financial Planning
- Tracking Petty Cash
- Entering Purchase Orders
- Organizing Outgoing Purchase Orders
- Analyzing Accounts Receivable
- Maintaining Letters of Credit
- Reporting Business Expenses
- Managing Debits and Credits
- Examining Leased Inventory Trends
- Tracking Fixed Assets
- Planning Commercial Real Estate Investment

Whether you're a newcomer learning Reflex basics or an experienced "power user" looking for tips, Reflex: The Workshop will help you quickly become an expert database analyst.

Minimum system configuration: IBM PC, AT, and XT, and true compatibles. PC-DOS (MS-DOS) 2.0 or greater. 384K RAM minimum. Requires Reflex: The Database Manager, and IBM Color Graphics Adapter, Hercules Monochrome Graphics Card or equivalent.

BORLAND
INTERNATIONAL

**Suggested Retail Price: $69.95
(not copy protected)**

TURBOPASCAL®

Version 3.0 with 8087 support and BCD reals

Free MicroCalc Spreadsheet With Commented Source Code!

FEATURES:

One-Step Compile: No hunting & fishing expeditions! Turbo finds the errors, takes you to them, lets you correct them, and instantly recompiles. You're off and running in record time.

Built-in Interactive Editor: WordStar®-like easy editing lets you debug quickly.

Automatic Overlays: Fits big programs into small amounts of memory.

MicroCalc: A sample spreadsheet on your disk with ready-to-compile source code.

IBM® PC Version: Supports Turtle Graphics, color, sound, full tree directories, window routines, input/output redirection, and much more.

THE CRITICS' CHOICE:

"Language deal of the century . . . Turbo Pascal: it introduces a new programming environment and runs like magic."
—**Jeff Duntemann, PC Magazine**

"Most Pascal compilers barely fit on a disk, but Turbo Pascal packs an editor, compiler, linker, and run-time library into just 39K bytes of random access memory."
—**Dave Garland, Popular Computing**

"What I think the computer industry is headed for: well-documented, standard, plenty of good features, and a reasonable price."
—**Jerry Pournelle, BYTE**

LOOK AT TURBO NOW!

- ☑ More than 500,000 users worldwide.

- ☑ Turbo Pascal is the de facto industry standard.

- ☑ Turbo Pascal wins PC MAGAZINE'S award for technical excellence.

- ☑ Turbo Pascal named "Most Significant Product of the Year" by PC WEEK.

- ☑ Turbo Pascal 3.0—the fastest Pascal development environment on the planet, period.

Suggested Retail Price: $99.95; CP/M®-80 version without 8087 and BCD: $69.95

Features for 16-bit Systems: 8087 math co-processor support for intensive calculations. Binary Coded Decimals (BCD): eliminates round-off error! A *must* for any serious business application.

Minimum system configuration: 128K RAM minimum. Includes 8087 & BCD features for 16-bit MS-DOS 2.0 or later and CP/M-86 1.1 or later. CP/M-80 version 2.2 or later 48K RAM minimum (8087 and BCD features not available). 8087 version requires 8087 or 80287 co-processor.

BORLAND
INTERNATIONAL

Turbo Pascal is a registered trademark of Borland International, Inc. CP/M is a registered trademark of Digital Research Inc. IBM is a registered trademark of International Business Machines Corp. MS-DOS is a registered trademark of Microsoft Corp. WordStar is a registered trademark of MicroPro International. Copyright 1987 Borland International BOR 0061B

TURBO PASCAL
TURBO TUTOR®

VERSION 2.0

Learn Pascal From The Folks Who Created The Turbo Pascal® Family

Borland International proudly presents Turbo Tutor, the perfect complement to your Turbo Pascal compiler. Turbo Tutor is really for everyone— even if you've never programmed before.

And if you're already proficient, Turbo Tutor can sharpen up the fine points. The manual and program disk focus on the whole spectrum of Turbo Pascal programming techniques.

- **For the Novice:** It gives you a concise history of Pascal, tells you how to write a simple program, and defines the basic programming terms you need to know.

- **Programmer's Guide:** The heart of Turbo Pascal. The manual covers the fine points of every aspect of Turbo Pascal programming: program structure, data types, control structures, procedures and functions, scalar types, arrays, strings, pointers, sets, files, and records.

- **Advanced Concepts:** If you're an expert, you'll love the sections detailing such topics as linked lists, trees, and graphs. You'll also find sample program examples for PC-DOS and MS-DOS.®

10,000 lines of commented source code, demonstrations of 20 Turbo Pascal features, multiple-choice quizzes, an interactive on-line tutor, and more!

Turbo Tutor may be the only reference work about Pascal and programming you'll ever need!

Suggested Retail Price: $39.95 (not copy protected)

Minimum system configuration: Turbo Pascal 3.0. PC-DOS (MS-DOS) 2.0 or later. 192K RAM minimum (CP/M-80 version 2.2 or later: 64K RAM minimum).

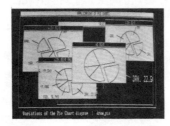

TURBO PASCAL
EDITOR TOOLBOX®

It's All You Need To Build Your Own Text Editor Or Word Processor

Build your own lightning-fast editor and incorporate it into your Turbo Pascal® programs. Turbo Editor Toolbox gives you easy-to-install modules. Now you can integrate a fast and powerful editor into your own programs. You get the source code, the manual, and the know-how.

Create your own word processor. We provide all the editing routines. You plug in the features you want. You could build a WordStar®-like editor with pull-down menus like Microsoft's® Word, and make it work as fast as WordPerfect.®

To demonstrate the tremendous power of Turbo Editor Toolbox, we give you the source code for two sample editors:

Simple Editor   A complete editor ready to include in your programs. With windows, block commands, and memory-mapped screen routines.

MicroStar   A full-blown text editor with a complete pull-down menu user interface, plus a lot more. Modify MicroStar's pull-down menu system and include it in your Turbo Pascal programs.

The Turbo Editor Toolbox gives you all the standard features you would expect to find in any word processor:

- Wordwrap
- UN-delete last line
- Auto-indent
- Find and Find/Replace with options
- Set left and right margin
- Block mark, move, and copy
- Tab, insert and overstrike modes, centering, etc.

MicroStar's pull-down menus.

And Turbo Editor Toolbox has features that word processors selling for several hundred dollars can't begin to match. Just to name a few:

- ☑ **RAM-based editor**. You can edit very large files and yet editing is lightning fast.
- ☑ **Memory-mapped screen routines.** Instant paging, scrolling, and text display.
- ☑ **Keyboard installation.** Change control keys from WordStar-like commands to any that you prefer.

- ☑ **Multiple windows.** See and edit up to eight documents—or up to eight parts of the same document—all at the same time.
- ☑ **Multitasking.** Automatically save your text. Plug in a digital clock, an appointment alarm—see how it's done with MicroStar's "background" printing.

Best of all, **source code is included for everything in the Editor Toolbox.**

Suggested Retail Price: $69.95 (not copy protected)

Minimum system configuration: IBM PC, XT, AT, 3270, PCjr, and true compatibles. PC-DOS (MS-DOS) 2.0 or greater. 192K RAM. You must be using Turbo Pascal 3.0 for IBM and compatibles.

TURBO PASCAL GAME WORKS®

Secrets And Strategies Of The Masters Are Revealed For The First Time

Explore the world of state-of-the-art computer games with Turbo GameWorks. Using easy-to-understand examples, Turbo GameWorks teaches you techniques to quickly create your own computer games using Turbo Pascal.® Or, for instant excitement, play the three great computer games we've included on disk—compiled and ready to run.

TURBO CHESS

Test your chess-playing skills against your computer challenger. With Turbo GameWorks, you're on your way to becoming a master chess player. Explore the complete Turbo Pascal source code and discover the secrets of Turbo Chess.

"What impressed me the most was the fact that with this program you can become a computer chess analyst. You can add new variations to the program at any time and make the program play stronger and stronger chess. There's no limit to the fun and enjoyment of playing Turbo GameWorks Chess, and most important of all, with this chess program there's no limit to how it can help you improve your game."

—George Koltanowski, Dean of American Chess, former President of the United Chess Federation, and syndicated chess columnist.

TURBO BRIDGE

Now play the world's most popular card game—bridge. Play one-on-one with your computer or against up to three other opponents. With Turbo Pascal source code, you can even program your own bidding or scoring conventions.

"There has never been a bridge program written which plays at the expert level, and the ambitious user will enjoy tackling that challenge, with the format already structured in the program. And for the inexperienced player, the bridge program provides an easy-to-follow format that allows the user to start right out playing. The user can 'play bridge' against real competition without having to gather three other people."

—Kit Woolsey, writer of several articles and books on bridge, and twice champion of the Blue Ribbon Pairs.

TURBO GO-MOKU

Prepare for battle when you challenge your computer to a game of Go-Moku—the exciting strategy game also known as Pente.® In this battle of wits, you and the computer take turns placing X's and O's on a grid of 19✕19 squares until five pieces are lined up in a row. Vary the game if you like, using the source code available on your disk.

Suggested Retail Price: $69.95 (not copy protected)

Minimum system configuration: IBM PC, XT, AT, Portable, 3270, PCjr, and true compatibles. PC-DOS (MS-DOS) 2.0 or later. 192K RAM minimum. To edit and compile the Turbo Pascal source code, you must be using Turbo Pascal 3.0 for IBM PCs and compatibles.

BORLAND
INTERNATIONAL

TURBO
PROLOG™

the natural language of Artificial Intelligence

Turbo Prolog brings fifth-generation supercomputer power to your IBM®PC!

Turbo Prolog takes programming into a new, natural, and logical environment

With Turbo Prolog, because of its natural, logical approach, both people new to programming *and* professional programmers can build powerful applications such as expert systems, customized knowledge bases, natural language interfaces, and smart information management systems.

Turbo Prolog is a *declarative* language which uses deductive reasoning to solve programming problems.

Turbo Prolog provides a fully integrated programming environment like Borland's Turbo Pascal,® the *de facto* worldwide standard.

You get the complete Turbo Prolog programming system

You get the 200-page manual you're holding, software that includes the lightning-fast Turbo Prolog six-pass compiler and interactive editor, and the free GeoBase natural query language database, which includes commented source code on disk, ready to compile. (GeoBase is a complete database designed and developed around U.S. geography. You can modify it or use it "as is.")

Turbo Prolog's development system includes:

- ☐ A complete Prolog compiler that is a variation of the Clocksin and Mellish Edinburgh standard Prolog.
- ☐ A full-screen interactive editor.
- ☐ Support for both graphic and text windows.
- ☐ All the tools that let you build your own expert systems and **AI** applications with unprecedented ease.

Minimum system configuration: IBM PC, XT, AT, Portable, 3270, PCjr and true compatibles. PC-DOS (MS-DOS) 2.0 or later. 384K RAM minimum.

Suggested Retail Price: $99.95 (not copy protected)

Turbo Prolog is a trademark and Turbo Pascal is a registered trademark of Borland International, Inc. IBM, AT, XT, and PCjr are registered trademarks of International Business Machines Corp. MS-DOS is a registered trademark of Microsoft Corp. Copyright 1987 Borland International   BOR 0016D

TURBO PROLOG™
TOOLBOX

Enhances Turbo Prolog with more than 80 tools and over 8,000 lines of source code

Turbo Prolog, the natural language of Artificial Intelligence, is the most popular AI package in the world with more than 100,000 users. Our new Turbo Prolog Toolbox extends its possibilities.

The Turbo Prolog Toolbox enhances Turbo Prolog—our 5th-generation computer programming language that brings supercomputer power to your IBM PC and compatibles—with its more than 80 tools and over 8,000 lines of source code that can be incorporated into your programs, quite easily.

Turbo Prolog Toolbox features include:

- ☑ Business graphics generation: boxes, circles, ellipses, bar charts, pie charts, scaled graphics
- ☑ Complete communications package: supports XModem protocol
- ☑ File transfers from Reflex,® dBASE III,® Lotus 1-2-3,® Symphony®
- ☑ A unique parser generator: construct your own compiler or query language
- ☑ Sophisticated user-interface design tools
- ☑ 40 example programs
- ☑ Easy-to-use screen editor: design your screen layout and I/O
- ☑ Calculated fields definition
- ☑ Over 8,000 lines of source code you can incorporate into your own programs

---

Suggested Retail Price: $99.95 (not copy protected)

Minimum system configuration: IBM PC, XT, AT or true compatibles. PC-DOS (MS-DOS) 2.0 or later. Requires Turbo Prolog 1.10 or higher. Dual-floppy disk drive or hard disk. 512K.

BORLAND
I N T E R N A T I O N A L

Turbo Prolog Toolbox and Turbo Prolog are trademarks of Borland International, Inc. Reflex is a registered trademark of Borland/Analytica, Inc. dBASE III is a registered trademark of Ashton-Tate. Lotus 1-2-3 and Symphony are registered trademarks of Lotus Development Corp. IBM, XT, and AT are registered trademarks of International Business Machines Corp. MS-DOS is a registered trademark of Microsoft Corp.   BOR 0240

TURBO BASIC®

The high-speed BASIC you've been waiting for!

You probably know us for our Turbo Pascal® and Turbo Prolog.® Well, we've done it again! We've created Turbo Basic, because BASIC doesn't have to be slow.

If BASIC taught you how to walk, Turbo Basic will teach you how to run!

With Turbo Basic, your only speed is "Full Speed Ahead"! Turbo Basic is a complete development environment with an *amazingly fast compiler,* an *interactive editor* and a *trace debugging system*. And because Turbo Basic is also compatible with BASICA, chances are that you already know how to use Turbo Basic.

Turbo Basic ends the basic confusion

There's now one standard: Turbo Basic. And because Turbo Basic is a Borland product, the price is right, the quality is there, and the power is at your fingertips. Turbo Basic is part of the fast-growing Borland family of programming languages we call the "Turbo Family." And hundreds of thousands of users are already using Borland's languages. So, welcome to a whole new generation of smart PC users!

Free spreadsheet included with source code!

Yes, we've included MicroCalc,™ our sample spreadsheet, complete with source code. So you can get started right away with a "real program." You can compile and run it "as is," or modify it.

A technical look at Turbo Basic

- ☑ Full recursion supported
- ☑ Standard IEEE floating-point format
- ☑ Floating-point support, with full 8087 coprocessor integration. Software emulation if no 8087 present
- ☑ Program size limited only by available memory (no 64K limitation)
- ☑ EGA, CGA, MCGA and VGA support
- ☑ Full integration of the compiler, editor, and executable program, with separate windows for editing, messages, tracing, and execution
- ☑ Compile and run-time errors place you in source code where error occurred
- ☑ Access to local, static and global variables
- ☑ New long integer (32-bit) data type
- ☑ Full 80-bit precision
- ☑ Pull-down menus
- ☑ Full window management

Suggested Retail Price: $99.95 (not copy protected)

Minimum system configuration: IBM PC, AT, XT, PS/2 or true compatibles. 320K. One floppy drive. PC-DOS (MS-DOS) 2.0 or later.

Turbo Basic, Turbo Prolog and Turbo Pascal are registered trademarks and MicroCalc is a trademark of Borland International, Inc. Other brand and product names are trademarks or registered trademarks of their respective holders.
Copyright 1987 Borland International

BOR 0265B

EUREKA: THE SOLVER™

The solution to your most complex equations—in seconds!

If you're a scientist, engineer, financial analyst, student, teacher, or any other professional working with equations, Eureka: The Solver can do your Algebra, Trigonometry and Calculus problems in a snap.

Eureka also handles maximization and minimization problems, plots functions, generates reports, and saves an incredible amount of time. Even if you're not a computer specialist, Eureka can help you solve your real-world mathematical problems fast, without having to learn numerical approximation techniques. Using Borland's famous pull-down menu design and context-sensitive help screens, Eureka is easy to learn and easy to use—as simple as a hand-held calculator.

$X + exp(X) = 10$ solved instantly instead of eventually!

Imagine you have to "solve for X," where $X + exp(X) = 10$, and you don't have Eureka: The Solver. What you do have is a problem, because it's going to take a lot of time guessing at "X." With Eureka, there's no guessing, no dancing in the dark—you get the right answer, right now. (PS: $X = 2.0705799$, and Eureka solved that one in .4 of a second!)

How to use Eureka: The Solver

It's easy.
1. Enter your equation into the full-screen editor
2. Select the "Solve" command
3. Look at the answer
4. You're done

You can then tell Eureka to
- Evaluate your solution
- Plot a graph
- Generate a report, then send the output to your printer, disk file or screen
- Or all of the above

Some of Eureka's key features

You can key in:
- ☑ A formula or formulas
- ☑ A series of equations—and solve for all variables
- ☑ Constraints (like X has to be $<$ or $= 2$)
- ☑ A function to plot
- ☑ Unit conversions
- ☑ Maximization and minimization problems
- ☑ Interest Rate/Present Value calculations
- ☑ Variables we call "What happens?," like "What happens if I change this variable to 21 and that variable to 27?"

Eureka: The Solver includes

- ☑ A full-screen editor
- ☑ Pull-down menus
- ☑ Context-sensitive Help
- ☑ On-screen calculator
- ☑ Automatic 8087 math co-processor chip support
- ☑ Powerful financial functions
- ☑ Built-in and user-defined math and financial functions
- ☑ Ability to generate reports complete with plots and lists
- ☑ Polynomial finder
- ☑ Inequality solutions

Minimum system configuration: IBM PC, AT, XT, PS/2, Portable, 3270 and true compatibles. PC-DOS (MS-DOS) 2.0 and later. 384K.

Suggested Retail Price: $167.00 (not copy protected)

SIDEKICK®: THE DESKTOP ORGANIZER *Release 2.0*

Macintosh™

The most complete and comprehensive collection of desk accessories available for your Macintosh!

Thousands of users already know that SideKick is the best collection of desk accessories available for the Macintosh. With our new Release 2.0, the best just got better.

We've just added two powerful high-performance tools to SideKick—Outlook™: The Outliner and MacPlan™: The Spreadsheet. They work in perfect harmony with each other and *while* you run other programs!

Outlook: The Outliner

- It's the desk accessory with more power than a stand-alone outliner
- A great desktop publishing tool, Outlook lets you incorporate both text and graphics into your outlines
- Works hand-in-hand with MacPlan
- Allows you to work on several outlines at the same time

MacPlan: The Spreadsheet

- Integrates spreadsheets and graphs
- Does both formulas and straight numbers
- Graph types include bar charts, stacked bar charts, pie charts and line graphs
- Includes 12 example templates free!
- Pastes graphics and data right into Outlook creating professional memos and reports, complete with headers and footers.

SideKick: The Desktop Organizer, Release 2.0 now includes

- ☑ Outlook: The Outliner
- ☑ MacPlan: The Spreadsheet
- ☑ Mini word processor
- ☑ Calendar
- ☑ PhoneLog
- ☑ Analog clock
- ☑ Alarm system
- ☑ Calculator
- ☑ Report generator
- ☑ Telecommunications (new version now supports XModem file transfer protocol)

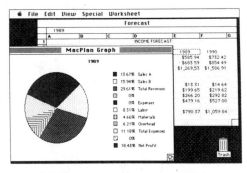

MacPlan does both spreadsheets and business graphs. Paste them into your Outlook files and generate professional reports.

Suggested Retail Price: $99.95 (not copy protected)

Minimum system configurations: Macintosh 512K or Macintosh Plus with one disk drive. One 800K or two 400K drives are recommended. With one 400K drive, a limited number of desk accessories will be installable per disk.

BORLAND
INTERNATIONAL

SideKick is a registered trademark and Outlook and MacPlan are trademarks of Borland International, Inc. Macintosh is a trademark of McIntosh Laboratory, Inc. licensed to Apple Computer, Inc. Copyright 1987 Borland International

BOR 0069D

REFLEX:® THE DATABASE MANAGER

**The easy-to-use relational database that thinks like a spreadsheet.
Reflex for the Mac lets you crunch numbers by entering formulas and link
databases by drawing on-screen lines.**

5 free ready-to-use templates are included on the examples disk:

- A sample 1040 tax application with Schedule A, Schedule B, and Schedule D, each contained in a separate report document.
- A portfolio analysis application with linked databases of stock purchases, sales, and dividend payments.
- A checkbook application.

- A client billing application set up for a law office, but easily customized by any professional who bills time.
- A parts explosion application that breaks down an object into its component parts for cost analysis.

Reflex for the Mac accomplishes all of these tasks without programming—using spreadsheet-like formulas Some other Reflex for the Mac features are:

- Visual database design.
- "What you see is what you get" report and form layout with pictures.
- Automatic restructuring of database files when data types are changed, or fields are added and deleted.
- Display formats which include General, Decimal, Scientific, Dollars, Percent.

- Data types which include variable length text, number, integer, automatically incremented sequence number, date, time, and logical.
- Up to 255 fields per record.
- Up to 16 files simultaneously open.
- Up to 16 Mac fonts and styles are selectable for individual fields and labels.

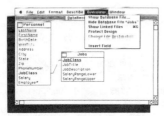

After opening the "Overview" window, you draw link lines between databases directly onto your Macintosh screen.

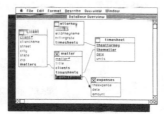

The link lines you draw establish both visual and electronic relationships between your databases.

You can have multiple windows open simultaneously to view all members of a linked set—which are interactive and truly relational.

Critic's Choice

". . . a powerful relational database . . . uses a visual approach to information management." **InfoWorld**

". . . gives you a lot of freedom in report design; you can even import graphics." **A+ Magazine**

". . . bridges the gap between the pretty programs and the power programs." **Stewart Alsop, PC Letter**

BORLAND
INTERNATIONAL

**Suggested Retail Price: $99.95
(not copy protected)**

Minimum system configuration: Macintosh 512K or Macintosh Plus with one disk drive. Second external drive recommended.

Reflex is a registered trademark of Borland/Analytica, Inc. Macintosh is a trademark of McIntosh Laboratory, Inc. and is used with express permission of its owner.
Copyright 1987 Borland International

BOR0149A

TURBO PASCAL MACINTOSH™

The ultimate Pascal development environment

Borland's new Turbo Pascal for the Mac is so incredibly fast that it can compile 1,420 lines of source code in the 7.1 seconds it took you to read this!

And reading the rest of this takes about *5 minutes*, which is plenty of time for Turbo Pascal for the Mac to compile at least *60,000 more lines* of source code!

Turbo Pascal for the Mac does both Windows and "Units"

The *separate* compilation of routines offered by Turbo Pascal for the Mac creates modules called "Units," which can be linked to any Turbo Pascal program. This "modular pathway" gives you "pieces" which can then be integrated into larger programs. You get a more efficient use of memory and a reduction in the time it takes to develop large programs.

Turbo Pascal for the Mac is so compatible with Lisa° that they should be living together

Routines from Macintosh Programmer's Workshop Pascal and Inside Macintosh can be compiled and run with only the subtlest changes. Turbo Pascal for the Mac is also compatible with the Hierarchical File System of the Macintosh.

The 27-second Guide to Turbo Pascal for the Mac

- Compilation speed of more than 12,000 lines per minute
- "Unit" structure lets you create programs in modular form
- Multiple editing windows—up to 8 at once
- Compilation options include compiling to disk or memory, or compile and run
- No need to switch between programs to compile or run a program
- Streamlined development and debugging
- Compatibility with Macintosh Programmer's

- Workshop Pascal (with minimal changes)
- Compatibility with Hierarchical File System of your Mac
- Ability to define default volume and folder names used in compiler directives
- Search and change features in the editor speed up and simplify alteration of routines
- Ability to use all available Macintosh memory without limit
- "Units" included to call all the routines provided by Macintosh Toolbox

---

Suggested Retail Price: $99.95   (not copy protected)

Minimum system configuration: Macintosh 512K or Macintosh Plus with one disk drive.

BORLAND
INTERNATIONAL

Turbo Pascal and SideKick are registered trademarks of Borland International, Inc. and Reflex is a registered trademark of Borland/Analytica, Inc. Macintosh is a trademark of McIntosh Laboratories, Inc. licensed to Apple Computer with its express permission. Lisa is a registered trademark of Apple Computer, Inc. Inside Macintosh is a copyright of Apple Computer, Inc.
Copyright 1987 Borland International BOR 0167A

Borland
Software
ORDER TODAY

BOR 0234